JEWS, JUSTICE AND JUDAISM

RELIGION IN AMERICA SERIES
Edited by Charles W. Ferguson

Books by Robert St. John

JEWS, JUSTICE AND JUDAISM

ROLL JORDAN ROLL

THE MAN WHO PLAYED GOD

THEY CAME FROM EVERYWHERE

ISRAEL: LIFE WORLD LIBRARY

THE BOSS

BUILDER OF ISRAEL

BEN-GURION

FOREIGN CORRESPONDENT

THROUGH MALAN'S AFRICA

THIS WAS MY WORLD

TONGUE OF THE PROPHETS

SHALOM MEANS PEACE

THE SILENT PEOPLE SPEAK

IT'S ALWAYS TOMORROW

FROM THE LAND OF SILENT PEOPLE

ROBERT ST. JOHN

JEWS, JUSTICE AND JUDAISM

A Narrative of the
Role Played by the
Bible People in
Shaping American History

Garden City, New York
DOUBLEDAY & COMPANY, INC.
1969

Library of Congress Catalog Card Number 68–17804
Copyright © 1969 by Robert St. John

To Jewish leaders,
rabbis and laymen alike,
who have fought prejudice,
stupidity, intolerance,
intimidation and fanaticism
in their struggle for
social justice in America,
this book is humbly dedicated.

Contents

AUTHOR'S NOTE

All quotations from the Bible are worded as in the 1959 translation of the Holy Scriptures published by The Jewish Publication Society of America.

The spellings of Hebrew words and religious terms are as in the Standard Jewish Encyclopedia, Cecil Roth, editor-in-chief; Doubleday & Co., 1966.

ACKNOWLEDGMENT

Appreciation is expressed to the author and the publisher for permission to quote the passage in Chapter 28 from *Giants of Justice*, Albert Vorspan, Union of Hebrew Congregations, New York, 1960.

A PRELIMINARY NOTE TO THE READER

AMERICAN history is a great tapestry—a never-ending series of scenes and episodes, continuously being woven out of the dreams and the nightmares, the follies and the ambitions of a determined people. Through the fabric run certain definable threads, some of striking colors. These represent Judaism's contributions to the American panorama. Without these threads there still would be the tapestry, but it would not be so rich or nearly so significant.

From the day that a member of the first Jewish colony in America petitioned New Amsterdam authorities for the right to practice his religion, until just yesterday, when some young rabbi somewhere called on his congregation to join in the local campaign for open-housing, American Jews have been contributing to the moral fiber of the nation.

The millions of Jews who have immigrated to the United States in the last 314 years from every point of the compass brought with them, regardless of their country of origin, a common belief in the principles of Judaism. As they have taken their places in the American scene, they have continuously influenced the national action by adhering to those principles.

It is highly significant that 3 percent of a country's population, united only by religion, has contributed ethical principles that have become such an integral part of America.

Every religious segment in the country, of course, has helped in weaving the tapestry. Justice in its many manifestations has been the golden thread that Judaism has contributed.

It is seen in the wording of the legal code of the Massachusetts Bay Colony, called *A Body of Liberties*. It is seen in the early

American struggle for freedom of thought and religion. It is seen in the fight for the right of any minority member to vote, to hold public office, to live the free life. It is seen in the defeat of those who have tried to oppose civil liberties, civil rights, and social justice for all men.

The theme of this narrative is: Who are the Jews of America, how and why did they come here, what were the various religious ideas they brought with them, how were they welcomed and how were they treated, what changes did America effect in their religious practices, and in what manner did they make their specific contributions to America.

It is hoped that among the readers there will be many non-Jews to whom some of the facts will be new and some of the terminology strange. Accordingly, any words not in general American usage are explained parenthetically when they appear for the first time.

Literally tens of thousands of books have been published, publicly or privately, on the subjects of Jews, justice, and Judaism in the United States. This volume does not pretend to be a definitive narrative. It aims only at introducing the reader to a subject which is rich in rewards for anyone who pursues it further.

Some but not all of the great figures of American Judaism appear in these pages, such as Solomon Schechter, the outstanding leader of Conservative Judaism in America; Isaac Mayer Wise, leader of the Reformists; Jacob Joseph, who came from Vilna to be Chief Rabbi of the Orthodox synagogues of New York, as well as such provocative characters as Mordecai Kaplan, who construed Judaism as a civilization; Rabbi Stephen Wise, who championed freedom of the pulpit, and such non-clerical giants as Louis D. Brandeis, Benjamin N. Cardozo, Louis Marshall, David Dubinsky, Hannah G. Solomon, Samuel Gompers, Felix Frankfurter, and the Szolds, father and daughter.

Some minor but colorful characters are introduced in order to show that the justice of Judaism is practiced on the byways as well as along the major highways of America.

ROBERT ST. JOHN

June 1968
Washington, D.C.

JEWS, JUSTICE AND JUDAISM

I

UNWELCOME PIONEERS

ONE windy morning in early September 1654, a French ship, the *St. Charles*, put in to the port of New Amsterdam. Among the passengers taken ashore in small boats were twenty-three sea-weary Jews—people without a home, without a destination. They were to create the first Jewish colony on the soil of North America, yet they had come to this particular spot not at all by choice. They were symbols of what had been happening to Jews for 1584 years—since the destruction of the Second Temple. They were refugees from religious persecution that was forever catching up with them. For a time they had known peace, prosperity and freedom of worship in Brazil, but then the long arm of the Inquisition had reached out, and now they were refugees again. As they left the small boats and put foot to soil, they looked around nervously. What sort of place was this? Would the people here treat them with the religious toleration they had experienced briefly under the Dutch in Recife, or would they be forced to move on? If so, where could they possibly find open doors and a welcome? Would it always and forever be thus . . . this eternal wandering . . . the endless wonder and worry about tomorrow?

Once There Was a Golden Age

But that is not the proper place to begin the story of the Old Testament People and America. It must start back in Spain, where, during certain of the medieval centuries, Jews had their golden age.

Because of the tolerance of Moslem Moorish rulers, they became doctors, lawyers, teachers, mathematicians, poets, philosophers, and merchant princes. They built exquisite palaces and great synagogues, and life was good. But when the Christian kingdoms of what is now Spain began uniting to drive out the Moors, Spain's Jews were also the victims. Cordova's magnificent synagogue was burned to the ground. The Jews of Toledo were massacred. There were pogroms in a hundred cities and towns of Castile alone. Fanatical Christians, armed with sword and firebrand, burned, looted, and slaughtered. Tens of thousands of Jews were killed. Monks, holding aloft crucifixes, gave the Jews a choice: conversion or death. Thus the inhabitants of entire towns were converted *en masse*, hundreds of thousands in all. Some in time were absorbed into the Christian family and were lost as Jews. Others, while putting on the robe of conformity, kept their religion, remaining faithful to Judaic tradition. But life for them became more precarious. If they lit candles on the eve of the Jewish sabbath, or celebrated a feast day, or merely abstained from eating food forbidden by the rules of Judaism, they risked being reported by a malicious neighbor. All Jews who had undergone conversion—even those who had intermarried and conscientiously were trying to be faithful Christians—were termed Marranos, from the Spanish word for pig, *marrano*.

Starting in 1480, life under the Inquisition became almost intolerable for the Marranos. Every move they made was watched. Ingenious traps were devised to catch them in some act of commission or omission that could be branded heretical. The penalty was death by burning at the stake.

Isabella of Castile came to the throne with grandiose ambitions to make Spain outshine any power the world had ever known. Because she was obsessed with the idea that Jews were a liability rather than an asset to Spain, a decree was issued: in three months every Jew must be out of the country. The deadline was August 2, 1492. To most American schoolboys, 1492 may be the year that "Columbus sailed the ocean blue" but for Jews, 1492 was not a year to be remembered happily. Castile and Aragon finally had been united, a political fact that enabled the expulsion to be effective, for now the Jews could no longer flee from kingdom to kingdom, playing one against the other.

Was Columbus a Jew?

There are many historical ironies in the fact that Christopher Columbus sailed from Spain for the New World on August 3, the day after the last Jew was supposed to be out of Spain. The nationality and religion of the explorer will probably forever remain a matter of controversy, although there are historians who cite what they term "adequate proof" that his real name was Cristóbal Colón and that he was a Spanish Jew, not an Italian Catholic. If this was true, Columbus himself was struck by the irony of the situation, for he began his journal of the adventure in these words: "After the Spanish monarchs had expelled all the Jews from their kingdoms and lands . . . in that same month they commissioned me to undertake the voyage to India with a properly equipped fleet."

Five of the men who manned Columbus' ships were Jews. One of them, Rodrigo de Triana, was the first to sight land. Another held the important post of fleet physician. The great Marrano theologian, Diego de Deza, was one of Columbus' principal supporters, as were Juan Cabrero, Gabriel Sanchez, and Alfonso de la Caballeria, all Marranos. Columbus obtained considerable help from Abraham Senior and Isaac Abravanel, royal contractors, who were also Jews. Abraham Zacuto, a learned Jewish astronomer, publicly supported the adventure and gave Columbus the astronomical tables he used in his navigation. And what motivated Columbus to send the first news of his success from the Canary Islands early in 1493 not to the king or queen directly, but to a Jewish friend and supporter, Luis de Santangel, chancellor of the royal household?

The First Jew in the New World

Although it may have been coincidence, it is interesting that when Columbus reached what he thought was the mainland of Asia (actually Cuba) one of the two men he sent ashore to try to find the palace of the Khan, of whom Marco Polo had told such tales, was Luis de Torres, a Marrano who had been named the expedition's interpreter because of his knowledge of many languages. De Torres thus earned the honor of being the first Jew to set foot on the soil of the New World. The first words of Hebrew spoken on this continent were questions the interpreter asked the copper-skinned natives in the language of his own biblical ancestors. Then he tried Arabic, which he also spoke fluently. The Arawak Indians were equally ignorant of Hebrew and Arabic, so the conversation had to take place in sign language.

It was more than 150 years later that a young minister, the Reverend Thomas Thorowgood, published a book in English entitled: *Jews in America, or Probabilities That the Americans Are of That Race*, which purported to prove that American redskins are actually descendants of the Lost Ten Tribes of Israel, a theory that had been advanced first in 1585 by Father Dwan in a history of New Spain, based on what he claimed was a resemblance between the religious rites of Jews and American Indians. The Thorowgood book inspired an Amsterdam rabbi, Merrasseh ben Israel, to write a pamphlet published in Latin under the title *Spes Israelis* and in English as *The Hope of Israel*, in which he, likewise, declared that the American aborigines were descendants of the ancient Israelites. Later William Penn had the same idea. He claimed that American Indians bore certain physical resemblances to the Jews he remembered seeing in his youth in the ghetto of his native city, London.

When Columbus sailed away in disappointment at not having found the palace of the Khan, Luis de Torres remained behind. He may have reasoned that here was one place no one would question his method of worship, that here no one had yet heard of the Inquisition. He spent the rest of his life in Cuba, the first Jewish settler in the New World. Unlike many of those who would follow, he was a settler not by either accident or compulsion, but entirely by choice.

To Spain, to Portugal, to Brazil

Meanwhile, thousands of the Jews forced out of Spain by Isabella and Ferdinand had gone to Portugal. There they were granted the rights of domicile upon payment of heavy refugee duties, but when Ferdinand and Isabella refused to permit their daughter to marry the

Crown Prince of Portugal unless the Marranos, as well as the Mohammedan refugees from Spain, were forced to move on, the ever-wandering Jews were required to pack up once again. Some went to Brazil early in the sixteenth century, braving tropical diseases, almost unbearable heat and other jungle conditions in return for the right to worship as they pleased.

But the arm of the Inquisition was long enough to reach across an ocean. Priests, missionaries, spies, and *agents provocateurs* arrived in the New World to convert the natives to Christianity and to apprehend Marranos, hundreds of whom were burned at the stake as a lesson to the Indians, who may have been more astounded than intimidated by such cruelty on the part of pale-faced men from across the water.

In Brazil, the bishop of the capital city, Bahia, was required by the Portuguese government to search out "secret Jews," as they were called, and send them back to Lisbon for trial. For years the Marranos there lived in fear, and no wonder, for any non-Jew who denounced a secret Jew was rewarded with a sizable percentage of the convicted man's property.

Temporary Freedom Under the Dutch

In 1624 an armed expedition sent out by the Dutch West India Company, one night under cover of darkness sailed into the harbor of the Brazilian city of Pernambuco, which the Dutch renamed Recife, and drove out the Portuguese. From a Jewish point of view this was fortuitous. Amsterdam had become known as New Jerusalem. Marranos who had fled there from Spain and Portugal had prospered. Some had established banking houses. Others had built factories or founded new industries. And so the arrival of the Dutch in Brazil was welcomed by the Jews there. For the next thirty years, under Dutch rule, they lived well, some becoming owners of plantations and sugar mills, traders, even engineers. As evidence of their freedom of worship, they built a two-story white stone synagogue, Zur Israel (the Rock of Israel).

But the Portuguese returned in 1654 and reconquered the colony, giving the Jews a choice: baptism or exile. Most of them, with little hesitation, chose exile. They were given three months in which to leave. There were by then 1500 Jews in the colony, Zur Israel counting 150 families in its congregation. There was not room aboard the Dutch ships sailing back to the Netherlands to accommodate everyone and so, eager to be rid of the unwanted people, the Portuguese put sixteen of their ships at the disposal of the Jews. One of the last to leave was the *Valk*. Aboard were twenty-three Brazilian Jews.

Pirates and Profiteers

After a stormy trip, the ship finally reached the Caribbean, but off the island of Jamaica it was boarded by Spaniards. The pirates were prevented from plundering the ship and harming the passengers by the timely intervention of a French privateer, the *St. Charles*. (In court records the ship is also called the *Saint Catrina*, or the *St. Catherine*.) Thus the Jews were rescued. But the French skipper demanded 2500 guilders (some over 100 guilders per head) to take them to the nearest Dutch port, New Amsterdam.

After six months at sea, the twenty-three travel-weary Jews finally went ashore at what would some day be called New York City and in another three centuries would have a Jewish population of almost two million. They were emaciated and bedraggled. They had been burned by the sun and the wind. (A New Amsterdam cleric described them as "healthy but poor.") They carried only a few possessions, but they all had hope—hope that here, maybe, they would be able to practice their religion proudly and freely.

New Amsterdam was small but cosmopolitan. The five hundred people on what is now Manhattan Island spoke eighteen languages, plus some Hebrew. They were governed by the son of a Christian minister, the irascible Peter Stuyvesant, who ten years earlier had lost a leg in battle on the island of St. Martin. A man of violent prejudices, he was intolerant of even Dutch Lutherans, some of whom he had already jailed. Baptists and Presbyterians who had drifted into New Amsterdam were required to move on. On his instructions, Quakers, whom he called "instruments of Satan," were arrested and expelled. A few were even tortured. One Quaker preacher was sentenced to two years at hard labor behind a wheelbarrow and when he rebelled at this indignity was brutally maltreated. Another "unwanted immigrant"—Stuyvesant's term for a Quaker—was tied to the rear of a cart and dragged down the road to the dock, simply because he had been trying to propagate his religious ideas.

The First Rosh Ha-Shanah

This was the atmosphere of the place to which the twenty-three Jews from Brazil had come, not entirely by choice. Captain Jacques de la Motthe, skipper of the *St. Charles*, led them from the ship to the *Stadthuys* or City Hall, where he explained to Stuyvesant that they owed him 1567 guilders, having paid only 933 of the 2500 guilders agreed on. Their answer was that they would pay the balance as soon as they could write to friends in the Netherlands and receive remittances from them. What then happened was symbolic of what lay ahead for Jews in America: cruelty, then kindness, then cruelty again—a confusing ambivalence. While some of the Dutch settlers were magnanimously offering temporary shelter to the homeless refugees, Stuyvesant and his magistrates decided that one way they could be forced to pay their debt to the ship captain would be for him to order a sale of their possessions. So a public auction was announced for the next day, September 12. Spokesmen for the twenty-three pleaded that September 12 and 13 were Rosh Ha-Shanah, the first and second days of their Hebrew New Year, which all religious Jews observe by attending synagogue services, or, if that is impossible, by reflecting in private on the events of the past year and praying for a good twelve months to come. They received their first surprise when their pleas were honored and the sale was postponed until September 14.

On the day of the auction a small crowd gathered around the auctioneer as he mounted his stand. The refugees had few possessions and much of what they did have was obviously of sentimental rather than monetary value. This was so clear to the Dutch burghers and their wives, who had come looking for bargains, that as the auctioneer held up first one item and then another, some spectator would make a ridiculously low bid and the others, as if by prearrangement, would remain silent. Then the successful bidder would turn his purchase back to the original owner.

Imprisoned for a Group Debt

Infuriated, Captain de la Motthe ordered the sale stopped and conferred again with Stuyvesant, who agreed that two of the refugees should be held in prison until the remainder of the debt was paid. But, said the wily governor, the skipper would have to pay prison authorities the room and board bill of the incarcerated men. Later, David Israel and Moses Ambrosius were chosen as the hostages.

Captain de la Motthe waited a month. Then rather than keep his ship and his entire crew idle any longer, he sailed away, with the refugees' promise that they would pay him as soon as they received money from abroad. (After he left they discovered that he had charged them three times the normal fare for such a trip.)

Stuyvesant, annoyed at having twenty-three unwanted immigrants on his hands, wrote to his employers, the Dutch West India Company, asking for permission to expel them. When the Jews heard this they sent a petition to Amsterdam asking for the right to remain. Then the leading Dutch Reformed minister in New Amsterdam, John Megapolensis, who had been born a Catholic but had become a Protestant by conversion, added his invective, writing on March 18, 1655, to Amsterdam that he was against permitting the Jews to remain because he felt "their greed" would hurt the colony economically and their religion would hurt the colony spiritually, for it would increase the number of creeds "bedeviling" New Amsterdam. He wrote: "These people have no other God than the Mammon of unrighteousness and no other aim than to get possession of Christian property, and to overcome all other merchants by drawing all trade toward themselves. Therefore we request your Reverences to obtain from the Messrs. Directors that these godless rascals, who are of no benefit to the country, but look at everything for their own profit, may be sent away from here. For as we now have here Papists, Menonites and Lutherans among the Dutch; also many Puritans or Independents, and many Atheists and various other servants of Baal among the English under this government, who conceal themselves under the name of Christians, it would create still greater confusion if the obstinate and immovable Jews came to settle here."

The Fight for the Right to Be Different

The next move came from seven Sephardic Jews, all important in Amsterdam's commercial life, who felt they could use their influence to persuade the Dutch West India Company to overrule Stuyvesant. In a petition to the company's directors they pointed out that the twenty-three Jews in New Amsterdam, whose fate the company was about to decide, were representative of a large body of their co-religionists who had loyally supported the Dutch in Brazil, not only with their wealth but some of them with their lives. They also argued that these twenty-three and other Jews who might follow them to the New Netherlands would help to make the colony prosper.

Stuyvesant countered that if he gave the Jews liberty and freedom "we cannot then refuse the Lutherans and the Papists." It thus follows that as the Jews of New Amsterdam fought for their own freedom of worship, they were, at the same time, helping to establish liberty for others—Lutherans, Catholics, Baptists, Presbyterians, and Quakers. This was in the Judaic tradition, for it is a fundamental of the religion that every group, in every community, in every period of civilization has the right to be different; that such differences must be respected by others; that the most fundamental difference to be honored is difference in religion.

Anti-Semitism in High Places

The winter of 1654–55 was so severe that the rivers which normally flowed so swiftly around New Amsterdam froze solid. There were about four hundred settlers in all on the island. Some befriended the refugees from Brazil; others resented that these people —"these foreigners"—had become charges of the community. But Stuyvesant outdid them all in his unfriendliness. Once he fumed that

Jews were notorious "for their usury and deceitful trading." Again he told his superiors in Amsterdam that "members of the deceitful race" should not be permitted to "infect and trouble this new colony." While awaiting a decision from the Dutch West India Company, Stuyvesant denied the people from Brazil even the most elementary economic and religious rights.

Finally spring came and a ship from the Netherlands brought mail, money, provisions, and permission from the Dutch West India Company for the Jews to remain. The communication said it would be unreasonable and unfair to deny their request, especially in view of their loyalty in defending Brazil against the Portuguese, and also "because of the large amount of capital this nation has invested in the shares of this company." And so—

"After many deliberations we have finally decided and resolved . . . that these Portuguese Jews may travel and trade to and in New Netherland and live and remain there provided the poor among them shall not become a burden to the company or to the community, but be supported by their own nation. You will govern yourself accordingly."

A Ghetto Called Jews' Alley

Stuyvesant had been overruled, but he continued to try in many ways to make life difficult for the Jewish immigrants. He suggested that they build their houses "as close together as possible." The implication was clear; they were to establish their own ghetto, even though they were in the freedom-loving New World. The street in which they now dwelt in close proximity to each other came to be called Jews' Alley.

Stuyvesant forbade the twenty-three to engage in any retail trade or to join any of the craft guilds, and the Dutch West India Company backed him up. In the spring of 1657 Jacob Cohen Henriques, one of the twenty-three, petitioned for the right to bake and sell bread. But even though he agreed to do so "with closed doors" (probably meaning he would only sell wholesale) his application for a permit was rejected.

The twenty-three from Brazil were not the first Jews on the North American continent. The Jewish historian Jacob Rader Marcus has written: "No Jew is ever the first Jew in any town; there is always one who had been there before him." In this case the one who had been there before was Jacob Barsimson of Holland, who arrived just one month before the French ship dropped anchor in the harbor of New Amsterdam. He had come on the ship *Peartree* with a party of immigrants sent by the Dutch West India Company. He cleared land, traded with the Indians, and for a time hired out as a manual laborer. He may not have been the first Jewish settler in North America, but at least he was responsible for the first case in which observance of the Jewish Sabbath was officially recognized as a valid reason for failing to answer a court summons. The record reads: "Though the defendant is absent yet no default is entered against him as he was summoned on his Sabbath."

(There is no record of what offense Barsimson had committed, why a summons against him was issued, or what the outcome of the case was.)

Permission to Pray—in Private

The greatest blow that the twenty-three religious Jews from Brazil had to bear was the news that they would not be permitted to erect a synagogue or even to pray together in public. It was two years after their arrival before they were given written permission to practice their religion "in all quietness within their homes." There was nothing at all anti-Semitic about the situation. It was simply that the New Netherland colony had a regulation prohibiting any public religious gatherings except by the Dutch Reformed Church, which alone was permitted to erect religious buildings. Even the Dutch Lutherans were discriminated against. But for the twenty-three Jews to be required to pray surreptitiously was almost as revolting as the conditions in Brazil from which they had fled.

Most of the refugees were Sephardim. After the destruction of the Second Temple and the Dispersal, those Jews who were scattered through Asia and Europe fell into two distinct groups: the Ashkenasim, being the Jews of Middle, Northern and Eastern Europe, especially of Germany, Poland, and Russia, who some time later were to play a major role in the story of American Judaism, and the Sephardim, being the Jews of Southern and Western Europe. (The word Sephardi derives from Sepharad, used as a place name in the Book of Obadiah and as the word for Spain in post-biblical Jewish literature.) Sephardim and Ashkenasim were all worshipers of the same god, but each group had a distinct literature, philosophy, and outlook on life. Their religious customs were also different. The Sephardic way of life had been affected by Babylonian, Persian, Greek, and Roman culture. For hundreds of years the Sephardim had set the patterns for European Jews in manners, morals, scholarship, and even dress.

Congregation Shearith Israel

Despite official obstruction, these forerunners of an ever-growing wave of Sephardic immigration to America were determined to reconstitute, here in the New World, the European-type religious community to which they were accustomed. Though they were forbidden to build a synagogue, they at least were free to organize a congregation, which they quickly proceeded to do, calling it Congregation Shearith Israel (Remnant of Israel).

When three of their number (Abraham De Lucena, Salvador Dandrada, and Jacob Cohen) petitioned Stuyvesant for the right to have a Jewish graveyard, the request was granted—but only in principle. They were told they could establish such a cemetery "when the need arises." On July 14, 1656, one of the *St. Charles* passengers died and the Jews were then given permission to use a certain tract of land for this and future burials.

Much to the annoyance of those residing in Jews' Alley, New Amsterdam copied the Motherland's system of excluding Jews between the ages of sixteen and sixty from military service, but instead required them to pay a tax of sixty-five stivers a month, which they considered a cruel combination of discrimination and humiliation. Only the affluent among the twenty-three could afford such a tax and few of them were affluent.

American Jewry's First Leader

The situation in New Amsterdam had already created a leader. Asser Levy van Swellem, an Ashkenazi Jew, was a native of Amsterdam, but had lived in Brazil until forced to flee. When he arrived in New Amsterdam he dropped his Dutch name and became known simply as Asser Levy. Objecting to the discriminatory military tax, he joined with Barsimson in petitioning for the right to stand guard in defense of the town, like any burgher. The Court of Burgomasters not only rejected the plea, but informed the two men that if they were discontent with the decision, they were hereby given permission "to depart whenever and whither it pleases them."

Undismayed, Asser night after night performed guard duty anyway and a year and a half later presented another petition, this time saying that as he had once been a burgher in Amsterdam, and as he had been keeping watch and ward like the other New Amsterdam citizens, he did hereby request full burgher status. Again the court turned down his request, but he was granted the right of appeal and finally the Council of the Colony ruled in his favor. Thus Asser Levy won not only for himself but for his fellow Jews the right to full citizenship in the New World.

For another thirteen years, until his death in 1680, Asser Levy played a leading role in the colony. Buying furs from the Indians was a profitable business, so Levy became a fur trader. Rivals tried to have him barred from this activity, but he finally succeeded in establishing for himself and all others the right to trade anywhere in New Netherland.

The Broadway Shambles Slaughterhouse

Only six butchers were permitted to have shops in New Amsterdam. Levy applied for and was granted one of the six licenses. He was excused from killing hogs "because of his religion." Then he opened a slaughterhouse so that "all persons should have the liberty to kill and hang meat therein." It was at the end of Wall Street, known as "the Broadway Shambles," the first Jewish slaughterhouse in North America. Levy probably served as the *shohet* or religious butcher, doing the slaughtering of cattle and fowl according to kosher Jewish regulations.

This unusual man also became the first Jew to own real estate in what was to become New York City—perhaps the first in what was to become the United States. He purchased a plot on South William Street, and then a plot in Albany, the site that the explorer Henry Hudson had chosen for a settlement. He also established and operated a tavern near his Wall Street slaughterhouse. Ten years after the arrival of the twenty-three Jews at New Amsterdam Asser Levy was rated one of the city's wealthiest citizens and even loaned municipal authorities the money needed to rebuild the city's defenses. Christian and Jew alike respected him. When the Lutherans needed money to construct their first church, it was Asser Levy who advanced them the necessary funds. Often a Christian friend would name him as the executor of his estate, and once a court appointed him custodian of certain goods over which two Christians were litigating. His reputation spread beyond the borders of New Netherland. When he intervened with Connecticut authorities on behalf of a Jewish friend who had been fined for breaking the Sabbath, the court halved the fine "as a token of respect for the said Asser Levy."

The "Abominable Religion" of "Unbelieving Jews"

By the time of his death Asser Levy was recognized throughout the colony as a distinguished citizen who had had more to do than any man with helping the handful of Jews on Manhattan Island win the right to engage in retail trade, to buy and sell real estate, to be exporters and importers, to deal in furs, and to be admitted to citizenship as burghers.

But what they wanted most was the privilege of worshiping together in public. So once again they petitioned Stuyvesant. In announcing his decision the governor said that "public exercise of their abominable religion has been refused." On another occasion, speaking of a shipment of Negro slaves he had just received from Curaçao, he said he preferred them to "unbelieving Jews."

2

INSPIRATION FOR THE PURITANS

Long before the arrival of the first Jew on Colonial soil, Judaism had exerted an indirect influence on the New World. The Puritans made no secret of their ambition to establish a theocratic state modeled on ancient Israel. They knew the history of the Jews better than they knew English history. Their popular heroes were Abraham, Isaac, Jacob, Moses, David, Solomon, and Jeremiah. Their preachers' sermons were nearly always based on Old Testament texts. They decided that because the Old Testament had been written in Hebrew, Hebrew must have been the mother tongue from which all other languages sprang.

Cotton Mather, Hebrew Scholar

If any one man personified Puritanism it was Cotton Mather, its most influential author and its most learned minister. His attitude toward Jews and their religion indicates how penetrating was the influence of Judaism in those early American days. At the age of twelve Cotton Mather began the study of Hebrew and in college became a master of the biblical language. He also was a student of the Talmud. Later in life he trained his eldest daughter to read Hebrew. Among his prolific writings was a six-volume history of the Jews. He was fascinated by the idea that Jews, of all the people in the world, had learned the will of God by direct communication. In his sermons and in the 450 books he wrote he liked to use stories by or about Jews—often stories from the Talmud—to illustrate important points he wished to make. He distinguished, however, between the ancient Israelites and the Jews of his day, whom he considered only as fit subjects for conversion.

What Cotton Mather and his fellow Puritans respected most about Judaism was its consistent emphasis on respect for learning. Intellectualism became their passion and resulted in the founding of Harvard College a few years after their settlement had been established. It may seem strange today but it was quite logical then that one of the important subjects in the curriculum should have been Hebrew, for, after all, was this not the language in which *The Book* had been written? For that reason many students began to spend one day each week for three years trying to become proficient in the language of the Bible. Freshmen used a textbook by a German professor bearing this challenging title: *The Hebrew Sun Dial, or Advice as to How the Elements of the Holy Language May Be Sufficiently Apprehended by College Students in a Space of 24 Hours.* For years all Harvard students were required to recite a verse from the Bible in Hebrew each day at morning prayers. In order to graduate it was necessary to demonstrate proficiency in reading the entire Bible in Hebrew. Until 1817 Harvard commencement exercises included an oration in Hebrew. It is important to know that at this time Hebrew was not studied in British universities. The Puritans had added it to their college curriculum as one more expression of their new freedom.

Hebrew Taught Direct by Mail

As other colleges were founded they followed the lead of Harvard and likewise made Hebrew a required subject. At Yale, Hebrew became such a popular course that classes were held in the largest lecture hall on the campus, and a Yale professor was so successful in establishing a Hebrew correspondence course that the local postmaster's salary had to be raised because of the quantity of mail received.

By the time Ezra Stiles was elected president of Yale, in 1777, Hebrew had become, in his own words, "essential to a gentleman's education." He personally drilled the Yale boys in Hebrew, especially in one of the Psalms which he thought "would be the first we should hear in heaven." One of his arguments for the study of Hebrew was the shame that any graduate of Yale would feel if "he should be entirely ignorant of the holy language when he got to heaven."

A commencement address Stiles delivered during the Revolution—entirely in Hebrew, as was his custom—was based on Ezra VII, 10: "For Ezra has set his heart to seek the law of the Lord, and to do it, and to teach in Israel statutes and ordinances." In his enthusiasm for Hebrew, Stiles declared it "a glorious language which throws more light on the Old Testament than all the Commentators."

Yale's seal, designed in the early eighteenth century by a now-anonymous scholar, is still in use, unchanged. It shows an open Bible inscribed with large black Hebrew letters spelling out the words Urim and Thummim, the sacred means of divination used by the early Hebrews, which were attached to the breastplate of the high priest. Many years later, when Yale wanted a coat of arms, the original seal was used. By this time few scholars any longer knew Hebrew, so it was suggested that the two Hebrew words should be translated into some more common language underneath the seal. The real meaning of Urim and Thummim was apparently in doubt. One suggestion was that they mean "light" and "truth" (an incorrect assumption) and so, accepting this version, Yale placed on its coat of arms under the shield the Latin words: *Lux et veritas.* The Dartmouth seal bears the Hebrew words *El Shaddi* (God Almighty).

The first public school of New Haven, Connecticut, was one of several in which Hebrew was a required subject, even for small children.

The New England Primer, the most noteworthy of Colonial textbooks (it eventually sold a total of more than 7,000,000 copies) taught the A-B-C's biblically, starting with A ("In Adam's fall we sinned.") to Z ("Zaccheus, he did climb a tree, His Lord to see.").

Hanging the Witches at Gaza

Knowledge of the language of the Israelites helped the Colonials capture the real meaning of the Bible, which in turn aided in the discipline of their minds and in the fortification of their will.

Not only did the New Englanders of those days know the Bible backward and forward, in and out, cover to cover, but they also knew the Talmud. Example: in the days when Cotton Mather was arousing the people of the Colonies against the evil work of alleged witches, he cited from the Talmud a tale about the hanging of eighty witches at Gaza.

The language of the Bible colored and permeated the thought, writings and speech of the new young land. The New Englanders frequently used biblical allusions when they descended to name-calling. Anne Hutchinson, the heretic, was branded "a wretched Jezebel." Many Hebrew words entered the everyday American language. Phrases from the Psalms became New World idioms. When parents christened their offspring, they often bypassed more familiar English names and called their children Ruth, Esther, Rachel, Benjamin, Joseph, Daniel, or Ezra. Such esoteric names as Zechariah often were used by the New Englanders, although in those days American Jews seldom used them. (Names of Christian saints were conspicuous by their absence.)

Settlements, towns, and cities, rivers and mountains were also given biblical names. Salem, which stems from the Hebrew word for peace, was the most popular. There are now twenty-six communities in the United States called Salem. There are also sixteen Sharons, eight Canaans, twelve Hebrons, seven Bethlehems, seven Jordans, six Jerichos, two Zebuluns, two Benjamins, and two Josephs, as well as Moses, New Mexico; Noah, Tennessee; Levy, New Mexico; Asher, Oklahoma; Sodom, New York; David, Kentucky; Daniel, Wyoming; Solomon, Kansas; Sinai, South Dakota; Abraham, Utah; Samson, Alabama; Gideon, Missouri; Uriah, Alabama, and Beersheba Springs, Tennessee.

America Had Its Moses

Although many of the original settlers of America may never have met a living Jew, they were Bible-loving people and in their struggle for religious freedom liked to compare themselves to the men and women Moses had led from Egyptian slavery to freedom in the promised land. King James was their Pharaoh, the Atlantic

Ocean their Red Sea, and America their Canaan. They likened many of their early leaders to Moses. Referring to John Winthrop, Cotton Mather wrote: "Accordingly when the noble design of carrying a colony of chosen people into an American wilderness was by some eminent persons undertaken, this eminent person was, by the consent of all, chosen for the Moses, who must be the leader of so great an undertaking; and indeed nothing but a Mosaic spirit could have carried him through the temptations to which either his farewell to his own land, or his travel in a strange land, must needs expose a gentleman of his education."

On John Cotton's tombstone were chiseled these words:

> But let this mourning flock be comforted,
>   Though Moses be, yet Joshua is not dead;
> I mean renowned Norton; worthy he
>   Successor to our Moses is to be,
> O happy Israel in America,
>   In such a Moses, such a Joshua.

They likened their own trouble with the Indians to the Israelites' trials and tribulations in the desert.

God's Chosen People

Bitterly persecuted as they were, the Pilgrims and the Puritans drew many parallels between themselves and the Jews. They, too, felt they had been chosen by God for the special task they had undertaken. The opening line of a poem from a life of Roger Williams reads:

> Like Israel's host, to exile driven,
>   Across the floods the Pilgrim fled;

A contemporary satirical verse contained these lines:

> New-England they are like the Jews,
>   As like as like can be.

Moses became the lawgiver of the Puritans, as he had been of the ancient Israelites. When they drew up their own laws they patterned them after the Mosaic Law. In the code of 1655 for the Colony of New Haven, half the statutes contained references to the Old Testament. Because Mosaic Law did not provide for trial by jury, the Puritans likewise rejected the principle of juries. In those days anyone in the Massachusetts Bay Colony charged with a serious crime was given this verse from Psalm XXVIII to read: "He that hideth his sin shall not prosper, but he that confesseth and forsaketh his sins shall find mercy."

In the early days of the Massachusetts Bay Colony the Puritans used the Old Testament as their statute book. Then, in 1641, a legal code called *A Body of Liberties* was framed, with forty-six of the forty-eight proposed laws drawn directly from the Old Testament.

Why They Abhorred a Monarchy

Whenever the early settlers discussed the ideal form of government—the form of government under which they wished to live permanently—they were influenced by their biblical knowledge. Moses cautioned his people that they should be responsible to no other king than God. Samuel delivered a long warning on the dangers and evils of a monarchy. And so from the start the Puritans abhorred the idea of a king and talked long and loud about separation of the colonies from monarchical England.

The religious life of the early Americans was also greatly influenced by Judaic teachings and practices. From this source they learned to fast. The first Thanksgiving, in 1621, resembling in many ways a Jewish feast, was a far cry from modern Thanksgiving celebrations. They recited a tale of their trials and wanderings, bearing more than a coincidental likeness to the *Haggadah*, the account of the Exodus used by Jews at their Passover meal, the *Seder*. They were convinced that a whole nation could have a covenant with God, as evidenced by Governor Winthrop's assurance to the people of the Massachusetts Bay Colony: "If wee keep this covenant wee shall finde that the God of Israell is among us, but if wee deal falsely with our God . . . wee be consumed out of the good land . . ."

So Much Like Judaism

Now, free from the centralized authority of the English church, the Puritans organized their religious as well as their secular life along Old Testament lines. Each of their churches was independent and autonomous, just as each Jewish synagogue is. No minister was thought to have supernatural powers, just as no rabbi (except the Hasidic *rebbe*) is believed to be invested with supernaturalism, and therefore the Colonial church leaders were chosen democratically, by the congregations themselves, just as rabbis were chosen.

The Puritans, like the Jews, began observing their Sabbath at sundown on the previous day. Also like the Jews, they did no manner of work from sundown on Sabbath eve to sundown on the Sabbath itself, refraining from even shaving, bedmaking, cooking, and dishwashing. They shunned any form of amusement and spent the entire holy day in prayer and religious contemplation. In those early New England days males and females sat separately in their churches, just as they still do in orthodox Jewish synagogues.

The idea that the American Indians may be descendants of the Ten Lost Tribes inflamed the imagination of the New England Puritans, who sought zealously for evidence.

Jews, Puritans, and Education

The Puritans had deep appreciation of the emphasis Judaism places on education, as evidenced by Cotton Mather's statement: "In every town among Jews, there was a school, whereat children were taught the reading of the law; and if there were any town destitute of a school, the men of this place did stand excommunicate, until they were erected: besides and beyond they had *midrashoth*, or divinity-schools, in which they expounded the law to their disciples. Whether the churches of New-England have been duly careful or not about their other schools, they have not been altogether careless about their *midrashoth;* and it is well for them that they have not."

One-tenth of One Percent

Despite this profound influence of Judaism on early America, Jews were rare in the thirteen colonies. Even by 1776, when the total Colonial population had reached about two and a half million, there were only 2500 to 3000 Jews among them. They comprised only about one-tenth of one percent of the total population, yet they and the religion which dominated their lives had an effect on young America that had little relationship to the mathematics of the situation.

There were never many Jews in the Massachusetts Bay Colony. Maybe this is why they escaped the fanatical treatment meted out to Catholics and Quakers. Or maybe it was because they were not regarded as public enemies. The worst thing Cotton Mather wanted to do to them was to convert them. This ambition dominated his thinking, his talking, and his actions. Yet he opposed the use of punishment or violence to enforce conformity, and he was loud in his condemnation of religious persecution.

"Ye Jew" in Massachusetts

Boston did not have a Jewish congregation until long after the Revolution, but the history of the Massachusetts colony is sprinkled with names of individual Jews. The first to be mentioned in legal documents is Solomon France, who, in 1649, five years before the arrival of the Brazilian Jews in New Amsterdam, asked the court in Massachusetts to help him collect a fee for supervising a shipment of goods from abroad for the major general of the colony. The magistrates denied his claim but granted him an allowance to tide him over until he could get passage back to the Netherlands.

The next Jew before the courts was named Sollomon. He apparently was of partial Negro descent, for the record describes him as a "Malata Jew." (The theory has been advanced that he may have been born to a slave mother and a Jewish father, who set him free.) In 1668, when it was an offense punishable by a month's prison sentence to be absent from church on Sunday, Sollomon was arrested for traveling toward New Hampshire on the Christian holy day. There is no record of the punishment meted out to him.

The Boston tax list in 1674 included the name of Rowland Gideon, "ye Jew." The next year he was co-plaintiff with another Jew in a lawsuit in which he won a judgment of 112 pounds. The defendant appealed. Gideon, in his reply, mentioned his Jewish origin and reminded the court that God had informed "owr Father (Moses) that the same Law should bee for the stranger & sojourner as for the Jssraellits." Apparently he felt he was being discriminated against because of his religion and therefore threw himself on the mercy of the judge and jury, "praing for the prosperity of yowr Gouermn, and that yow may bee further fathers of this scatered Nation."

There were only a few Jewish families in the Boston area in the early years of the eighteenth century. When a death occurred the body had to be shipped to Newport, Rhode Island, for burial in the Jewish cemetery there. But in the early 1700s two Boston Jews, Michael Asher and Isaac Solomon, partners in the snuff business, set aside a small plot of land as a cemetery "for the Jewish Nation."

Early in the 1700s a Jewish merchant, Isaac Lopez, was elected constable in Boston. The job involved maintaining public order and collecting taxes. The record shows that Lopez, after the election, decided to pay the fine that was provided for those declining to serve, rather than assume the onerous duties and the financial impositions of the post.

The first Jew to be granted a degree from Harvard—or from any other American college—was Judah Monis, who had had rabbinical training in Leghorn and Amsterdam before emigrating to America. He was given an honorary Master of Arts because he had just written a new Hebrew grammar. (Two years later Monis underwent the hoped-for conversion to Christianity and was appointed to the Harvard faculty.)

Jewish Names Are Readopted

In the Massachusetts Bay Colony the laws were so liberal that it was possible for immigrants who had been Marranos to give up the pretext of being Catholics and openly practice their own religion. Many also dropped their Spanish-sounding names and resumed their original more Jewish names.

Because both the Dutch and the British lay claim to the Connecticut Valley, great rivalry developed between them. Merchants from New Amsterdam who came into the valley were accused of selling firearms to the Indians. This led to a ban on the sale of any goods by foreigners. Those few Jews who emigrated from New Amsterdam to the Connecticut Valley during the 1700s were the victims of this xenophobia. They were discriminated against not because of their religion but because most of them came from New Amsterdam. One of the victims was a merchant from New Amsterdam, who is named in court records simply as "David the Jew." His business methods apparently landed him in the hands of the law, for the General Court in Hartford fined him twenty shillings for "going into houses when the heads of ye families were absent, and tradeing prvision with the children." Later, however, "David the Jew" was permitted to take up permanent residence in Hartford, despite the fact that Connecticut had a strictly enforced law which provided that no one would be accepted as an inhabitant of a town unless he was "of an honest conversation" and was accepted by a majority of the townspeople.

Considering He Is a Jew . . .

In 1670, in the case of another Jew, the Hartford court found "that the sayd Jacob Lucina hath been frequent and notorious in his lascivious daliance and wanton carriage & profers to severall women," and he was fined £20. The defendant appealed and the General Court in its finding stated: "The court see cause considering he is a Jew, to shew him what fauore they may, abate him teen pownds of his fine." But Lucina objected to paying even half the original fine and solicited the help of a friend, Asser Levy, the Jewish leader in New Amsterdam. A few months later the court again halved the fine, "as a token of their respect to the sayd Mr. Assur Levy."

A report on New Haven written in 1772 told of a family of

eight or ten Venetian Jews who conducted services each Sabbath in "a room that had been equipped with special fittings." This may have been the first synagogue in the Connecticut Valley, if it can properly be called a synagogue.

3

AT LAST, A RECOGNIZED RELIGION

Ten years after the *St. Charles* sailed into the harbor of New Amsterdam and disembarked the twenty-three Brazilian Jews, a fleet of British warships dropped anchor in the same harbor. Peter Stuyvesant surrendered the colony without a fight and almost overnight New Amsterdam became New York, title passing from the Dutch West India Company to His Royal Highness, James, Duke of York.

For those living in Jews' Alley, the question was what the new name, the new flag, and new laws would mean to *them*. During the past ten years they had won some rights, but still they were not permitted to pray together in public, to build a synagogue or to hold public office. They also were denied the right to engage in any handicrafts, and even though they paid taxes, their poor, their orphans, and their aged were not entitled to government aid.

At first the religious freedom the British granted residents of the colony applied only to "those who profess Christianity." It was many years before the Jews likewise benefited by an order which stated that "all persons of what Religion soever" were guaranteed against "any disturbance or disquiet whatsoever for and by reason of their differing opinions in matter of Religion" as long as they did not disturb the public peace or molest others "in ye free exercise of their Religion."

What's Important Is a Minyan

The Jews of New York, while still quietly coming together for prayer in private, periodically presented a petition for the right to build a synagogue. The British, like the Dutch before them, shunted such petitions from governor to mayor to aldermen, and back again, and always ended up saying an emphatic "No!" So the Jews did their praying under the trees or in private homes. After all, the *place* of the praying was irrelevant. What was important was that they have a *minyan*—the ten adult male Jews of any locality who, coming together in one place, comprise all that Judaism says is necessary for public worship. (Even the word *synagogue* does not mean what many suppose. It does not connote what *church* does to a Christian: "the Lord's house" or "a place of worship." Coming from the Greek word *synagoge*, it means "a bringing together; an assembly.") Under the laws of Judaism, the ten men can meet in a field, a cave, under the trees, in a rented room, or in a million-dollar temple; it makes no difference.

So they waited, and while they waited they prayed humbly. The records do not show exactly when the British authorities relented, but some years before 1700 the members of Shearith Israel began gathering for prayers in an old grist mill which had recently been used by the Dutch as a church. Then they rented for £8 a year, from a Dutch shoemaker, a one-and-a-half-story house on what is now Beaver Street, between Broadway and Broad. At that time there were 855 families in New York, only twenty of them, or less than two percent, Jewish. There were five Christian churches.

Why a Rabbi Is Not Essential

There was no possibility of employing a rabbi, for no qualified person was available in North America, and the congregation was financially unable to send abroad for one. However, in Judaism a rabbi is not essential to the conduct of religious services, as a priest is to the conduct of a Catholic Mass, or a minister to the conduct of most Protestant services. All Jewish men who have had a proper Jewish education are supposed to know the order of the services and the essentials of Jewish ritual. A rabbi is primarily a teacher and, as such, is essential for the religious well-being and spiritual growth of a community, but under unusual conditions, as in New York in Colonial days, it was possible for a Jewish community to function without such religious guidance. Instead of employing a rabbi, Shearith Israel engaged a *hazzan*. This is the Hebrew word for "superintendent" or "officer." In ancient times a *hazzan* was a temple functionary. In modern times he is the cantor, who chants the services and officiates at weddings, funerals, circumcisions, and similar religious functions. A *hazzan* preaches only by special request. In early Colonial days, because there were no rabbis, the *hazzanim* took on an untraditional importance. At first they were volunteers, serving without compensation. In Colonial times the civil authorities recognized the *hazzanim* as being of equal rank and importance to Protestant ministers. They were exempt from military service and were free of certain other civil obligations. Most early American Jewish communities also had a *shohet* or ritual slaughterer, and a *shammash* or beadle.

£50 Plus Cordwood and Matzah

The first paid official at Shearith Israel was Saul Pardo, a merchant who had been admitted to burgher rights in 1685 and who had translated Pardo (meaning "brown") into English and was listed in congregational records as Saul Brown. His title was *hazzan* and for reading the services he was paid £50 a year and given six cords of firewood and enough *matzah* (the unleavened bread used at Passover) for his entire family. A salary of £16 a year plus wood and *matzah* was paid to the *shammash* who assisted the *hazzan*, kept the rented quarters clean, and saw that candles were always on hand.

Leadership in this and other early Jewish communities in America was vested in a board of officers known as the *junta* or *adjunta* or *mahamad*, a standing committee headed by the *parnas* or president, who kept the synagogue records, maintained discipline, imposed fines, and awarded honors. Shearith Israel's first president was Luis Gomez, merchant, who was a generous supporter of the congregation's activities.

The Hazzan's Humble Petition

In 1710 Abraham De Lucena, a prominent merchant and ship-owner, who had taken over the duties of *hazzan*, dispatched the following very misspelled communication to the New York authorities:

> The humble petition of Abraham De Lucena, minister of the Jewish nation, resideing at the city of New York, sheweth that yo'r petitioner's predecessors, ministers of the Jewish nation, residing at the city of New York, by reason of their ministerial ffunction, have from time to time beene exempted by the government, not only from boarding any officer civil or military, within this city, but likewise beene excus'd from severall duties and services incumbent upon the inhabitants of this city.
>
> Wherefore yo'r petitioner most humbly beggs yo'r Excellencies care of him (in consideration of his ministeriall ffunction) that hee may likewise be excused from all such offices, duties, and services, and be allowed the like priviledges and advantages within this city, as have formerly beene granted to his said predecessors as ministers aforesaid, and that yo'r Excellencey will be pleased to give such directions in the premisses as to yo'r Excellencey shall deem meet.
>
> And yo'r Excellencies petitioner, as in duty bound, shall ever pray, etc.
>
> Abraham De Lucena.

In 1711 De Lucena and six other New York Jews contributed to a fund for building a steeple on Trinity Episcopal Church in New York. Some years later in Philadelphia a group of Christians helped pay off the mortgage on a synagogue there. While in Europe anti-Semitic hatred and persecution were still taking a toll of Jewish lives, here in the New World something perhaps unique in history was occurring: men of one religion were helping men of another build religious structures, out of a feeling that they were all struggling toward a common goal, no matter how different might be their methods and approaches. The contributions of De Lucena and his friends to the Trinity Church steeple fund also indicated that the New York Jews by now were so secure in their own rights that they could be the benefactors of others.

For £100, One Loaf of Sugar, One Pound of Tea

In 1729 Congregation Shearith Israel bought a piece of land on Mill Street, not far from their rented quarters, for £100, one loaf of sugar and one pound of tea. Because the law still did not permit a Jewish religious body to own property, the lot had to be purchased in the names of four individuals. A moving appeal for funds to build a synagogue was sent to individual Jews and Jewish communities, not only in the Colonies, but abroad. One that went to Jamaica, in Spanish, said in part:

> We earnestly request you all as well as you *haham* (rabbi) to communicate this petition to the members of your holy *Kaal* (congregation or assembly) so that they may contribute all they can to the building of a holy synagogue which we have decided with the help of God to erect. We have already purchased an appropriate site for the edifice and another for a cemetery, but for want of sufficient means, the *Yehudim* (Jews) here being but a few, we have not been able to carry out our intentions, and until our hopes are realized, we must continue for the present to congregate in a synagogue rented from a *goy* (non-Jew).
>
> May the Almighty grant our wish and may He move your hearts that you may to the best of your ability assist us in the matter, and also help us to build a fence around the cemetery. And we will ever pray that you may prosper and increase in holy service. Amen.

Financial assistance came from many sources. The chief rabbi of Curaçao sent 264 pieces of eight (Spanish coins) which he had collected from his congregants. Other gifts came from Amsterdam, Barbados, and Jamaica. But the major contributions were made by the Jews of New York themselves. Handmade bricks had to be imported from England and were so expensive that each member of the community agreed to buy a certain number of bricks. Others gave mortar, or windows, or even part of a window. One man offered to pay for engraving the Ten Commandments, one shilling per commandment.

The First in North America

The little brick synagogue was finally completed early in 1730. It was set back as far as possible from the street, following the European custom of thus protecting such a building from attack, and was surrounded by a white picket fence. The building was 35 feet long. Even though at one end there was a gallery for the women, the inside height was only 21 feet. The bricks of the walls were blue on the outside. A perpetual lamp burned in front of the Ark. This first synagogue in North America was no larger than a medium-sized room but the members of Shearith Israel were as proud of it as if it were a towering structure of stone and steel. Here was substantial proof, they knew, that Judaism now, for the first time, was a recognized religion in North America.

Jewish law requires that a Jewish boy shall be circumcized on the eighth day, but in the American Colonies there were few men qualified to perform the religious operation. Apparently Rhode Island had no *mohel* (circumciser), for in the archives there is a letter sent on August 8, 1756, by Abraham I. Abrahams, a New York merchant who doubled as a *mohel*, to Aaron Lopez in Newport, saying in part:

> I take it as a great honour in your presenting me with the circumcising your son. Shou'd been glad it had been sooner on acc't of my prentice being out of his time and gone and will make it difficult for me to go just now. And another reason, my Cousin Manuel and self have enter'd in the business of dstilling and tobacco manufactur. However, if I can possibly come in a little while hence will gladly do it, as nothing wou'd be more pleasure

than to see my good friends att your place which I realy long
to do. In my next will be more particular as to my coming. Till
then I am, with respect s'r

Your very hum'le ser't,
Abr'm I. Abrahams.
My spouse joins her complim'ts to you, spouse, & family.

Seventeen days later Mr. Abrahams again wrote to Mr. Lopez:

I am sorry to tell you that my bussiness will not admit of
my being with you yet. Hope my brother will be here soon as
have had an acc't of his arrival. However as it is very uncertain
when I shall be able to come, having two trades in mind, and
have hear'd that Doct'r Marks is releas'd out of gaol (jail). Believe
he wou'd willingly go if you was to write him. Think he gladly
go. Nothing wou'd give me more pleasure than to be with my
friends, but as yet I can't. Pray make my excuse to them for not
writing being in a great hurry of bussiness. My spouse joins
her best respects to you, family, Mr. Moses Lopez, Mr. Rivera, and
theirs, with, s'r,

Y'r very hum'le serv't,
Abr'm I. Abrahams.

It was not until mid-February of the next year that Abrahams
went to Newport and finally performed the rite.

On Foot, On Horseback to Study Judaism

In the days when Congregation Shearith Israel was renting the
shoemaker's building, a school was established called the *Yeshivath
Minhat Areb*. Later, when a wooden community house was built,
children came on foot and on horseback from all over Manhattan
Island to sit on bare wooden benches and study religious subjects.
In 1755 the school began offering instruction in both secular and
religious subjects, with "English Reading Writing & Cyphering" included in the curriculum. This was an innovation. Since the days
of the prophets, Judaism had always attached importance to learning

but the traditional Jewish school stressed Hebraic textual studies.

At first the one and only instructor was the *hazzan*, but in 1762 the Junta decided to employ a full-time teacher at a salary of £20 a year, "plus prerequisites." Parents who could afford it were to supplement this salary with individual contributions of £8 per child. The first full-time teacher was the *mohel*, Mr. Abrahams. The only Jew to be graduated before the Revolution from Kings College (which later became Columbia University) was Isaac Abrahams, who is presumed to have been the son of the schoolmaster and one of his pupils in the synagogue school. Under Abrahams the children studied Spanish, English composition, and arithmetic, but most of the six hours spent each day in the classroom was devoted to Hebrew. In some records Abrahams is called the *rabby* or *ribbi*, but he never actually was the rabbi of the congregation. The confusion grows out of the fact that in both Yiddish and Hebrew *reb* or *rebbi* or *rabbi* is used to signify a wise man or teacher, as well as the spiritual leader of a congregation.

If the Hazzan Does Not Misbehave

An insight into life in the New York congregation in the middle of the eighteenth century is provided by correspondence between the officers of Shearith Israel and a Sephardic congregation in London called *The Gate of Heaven*. The New Yorkers wrote that they wished to employ, as *hazzan*, a young, unmarried man of sound character, who knew Hebrew, English, and Spanish, who sang well, and who would be able to lead services as well as instruct the young. Some months later, in another letter, they restated their needs: ". . . wee have no objections to a marr'ed man, but would choose one rather if with a small family and not attended with much charge, as our congregation is small, and few that are able to contribute to support thereof.

"The salary of fifty pounds sterling is exclusive of voluntary offerings, and marriages and other things of that kind, also of the fees of those children whose parents are able to pay for thire schoolings. Should a proper person present, wee shall defray the reasonable expense of thire sea store and passage, which wee shall desire Mr. Moses Franks to supply. As to settling a salary for a term or years or returning at our expense, on any little disquit which he might take, it is not agreeable to the congregation, and wee presume might be attended with bad consequence, if the person so fixed should build thereon, and be the very means of producing some kiend of dislike which wee would willingly avoid. But wee think there will be no reason to doubt his continuance should he not misbehave, which wee hope will not happen, as wee are confident that your goodness would not recommend any but such as may appear proper and worthy thereof."

London finally supplied New York with a *hazzan* who served Shearith Israel well for seven years before getting homesick and returning to England.

Shearith Israel Spoke for All

Shearith Israel, having built the first synagogue in North America, was taken as a model. Other congregations, as fast as they were formed, looked to Shearith Israel as spokesman for the entire Jewish population in Colonial America.

Because most of the original twenty-three immigrants had a Sephardic background and all of them had most recently lived in Brazil, where Sephardic practices were followed, Shearith Israel was organized along Sephardic lines. This meant that the chanting of the services, the pronunciation of Hebrew, the very order of the service were all different from what was familiar to Jews with an Ashkenazic background.

During the first third of the eighteenth century, America saw the start of what someday would be a mass movement of Ashkenazic Jews to America. The first instinct of those already here was to welcome the newcomers with open arms. They were fellow Jews. They had been, like the Sephardim, victims of cruel persecution. Their numbers and their abilities were needed to help build a new civilization in this new world. They were also needed to help strengthen the various Jewish communities. But tensions quickly developed.

Ashkenazim Versus Sephardim

The word *Ashkenazi* comes from Genesis III: 10:3, which names *Ashkenaz* as one of the great-grandsons of Noah. It was first used by Jews with a Spanish background to describe German Jews, for to them Germany was the East. Later, German Jews used it in referring to Jews of Hungary, Rumania, Poland, and Russia. (One is reminded that New Yorkers think of Cleveland as Middle West, whereas Middle West to a Clevelander means Iowa, while the West has a much different meaning to people living east of the Hudson River than to Chicagoans.) Gradually the word *Ashkenazi* took on pejorative colorations, just as Northerner and Southerner, Yankee and Rebel—words innocent in their original meaning—did in America. The Sephardim tended to look upon themselves as aristocrats, members of an elite group. They boasted of their intellectual background. They had had centuries of Western orientation. As Marranos they had been on intimate terms with nobility and had been advisers to emperors. They had been the first to found Jewish colonies in the New World. They referred to the Ashkenazim as *Tudescos*, a word that simply means Germans, yet before long developed unfavorable overtones.

The Ashkenazim, living for hundreds of years in the dreary ghettos of Central and Eastern Europe, had concentrated on spiritual matters, with the Torah and the Talmud as their refuge in times of trouble and despair. The ghetto forced them to eschew secular learning and to withdraw from the developing intellectual world, thus widening the gap between themselves and their neighbors. Enforced physical isolation was followed by intellectual sterility. But the ghetto Jews found comfort in devoting their entire energies to the tradition, especially to the Talmud, and they became self-appointed guardians of the Jewish heritage. Few Ashkenazim had grown wealthy, or had been named advisers to royalty, or had had intercourse of any sort with nobility. Not many had submitted to forced conversion. There was no Ashkenazic equivalent of the Marrano.

In their two widely separated areas of Europe (and the Middle East) the Sephardim and the Ashkenazim had developed along quite different lines. After their dispersal by the Spaniards, the Sephardim continued to speak Medieval Spanish wherever they went, even in such places as Tunisia, Morocco, Algeria, and America. They called it Ladino. It was—and is—Medieval Spanish, the Spanish their ancestors spoke, to which some words have been added from Hebrew and the languages of the countries across which the Spanish Jews were scattered. Most of the Ashkenazim came to America speaking Yiddish, which started out as Medieval German, to which many Hebrew and Slav words have been added. Unlike Ladino, Yiddish is written in Hebrew characters.

Both Prayed in Hebrew, But . . .

Both Sephardim and Ashkenazim prayed in Hebrew, but their pronunciation was different enough to make a stranger wonder if they were speaking the same words. The difference was in the sound given to vowels, and the accent. Also, each group had a different way of chanting. Even more noticeable, the prayers themselves were different. Both groups lived by the same basic Mosaic law and agreed on all important theological points, but the Sephardim used in their service poems that were foreign to the Ashkenazim. Also, the Sephardim followed some religious customs utterly unknown to the Jews from Eastern Europe.

And so the Ashkenazim and the Sephardim met in such places as New York and attempted to amalgamate. For the next hundred years the story of Judaism in America would be interlaced with this Ashkenazic-Sephardic conflict, until finally it would be decided by simple mathematics.

When the twenty-three Brazilian Jews were given permission to remain in New Amsterdam the Dutch stipulated that they must care for their own sick, their own poor, their own aged. Later, the British, although taxing New York Jews like anyone else, still refused them the municipal services that others received. There is no evidence that Congregation Shearith Israel ever objected. Synagogue records show many expenditures for the needy, even payment of doctors' bills. When needy Jews arrived in New York from abroad or even from other colonies, they were boarded at the home of the *shammash*, with the congregation bearing the expense. There is no evidence that the Jewish community at any time in the Colonial period ever turned to the government for help. Instead, being steeped in Judaism, they looked upon it not only as a duty but a privilege to help their own people in distress. They had learned from Maimonides and their other learned men the rules of charity. In time this would become one of their major contributions to the new land to which they had come in search of freedom.

4

AND LET THEM MAKE ME A SANCTUARY

How came they here?

Henry Wadsworth Longfellow asked the question in a poem he wrote in 1852 about the Jewish cemetery in Newport, Rhode Island. The answer is that they came to Newport and made it into the second largest Jewish community in the Colonies principally because of Roger Williams, who therefore plays an important role in the story of American Judaism.

Williams advocated religious freedom as an inherent right of the people, rather than as a mere toleration that could be denied at the government's will. He called it God's desire that freedom of worship should be enjoyed by men of all nations, whether Christians, Moslems, Jews, or pagans.

Everywhere—in the Old World as well as the New—state and church in those days were at least linked. Often one dominated and controlled the other. Minorities were helpless victims of an almost intolerable situation. Williams, who had had years of experience as a member of a minority in England, championed the rights of all minorities. One biographer described him as "a rebel against all the stupidities that interposed a barrier betwixt men and the fellowship of their dreams." He not only bitterly opposed the idea of a church-state, but with bold and vivid phrases condemned forced conversions. He once stated his attitude toward militant proselytizing these words: "That cannot be a true religion which needs carnal weapons to uphold it." He even condemned white colonists for stealing land from the Indians.

The Promise of Absolute Religious Freedom

This young religious radical—bold, talented, and aggressive (his enemies called him "a troublesome fool")—began his fight for religious toleration in Massachusetts. When officials of that Colony threatened to send him back to England, he fled into the wilderness beyond Massachusetts, bought land from the Indians, and founded Providence. There he began putting his iconoclastic ideas into practice. In Providence absolute freedom of worship would be assured for everyone—for Christians of whatever hue and also for Jews. "I desire," said Williams, "not that liberty for myself which I would not freely and impartially weigh out to all the consciences of the world besides; therefore, I humbly conceive that it is the express and absolute duty of the civil powers to proclaim an absolute freedom of conscience in all the world."

In the Colony's charter of 1644 it was made clear that the will of the majority would prevail but "only in civil things." Anything to do with religion was not to be a matter of government competency. When a second charter was obtained in 1663, the Rhode Islanders were able to wring from Charles II a declaration that no one should be molested in the Colony because of his religion, provided he did not disturb the peace.

In a letter to a friend, Williams wrote that "the state is comparable to a heavily loaded passenger ship crossing the ocean. The Catholics, Protestants, Jews, and Turks on board are not required to attend the ship's religious services, nor are they forced to give up their own form of worship. However, the captain has the duty of maintaining order and discipline among passengers and crew alike."

Williams Champions English Jews

One of the vital issues of the period was whether England should open its doors to Jews, who, under Edward I, had been forced to flee Britain. There were those who wanted to keep England free of

Jews forever. Williams, on a visit home to England, pitted both voice and pen against this group. In a pamphlet he denounced the "oppressions, incivilities and inhumanities" of England toward the Jews and called on Christians to take the initiative in breaking down "that superstitious wall between us Gentiles and the Jews" and in making way for "their free and peaceable Habitation amongst us."

Williams' boldness in putting his ideas into practice drew the fire of critics on both sides of the ocean. The Dutch Reformed leader of New Amsterdam called the Rhode Island Colony "the receptacle of all sorts of riff-raff people . . . nothing else than the sewer of New England. All the cranks of New England retire hither."

Among those who went to this new haven were some Jews. They were drawn by the fact that here at last was a place to live that had no established church. Also, Williams had specifically invited Jews to settle in his Colony. He called frequently for "free and peaceable Habitation" of Jews and Christians together.

First Rabbi in New World

One of the first Jewish residents of Williams' colony was Mordecai Campanelli. When the Portuguese Jews living in Brazil under Dutch rule prospered to the extent that they could afford a rabbi, they asked friends and relatives in Amsterdam to select one for them. Isaac Aboab was the man chosen. He had the double distinction of being the first rabbi as well as the first Jewish author in the New World. He took with him to Brazil a young friend, Mordecai Campanelli, who, after the Portuguese reconquered Brazil, moved on to Rhode Island, attracted by Williams and his liberalism, and became one of the early settlers of Newport, the chief port of the new Colony. He changed his name to Campanal, a name that appears often in the history of Newport. One document (the authenticity of which has been questioned) tells how in 1658 the first Masonic meeting of record in the New World was held in Campanal's home in Newport. The document says: "Wee mett att y House off Mordecai Campunall and affter Synagof Wee gave Abm Moses the degrees of Macourie."

Isolation But Not in Death

Although many of the pioneer American Jews, without complaint, led isolated lives, in little contact with their own people, they had a dread of being alone in death. That was why the first request generally made by a new Jewish community in America was for a plot of land to serve as a common burial ground. In Newport a plot was purchased by Mordecai Campanal and Moses Pacheche, a native of Hamburg, Germany. It was to be used by "Jews and their Nation, Society or Friends." By Longfellow's day the graveyard was covered with stones bearing such names as Lopez, Rivera, Touro, Lucena, Pollak. It was those names, those stones, that inspired Longfellow to write:

> *How strange it seems! These Hebrews in their graves*
> *Close by the street of this fair seaport town,*
> *Silent beside the never-silent waves,*
> *At rest in all this moving up and down!*

Campanal sailed in 1678 to the Barbados to visit relatives and friends. This island, the easternmost bit of land in the West Indies, had been settled by the British in 1627. By now it was actively engaged in exporting molasses and rum to Europe and North America. Campanal's glowing stories of life in Rhode Island resulted in four or five families of Campanellis and several other Jewish families moving to Newport. They were all merchants, already experienced in trade between the Colonies of the New World, and it is no wonder that they prospered after reaching Newport. But their success led to trouble.

Civil Equality for Jews

Major William Dyer, whose mother, a Quaker, had been hanged in Boston as a heretic, was Surveyor-General of Customs for all the British Colonies, with headquarters in Boston. He seized ships and imposed fines in an arbitrary manner that made him both feared and hated. In 1685 he brought suit against eight Jewish merchants from Barbados—one woman and seven men, four bearing the name Campernell or Campanelli or Campanal or Campanell. They were charged with violating the Navigation Laws by trafficking as aliens in molasses and rum from overseas, the export-import business being closed to "foreigners." Pending trial, the property of all the defendants was seized. Dyer failed to appear on the day set but the trial was held anyway, with the court ruling in favor of the defendants. Dyer was obliged to pay the court costs and the property that had been seized was returned to the eight Jews. This case established the principle of civil equality for Jewish settlers in Rhode Island. A sequel to the story is that three years later Abraham Campanell, one of the defendants, was licensed as a freeman, the only Jew to be accorded this privilege in the entire history of Colonial Rhode Island. While there was no state religion in Roger Williams' colony and while each individual could worship God as he pleased, Catholics and non-Christians could neither vote nor hold office— except the unique Jew, Abraham Campanell.

The Campanells fanned out from Newport, some going to Boston, where one of them landed in trouble. In Colonial days inhabitants of any town had certain privileges, including the use of the town common for pasturing animals, and the right to be supported by the community in case of distress. There were strict regulations that determined just who was an inhabitant and who could remain in a town. One such law read:

> It is ordered that no inhabitant shall entertaine man or woman from any towne or countrye as a sojourner or inmate with an intent to remain here, butt shall give notice thereof to the Selectmen of the towne for their approbation within 8 days after their cominge to the towne upon penalty of twenty shillings.

Warned Out of Boston

When the town officials received such a notice they issued an order commanding the visitor to depart within a certain time limit. This was called a "warning out." In 1726 one David Campanell, who is described in the records as "a Jew from Rhode Island," was warned out of Boston. Instead of returning to Rhode Island, he continued north and east until he came to the farming-fishing community of Ipswich, where he settled down and raised a family. The town record of his death lists him as "David Campanell, a Jew," but some of his descendants, who scattered across New England, became converts to Christianity. Various branches of the family spelled the family name differently: Campernall, Campanal, Campnell, Campel, and even Campbell.

It was on the centenary of the settlement of the first Jews in Newport in 1658 that the Jewish community, calling itself Congregation Yeshuat Israel (Salvation of Israel), purchased for £1500 a piece of property 92 by 106 feet in what was then the outskirts of the city. Two of the three Jewish merchants whose names are on the deed had been interested in the construction of Newport's Redwood Library, a beautiful classical Colonial building. It had been designed by Peter Harrison, a British architect then living in Newport, to whom the Jewish leaders now turned with a request that he design their synagogue. While he worked on the plans, they addressed the following letter to Shearith Israel Congregation in New York:

Newport, R.I. Adar 22d 5519
(March 21, 1759)

Gent.

The Pious Intentions of a Congregation yet in its Infancy, we desire may plead a sufficient excuse, for this Address; sincerely desirous to establish a regular Congregation in this Town we therefor, have Lately purchased a suitable Lot of Land whereupon we design to Build a Sinaguogue; & for furthering our said Intentions, we have Likewise by Subscription raised a small Fund, wherewith to Begin, and carry on the Work and which in due Time, we hope to see fully compleated. At present finding our Abilities not equal to our wishes, for finishing the Work, in so short a Time as we desire, we have resolved to crave the Asstance of the several Congregations in America, and as the Feast of the Passover is near at Hand, a Time when there will be the greatest appearance of our Brethren at New York; we embrace this opportunity to acquaint you with our proceedings, and Intentions, relative thereto;

Intreating you to communicate the same, to the Congregation, at New York, & to supplicate for us, their charitable assistance, toward carrying on this work; either by a Freewill Offering in the Sinagogue; or by Subscription, or in any way which may be agreeable to you.

Wehn we reflect on how much it is our Duty, to Instruct Children, on the Path of Vertuous Religion & how unhappy the portions must be of those Children, and their Parents, who are thro necessity, educated in a place where they must remain almost Totally uninstructed, in our most Holy & Divine Law, our Rites & Ceremonies; & from which place, they may perhaps never have it in their power to depart; when we farther reflect on how much it is our Duty to assist the Distressed; & when we consider the extensive Usefullness of a Charity, like this for which we now supplicate assistance; we can entertain no Doubt of your Zeal to promote this good Work.

That God Almighty will be pleased to direct your Councils, prosper your Vertuous Axtions, and Intentions, give us Peace, and very soon the Redeemer of Zion, is and shall be the Devout Prayer of

Gent.

Your obedient & very hume Servts

Jacob Rods Rivera	Abm Rs Reveira
Jacob Isaacks	Isaac Polock
I. Hart	Moses Lopez
Aaron Lopez	Isaac Elizer
	Moses Levy

Within a few days they received this reply:

Gentn.

Conformable to your desire a *Nedaba* (offering) was made in our Synagogue the Seventh day of *Pesah* (Passover) when a contribution of £149:6 was offered towards building at New Port a place of worship to Almighty God. Your pious design was a sufficient inducement to promote the Success of your request, we heatly wish our mite may enable you to go on with the Holy building and that you may be a Religious & prosperous Congregation.

We must now desire you will send orders for the money.

We sincerely wish you success in all your Laudable undertakings,

and that our God may graciously enable his People to do *Mitzvot*
(meritorious action done in response to divine command) is the
unfeign'd prayer of

Gentn.

Appeals were also sent to the Jewish congregations in half a
dozen other cities in both the New World and Europe. The response
was generous. Ground was broken on August 1, 1759. Six corner-
stones were laid, so that the six largest subscribers could share the
honors. Four were for the synagogue itself and two for a Hebrew
school. The architect had warned them that attaching a school building to the synagogue would spoil the simplicity and beauty of his
original design, but they argued that education was an integral part
of their religion; that the children were more important than beauty.
Several weeks later 196,715 bricks for the outer walls arrived from
abroad. But twenty months after ground-breaking, the congregation
ran out of funds and an SOS was sent to Shearith Israel in New York.
Because of rising costs, said the letter, the building could not be
completed unless more outside help came from somewhere. Three
years after ground-breaking the following call went out for furnish-
ings:

Newport July 25, 1762.

Gent.

   As we have now contracted with Workmen, who are actually
at Work, to compleat the *Hechal* (the ark in which the Scrolls
of the Law are kept), *Tebah* (the reading platform), and Benches
of our Synagogue, are in great hopes same will be furnished by
Rosh Ha-Shanah (the Jewish New Year): We are getting ready
such furniture & Utensils as are needfull, for which reason our
Mahamad (body of trustees) desires me to address this to you,
Gentlemen, that you will be so kind as to make inquiry, who made
any offerings of Furniture & Ornaments toward this pious undertaking, to receive & forward the same to us with convenient speed;
that it may be here ready against the Time of Consecrating the
holy Fabrick. . . .

Your very hum. Servt.
Moses Lopez
Parnas.

In response to that appeal they received a *tamid* (the perpetual light that burns in front of the Ark), some candlesticks, a *tebah*, and 100 pounds of wax. From Amsterdam came a *Torah* scroll 200 years old.

About the time of the ground-breaking, Isaac de Abraham Touro, who had studied in some of the most celebrated academies in Europe, arrived in Newport from Jamaica and was engaged as *hazzan*.

Strangely, the best historical account of Jewish life in Newport has come down to us from a man who not only was not a Jew himself, but was the Congregational minister in Newport and later became president of Yale University, the Reverend Ezra Stiles. He became a close friend of Touro, whom he plied with questions, noting the answers in a diary he kept meticulously. Also, in this diary he noted the result of a census he took in Newport in 1760: fifteen Jewish families, a total of fifty-eight people.

In these times there was no ordained rabbi in all of North America, but transient rabbis often stopped off in the Colonies, either to raise funds for needy Jews in Palestine, or on their way to accept posts in Jewish communities in the Caribbean, which, because of their size and wealth, could afford the services of such European-trained scholars. Whenever a rabbi came through Newport the Reverend Mr. Stiles would seek him out and try to engage him in a discussion of profound theological matters, and then he would summarize the conversation in his diary. Before his departure for Yale put an end to these indulgences, he noted in his diary such conversations with six visiting rabbis.

Synagogue Yeshat Israel Dedicated

The Newport synagogue was dedicated on December 2, 1763, the first day of Hanukkah, the Festival of Lights. Some Christians, not ever having seen a synagogue until now, attended the dedication, curious about what a Jewish religious service was like. The Congregational minister, who was in the audience, gave this description of the building in an entry in his diary: "The Synagogue is about perhaps fourty feet long & 30 wide, of Brick on a Foundation of free stone; it was begun about two years ago, & is now finished except the Porch & the Capitals of the Pillars. The Front representation of the holy of holies, or its Partition Veil, consists only of wainscotted Breast Work on the East End, in the lower part of which four long Doors cover an upright Square Closet the depth of which is about a foot or the thickness of the Wall, & in this Apartment (vulgarly called the Ark) were deposited three Copies & Rolls of Pentateuch, written on Vellum or rather tanned Calf Skin; one of these rolls I was told by Dr. Touro was presented from Amsterdam & is Two Hundred years old, the Letters have the Rabbinical Flourishes.

"A Gallery for the Women runs round the whole inside, except the East End, supported by Columns of Ionic order, over which are placed correspondent Columns of the Corinthian order supporting the Ceiling of the Roof. The Depth of the Corinthian Pedestal is the height of the Balustrade which runs round the Gallery. The Pulpit for Reading the Law, is a raised Pew with an extended front table; this placed about the center of the Synagogue or nearer, the West End, being a Square embalustraded Comporting with the Length of the Indented Chancel before & at the Foot of the Ark.

"On the Middle of the North Side & Affixed to the Wall is a raised seat for the Parnas or Ruler, & for the Elders; the Breast and Neck interlaid with Chinese Mosaic Work. A Wainscotted Seat runs around Side of the Synagogue below, & another in the Gallery. There are no other Seats or Pews. There may be Eighty Souls of Jews or 15 families now in Town. The Synagogue has already cost Fifteen Hundred Pounds Sterling. There are to be five Lamps pendant from a lofty Ceiling."

That is a good technical description, yet it fails to convey any sense of the beauty and charm of this architectural gem. The white simplicity of the interior gave the synagogue an impression of clean freshness that it would still retain hundreds of years later. The cushions on the white wooden seats were of deep wine-red velvet. The ceiling was painted a celestial blue. Illumination came from white sperm candles in brass chandeliers. A hidden stairway led from the *bimah* (reader's table) to the basement. (It apparently was difficult for people who had been forced for so long to pray in secret to readjust completely to the freedom they enjoyed in Newport.)

America's Oldest Jewish Edifice

Newport was proud then and is still proud of the Touro Synagogue, which today has the distinction of being the oldest Jewish edifice in America still standing. It has the dignity and simplicity of the Jefferson and Lincoln Memorials in Washington, D.C. It was built to blend harmoniously with the Newport architecture of the day, and this was significant. The Jews of Newport were not required to live apart from the rest of the community, in a ghetto, as their ancestors had been forced to do in Europe, and as the original Jewish settlers of Jews' Alley, New Amsterdam, had lived. They were free citizens of a Colony in which religious liberty was of prime importance. They lived in the same sort of houses as their Christian neighbors, with whom they were working, hand in hand, to build a free and prosperous community. It was therefore fitting that their synagogue should have been built to blend in harmoniously with its architectural surroundings, symbolizing the role Judaism would play in an integrated American society. It was an indication of how this body of Jews had taken root in the New Land.

Shortly before the Reverend Mr. Stiles left to take up his duties at Yale, one more itinerant rabbi came to Newport—Haim Isaac Carigal, a native of Hebron, Palestine, who had been ordained a rabbi in 1750 at the age of seventeen and a few years later had begun extensive travels through the Middle East, Europe, and the West Indies. Now he was about forty, had a long beard and wore a "high furr cap." Stiles found him "learned and truly modest, far more so than I ever saw a Jew." Such a warm friendship developed between the Christian minister and the Jewish rabbi that after Carigal left Newport they engaged in a frequent and lengthy correspondence, one of Stiles' letters running to twenty-nine pages—all in Hebrew! After Carigal's death Stiles, now president of Yale, commissioned a painter to do a portrait of the rabbi which was hung in the Yale Library.

The First Jewish Sermon in Print

While still in Newport the rabbi was invited to preach the Shavuot sermon in the synagogue. He spoke for 47 minutes, all in Spanish, interspersed with Hebrew. The congregation, being predominantly Ashkenazic, probably understood little of what he said, but they were intrigued by his gestures, his oratory and his appearance, for, in the words of Stiles, "he was dressed in his furr cap, scarlet robe, green silk damask vest, and chintz undervest, girt with a sash or Turkish girdle, besides the alb with tzizith (fringes attached to undershirt)." They were probably also impressed, as Stiles was, with his "dignity and authority . . . mixt with modesty."

Later that year the sermon was translated into English, and printed and sold in Newport under the rather lengthy title: "A Sermon Preached at the Synagogue, in Newport, Rhode-Island, Called *The Salvation of Israel,* on the Day of Pentecost, or Feast of Weeks, the 6th. Day of the Month Sivan, the Year of the Creation, 5533, or, May 28, 1773, Being the Anniversary of Giving the Law at Mount Sinai: by the Venerable Hocham, the Learned Rabbi, Haijm Isaac Karigal, of the City of Hebron, near Jerusalem, in the Holy Land."

The sermon had the distinction of being the only one ever delivered in Colonial America by a Jew that was put into print. At one point in the sermon Rabbi Carigal cautioned his listeners: "Let us not pretend to be angels, while we are only men. . . ."

The Merchant Prince of New England

Just a few years before the purchase of ground for the synagogue, a young Marrano and his wife and children fled from Portugal to Newport, joining a half-brother who had been living in the seaport city for some years. It was a custom in the New World for Marranos to drop any Spanish names they might have acquired and to be remarried in a religious ceremony. Thus Duarte Lopez and his wife were married again and he changed his name to Aaron Lopez. Several years later Lisbon was hit by an earthquake. Among the thousands of people who fled the devastation were a group of Marranos who headed for Virginia. But a storm drove their ship into the harbor of Newport, where they decided to remain. Other Jewish immigrants came from Holland, Spain, and Poland. Many began as candlemakers, silversmiths, brass workers, and soap makers. Some brought from Portugal a knowledge of how to make candles from the sperm of whales, which were greatly superior to those made from tallow. Lopez and his father-in-law, Jacob Rodriguez Rivera, two of the most prominent leaders of the Newport Colony, established factory after factory for the manufacture of sperm candles, until they finally owned seventeen in all. Then Rivera invented a sperm oil lamp. Lopez concentrated on shipping. Before long he was being called "the merchant prince of New England." His thirty transatlantic vessels and more than one hundred coastal ships carried to distant places the output of Newport's many factories.

Although actually few in total number, the members of Congregation Jeshuat Israel played important roles in helping to make Newport one of the most important commercial cities of the Colonies, surpassed only by Boston and Philadelphia.

One of the basic precepts of Judaism is charity. At one time, when Amsterdam counted 22,000 Jews among its population, 4000 of them by regular charitable contributions were wholly or partially supporting the other 18,000. In like manner the Newport Jews demonstrated in many ways their concern for those less fortunate, assisting both new immigrants and prospective immigrants.

Penalized for Being a Jew

When Aaron Lopez was informed that the Portuguese Inquisition was becoming more active in its persecution of Jews, he realized that his own brother, then in Lisbon, was in a precarious situation, being related to a man who had publicly reverted to Judaism, so he sent one of his ships to Lisbon to pick up his brother, his brother's wife, and their three children.

Nine years after settling in Newport, Aaron Lopez and a friend, Isaac Eliezer, applied to the Superior Court of Rhode Island for naturalization. Failing there, they petitioned the General Assembly.

The lower house voted its approval, but on one condition: "Inasmuch as the said Aaron Lopez hath declared himself by religion a Jew, this Assembly doth not admit himself nor any other of that religion to the full freedom of this Colony. So that the said Aaron Lopez nor any other of said religion is not liable to be chosen into any office in this Colony nor allowed to give vote as a free man in choosing others."

But the upper house decided that it was not a matter for the Assembly, so Lopez and Eliezer appealed again to the courts. Ezra Stiles, because of his friendship for Jews in general and Lopez in particular, was in court the day the decision was handed down and described it thus in his diary:

"And on the Eleventh Day of March 1762 Sentence was pronounced upon the Criminals successively brot to the Bar; first upon Jno. Sherman a noted Thief & Burglar for Burglary, sentenced to be hanged; secondly upon Fortune an abandoned Negro who set Fire to the Warehouses at End Long Wharf 19th Febr. which did damage £5,000 ster. & endangered the Conflagration of the Town, sentenced to be hanged; Thirdly upon—Lawton for Perjury in swearing to an accot. which he had falsely forged against another, sentenced to the Pillory & . . . And then the Jews were called to hear their almost equally mortifying sentence and Judgt: which dismissed their Petition for Naturalization. Whether this was designedly, or accidental in proceeding upon the Business of Court I don't learn."

For the Mortification of Jews

The decision shocked Ezra Stiles as much as it did everyone else who thought of the Colony founded by Roger Williams (dead for the past seventy-nine years) as a place of religious freedom. The pertinent paragraph of the decision reads:

"Further by the charter granted to this Colony, it appears that the free and quiet enjoyment of the Christian religion and a desire of propagating the same were the principal views with which this Colony was settled, and by a law made and passed in the year 1663, no person who does not profess the Christian religion can be ad-

mitted freely in this Colony. This court, therefore, unanimously dis-
miss this petition as wholly inconsistent with the first principles
upon which the Colony was founded and a law of the same now in
force."

Stiles synthesized his opinion of the sentence in these words: "I
remark that Providence seems to make every Thing to work for
Mortification to the Jews, & to prevent their incorporating into any
Nation; that thus they may continue a distinct people."

The Jewish merchants of Newport took their religion so seriously
that they had to guard against it dominating even their social life.
In 1761 nine of them organized the first social club in America.
Every Wednesday night during the winter the members would
gather for card-playing, followed by an elaborate dinner of many
courses, during which numerous toasts were drunk in wine that had
been brought to the Colony in members' ships from remote parts of
the world. Strict rules governed even what could be discussed. The
eighth rule read: ". . . none of the members shall, during a dinner,
hold conversation relating to synagogue affairs, on the forfeit of four
bottles of good wine."

At Last a Really Free College

A few years before the Revolution, the Rhode Island General
Assembly issued a charter for the founding of the College of Rhode
Island (later renamed Brown University) in which all religious
tests were prohibited and students were assured of "full free Absolute
and uninterrupted Liberty of Conscience." Religious instruction of a
sectarian nature was prohibited, even though the college was founded
by and was under the direction of Baptists. The college began with
one student in 1765. Four years later only twenty-nine students had
matriculated. The institution needed not only students but money.
One of those who responded to an appeal for funds was Moses
Lindo, a prominent Jew of Charleston, South Carolina, who, in sending a generous contribution, wrote: "The Reason that induces me
to be a Benefactor to this College is your having no objection in
Admitting the Youth of our Nation without Interference in Prin-

ciples of Religion. If so my donation shall exceed beyond the limits of your Imagination."

At their next annual meeting the college trustees voted that: ". . . the children of Jews may be admitted into this Institution and entirely enjoy the freedom of their own religion without any Constraint or Imposition whatever."

At a later date a college law was adopted which said:

". . . if any student of this College shall deny the being of a God, the Existence of Virtue and Vice; or that the books of the old and new Testament are of divine Authority, or Suggest any Scruples of Nature or circulate Books of such pernicious Tendency, or frequent the Company of those who are known to favour such fatal Errors, He shall for the second Offense be absolutely and forever expelled from this College. Young gentlemen of the Hebrew nation are to be excepted from this Law."

The story of Rhode Island, from its founding to the Revolution, is one of the relatively happy chapters in the history of Judaism in America.

5

OUTPOSTS OF JUDAISM

Some Pennsylvania Jews bartered furs with the Indians on the fringes of civilization. Others, hungry for learning, flocked to Philadelphia when it became one of the educational centers of the New World. Jews with imagination and vision initiated vast projects in the field of trade and land development. For more than eighty years their individual names were scattered through the records of Colonial Pennsylvania. A German visitor to Philadelphia in 1734 reported that he had found the city "a seat of all religions and sects," among which he named Dumplers, Sabbatarians, Boehmites, Schwenckfelders, Trichtfelders, Wohlwunschers (Well-Wishers), Jews, and heathens. The first indication that Jews had grouped together and formed a community came in 1738 when they acquired a burial ground in Philadelphia in the name of Nathan Levy, son of the well-known New York merchant and shipowner. It was Levy who later put the following advertisement in the Franklin (Pa.) *Gazette:*

"Whereas many unthinking people have set up marks, and fir'd several shots against the fence of the Jewish burying-ground, which not only destroyed said fence, but also a tomb-stone inclosed in it; there being a brick-wall now erected, I must desire those sportsmen to forbear (for the future) firing against the said wall. If they do, whoever will inform, so that the offender be convicted thereof before a magistrate, shall have twenty shillings reward, paid by Nathan Levy."

The Faithful Observed Shabbat

By this time there were also Jewish groups in Easton, Reading, Heidelberg, and many other localities. The ten Jewish families of Lancaster, a frontier post in the fur trade that was soon to become the largest inland city in North America, also acquired a cemetery about this time. Religious services were occasionally held in private homes. Several diaries indicate that the Jews of Lancaster followed the Jewish dietary laws, and refused to do business on the Sabbath.

The Philadelphia congregation, as yet unnamed, met for prayers in a rented room on Sterling Alley. Then, in 1747, they organized formally, choosing the name *Mikveh Israel* (the Hope of Israel).

Two of the most illustrious Jewish families of Colonial Philadelphia were the Gratzes and the Franks. Bernard Gratz became a wealthy merchant and shipowner. At one time he owned most of what is now Chicago. With a brother, Michael, Bernard Gratz operated barges and pack trains that took manufactured goods to every inhabited corner of North America, helping to push the frontier farther and farther west. They also shipped furs, lumber, grain, and cattle abroad.

The Philadelphia Jews delayed so long in building a synagogue that when the news was conveyed to Bernard Gratz in 1761 that some definite building plans had finally been made, his informant wrote incredulously that "Eternity is nigh at hand." Sarcastically he speculated on whether the Philadelphia synagogue would use London Ashkenazic ritual or would follow the Prague or Polish style. His own conclusion was that they would probably follow "the Quaker ritual"—meaning that there would be no ritual at all. He ended his letter to Gratz with the wish that "I myself shall have the pleasure to see it built."

The synagogue was not built that year, although the Philadelphians sent a messenger to New York to get a Scroll of the Law on permanent loan. The New York congregation also presented the Philadelphians with a *yad* or silver pointer and some prayer books. Thus they gradually obtained the religious articles needed to carry on services. It was not until 1777, however, that enough money was finally collected to build a synagogue in the center of the city, on Cherry Alley.

Rachel's Way and Aaron Square

The Philadelphia Jewish community was unusual in its variety. Some members had been born in New York. Others were from England. Still others were Polish-speaking Prussians. But the majority were recent arrivals from Germany who, knowing that Shearith Israel in New York was Sephardic, assumed that to be Sephardic was to be American, and so, wanting to become thoroughly American as quickly as possible, they decided to adopt the Sephardic ritual and manner of organization. Although they wrote their constitution in Yiddish, they borrowed not only words and phrases but the whole organizational system from the constitution of the Sephardim in New York.

One of the Pennsylvania pioneers was Aaron Levy, who bought a tract in the north-central part of the state which he called Aaronsburg. He named one street after his wife—Rachel's Way—and an intersecting street for himself—Aaron's Square. Aaronsburg never became a metropolis, but it still exists, a town of a few hundred people. (Other places named after Jewish pioneers include: Altman, Georgia; Altheimer, Arkansas; Levy, New Mexico; Mayer, Arizona; Newman, California; Solomon, Kansas.)

How Georgia Was Settled

Georgia was settled partly because of British humanitarianism, partly out of a desire to rid London of thousands of paupers languishing in debtors' prisons. The first Jewish settlers in Georgia were sent there partly because of Jewish humanitarianism, partly out of a desire to rid London of thousands of destitute German and Polish Jews who had become a burden on the Sephardic community.

After James Oglethorpe obtained a charter for the new Colony from George II, a Board of Trustees was formed, which several times debated whether to include Jews in the human shipments they proposed to send across the Atlantic. Each time a majority voted against it, fearing the Jews would be a liability and would lessen the

value of the Colony. Georgia was to be one hundred percent Protestant Christian. Three Jewish canvassers employed by the trustees
to raise funds for the colonization had obtained from Jewish sources
a considerable sum of money, which they now felt justified in using
to charter a ship on which they sent to Georgia forty-three Jews
they managed to smuggle out of England. A majority of them were
Ashkenazim. This was in 1733. When they arrived in Savannah,
Oglethorpe was so displeased that he sought legal advice as to
whether he had the right to send them back whence they had come.
When he was advised against it, he gave them the forty-three plots
of land in Savannah.

A Shipload of Jews to the Rescue

Six months later another chartered ship brought forty more Jews,
almost all Sephardim. They had paid their own passage. The Earl
of Edgemont, a friend of Oglethorpe, left this written account of
what this second shipload of Jews found awaiting them: "The people were fallen to drinking rum, whereby we had lost twenty persons,
and their sickness was grown contagious, so that those who attended
them, nurses, etc., were all dead, but a ship of forty Jews arriving
with a physician, he entirely put a stop to it, so that not one died
afterwards."

The hero of this episode was Samuel Nuñez, who had been a
physician at the court in Lisbon and whose descendants changed the
family name to Noah.

Back in London, when the trustees heard that a shipload of Jews
had arrived at Savannah, they promptly dispatched a message to
Oglethorpe, hoping that the Jews "will meet with no sort of encouragement."

News of the good works of Dr. Nuñez failed to change their
minds. They wrote Oglethorpe that they were "much pleased with
the Behaviour of the Jewish Physician," yet hoped that Oglethorpe
had not "taken any other Method of rewarding him than in granting
of Lands."

Grapes That Were Almost Pellucid

The eighty-three Jews who arrived in Georgia in 1733 constituted the first and only mass migration of Jews to Colonial America, if it can be called that. They made up fourteen percent of the total population of the colony. In the first month after their arrival they established a congregation which they called *Mikyeh Israel* (the Hope of Israel).

One of the Sephardim, Abraham de Lyon, who had been a wine grower in his native Portugal, had brought with him some choice grape vine cuttings and after several years succeeded in producing grapes that were described as being "as big as a Man's Thumb, almost pellucid."

Oglethorpe, to his credit, from the start placed the Jews on an equal footing with the other settlers. John Martin Bolzius, a Christian minister in the town of Ebenezer, wrote in his journal: "Even the Jews, of whom several families are already in the country, enjoy all privileges the same as other colonists."

He added that they had the right to "carry muskets like the others in military style." Another cleric wrote that "they all in general behave themselves very well and are industrious in their business."

One reason for the lack of discrimination against the Jews of Savannah was that the other early settlers were such a mixed lot themselves, among them being Irish, Germans, Scotsmen, Salzburgers, and Moravians, even though it was an English Colony. Another reason was that the early Jewish settlers were men of zeal and industry, qualities that were welcome in burgeoning America.

More Religious Than the Christians

It was twenty years after the founding of Oglethorpe's Colony before any religious building was erected. Three reasons were given for the failure of the Jews to build a synagogue: general religious apathy among Christians and Jews alike; a schism between Sephardim and

Ashkenazim; a belief that pride would keep the authorities from giving permission for the erection of a Jewish religious building before any Christian church was built.

However, the Jewish settlers had brought with them a Scroll of the Law and circumcision equipment, and before long they received from abroad a *menorah* (candelabrum), some prayer books and other religious items.

Despite the lack of a synagogue, many met together in private homes for prayers. They also celebrated the Jewish holidays and lived by Jewish religious rules, thus earning the praise of John Wesley, founder of Methodism, who spent two years in Savannah and wrote that he found the Jews more religious than some of his own co-religionists.

Later, according to Bolzius, whose *Journal* is the best source on Savannah Jews in the early days, services were conducted in the Ashkenazic tradition in a ramshackle cabin "where men and women are completely separated." He also reported that they had a lay reader, "a youth who understands many languages, particularly Hebrew . . . and is paid by them." Still later they rented a house on Market Square for their religious gatherings.

While castigating the Christians of Savannah for their Godlessness, Bolzius indirectly praised the Jews, writing that "they (the Christians) drink, play, walk and pursue all worldly amusements with them (the Jews); indeed they desecrate Sunday with the Jews, which no Jew whatever would do on his Sabbath to please the Christians."

The first Jewish settlement in Georgia was not a great success. By 1740 only three or four families remained. Those who fled did so for the same reason most of the non-Jews left: no cheap labor was available, slavery was prohibited, land tenure was restricted, and distant fields looked greener. Also there was the threat that the Spanish, now in Florida, might push as far north as Savannah. Portuguese Jews, some of whom had had intimate experience with the Inquisition, feared for their lives, knowing that they might be burned at the stake as heretics if the Spaniards laid hands on them.

Later, a much more permanent settlement of Jews in Georgia was built up. By 1770 the total population of Savannah was 1175, among whom were seven Jewish families, including twenty-seven male adults—many more than were needed for a *minyan*.

Land for a Graveyard

In 1733 Oglethorpe had given the original Jewish settlers a lot for the burial of their dead, but its limits had never been exactly defined. Some twenty-nine years later the Jewish community petitioned for an additional piece of land, and the right to surround the cemetery with a fence. It was not until 1770 that the lower house of the legislature finally passed an act granting the Jews part of the Savannah Common for burial purposes. When the bill finally came before the upper house a group of taxpayers in a petition urged its defeat on the ground that surrounding property values would be reduced, as "no Person would choose to buy or rent an House whose Windows looked into a Burial Ground of any kind, particularly one belonging to a People who might be presumed from Prejudice of Education to have imbibed Principles entirely repugnant to those of our most holy Religion." After the bill was killed in the upper house, Mordecai Sheftall, a member of the Sephardic group, conveyed five acres of land to ten trustees, all merchants, on the understanding that the plot would be used forever as a burial ground "for all persons whatever professing the Jewish religion." It was also to be a site for a synagogue, but a synagogue was not built until many years later. Meanwhile, Sheftall furnished a room in his own house for group prayer. Sheftall was the first white child born in Savannah and the first Jewish child born anywhere in the South. As a young man he became the Jewish founding member of the Union Society, the first cooperative charity undertaking in America, which united Jews, Protestants, and Catholics in a common social cause.

Carolina, a Haven for Minorities

People of many different faiths flocked to the land called Carolina, which Charles II had granted to eight English noblemen in 1663. They were attracted by words—powerful words, words pregnant with promise. John Locke, British philosopher, who drew up a constitution for the new Colony, wrote into it a special provision designed to protect minorities: "No person whatsoever shall disturb, molest or persecute another for his speculative opinions in religion or his way of worship."

Referring specifically to Jews, Locke wrote: "If we allow the Jews to have private houses and dwelling places among us, why should we not allow them to have synagogues?"

While Locke's constitution provided that all taxpayers would be required to support the Church of England financially, it also stated that "seven persons agreeing in any religion shall constitute a church." Referring to the Indians, Locke said the settlers had "no right to expel them or use them ill" just because they did not happen to be Christians. He also argued against barring any prospective settlers because of their religion. "Jews, Heathens and other dissenters," he wrote, "should be well treated in the hope of eventually converting them."

Jews Voted in 1703

Locke's proposed constitution, while outlawing atheism and requiring everyone over seventeen years of age to identify himself with some particular religious group, at the same time granted complete freedom in choosing the group with which one wished to identify.

Despite the questionable motive for treating non-Christians well—to encourage conversion—Locke's liberality was welcome. While his proposed constitution was never actually adopted, his suggestions did much to foster a spirit of toleration for—if not understanding of—minority views and practices. South Carolina created a better religious, cultural, political, and economic climate, from the Jewish point of view, than any other Colony. In 1703 in South Carolina Jews voted in an election, probably for the first time anywhere in the western world. In South Carolina, Jews participated actively and freely in almost every area of life. South Carolina was the first Colony to elect a Jew to high public office.

Fifteen years after the founding of Charleston, the governor used a Jew (apparently a Sephardi) as an interpreter in the questioning of four Spanish-speaking Indians from Florida who had been taken prisoner. In Charleston, Jews had the right to worship as they pleased and to work at any occupation they chose, or to conduct any type of business, or to engage in any form of trade, without restriction. This was the sort of freedom that persecution-weary Old World Jews were seeking.

The House of God and the Mansion of Peace

In 1697 South Carolina passed a naturalization law providing that "all Aliens, male and female, of what nation whoever, which are now inhabitants of S. Car." should have the same rights as anyone born of English parents. This was of great importance to any Jews already living in South Carolina. How many there were is uncertain. It is known that among those naturalized almost immediately were four merchants, all believed to have been Jews.

Only a trickle of Jews reached South Carolina until the mid-1700s; then many came from England and others from the West Indies. Also, some of the original settlers of Savannah, disillusioned with not finding Utopia there, moved up into South Carolina. Finally the Jewish community was large enough to form a congregation, and so during the high holidays of 1749 they organized *Congregation Beth Elohim Unveh Shallom* (the House of God and the Mansion of Peace). In less than ten years they had the funds to acquire a synagogue—although only a converted dwelling place. The congregation selected from among its own number a president, a *hazzan*, and a third official they called a *rabbi*. This title went to Moses Cohen, a shopkeeper, whose name had appeared in local records some years earlier when he advertised for a ten-year-old Dutch runaway servant girl. The *hazzan* was Isaac Da Costa, a local merchant, who was a member of one of the best-known and wealthiest Spanish families, with branches in all parts of Europe. Among his qualifications for the post was his intensive religious training in London and his possession of some of the works of Maimonides, the twelfth-century Jewish physician-philosopher-theologian.

In South Carolina, in these times, farmers were growing a plant native to India called indigo, used in the manufacture of dye. Moses Lindo, a Jewish merchant and broker, who arrived in Charleston from London in 1756 to buy indigo, was so impressed with the political and civil rights Jews were accorded there that he decided to remain. He taught the planters around Charleston how to improve their yield, was appointed Surveyor-General of Indigo for the entire Colony, and had much to do with the economic development of South Carolina. In 1769 a New England minister came to Charleston to raise money for Rhode Island College, which had opened several years earlier. Because of the fund-raiser's promise about the freedom the college would grant to Jewish students, Charleston Jewry was generous in its contributions, Lindo even more so than the others.

Maryland, for Christians Only

Catholics were the most persecuted people in England in the 1700s. They were not permitted to live within ten miles of London and if they wished to travel more than five miles from their place of residence they needed a special permit. In early America they were also the most discriminated against group. One Colony after another denied them the right to practice their religion, to vote, to become freemen, or even, in some cases, to own property. When Maryland was founded by Lord Baltimore, a Roman Catholic, he ordered his co-religionists to worship in private and to treat Protestants, who considerably outnumbered the Catholics in the Colony, "with as much mildness and favor as Justice will permit."

In 1649 the General Assembly passed "An Act Concerning Religion" which provided that anyone who should "blaspheme God, that is Curse him, or deny our Savior Jesus Christ to be the sonne of God, or shall deny the Holy Trinity . . . or shall use or utter any reproachfull Speeches, words or languages concerning the said Holy Trinity . . . shall be punished with death and confiscation or forfeiture of all his or her lands and goods to the Lord Proprietary and his heiress." One victim of the law was Jacob Lumbrozo, described in the records as "the Jew doctor." He was a Sephardi from Lisbon, who was at one and the same time not only a doctor but an innkeeper, merchant, farmer, and trader, and apparently a respected member of the community. But on February 23, 1658, Lumbrozo was charged in the provincial court with "uttering words of blasphemy against our Blessed Savior Jesus Christ," having been prodded into answering some tricky theological questions by a visiting Christian missionary. Somehow he escaped the death penalty, perhaps because the governor about that time proclaimed a general amnesty.

Priests and Jews, £200 Tax

After Maryland became a royal province, in 1691, Catholics were relentlessly oppressed. One of the many discriminatory measures adopted was a special head tax of £5 for every Catholic immigrant; £200 for priests and Jesuits. Jews were also treated as inferior people, ineligible to vote, hold office or worship together in public. Their head tax was also £200.

One of the most liberal Colonial constitutions was the one drawn up for the settlers living between the Hudson and Delaware rivers, in what then was called West New Jersey (now the State of New Jersey). One article declared that "no men, nor number of men upon earth, hath power or authority to rule over men's consciences in religious matters." No one was to be penalized or even harassed "for the sake of his opinion, judgement, faith or worship towards God." It was, therefore, not surprising that New Jersey attracted many Jewish settlers.

Not the Promised Land

As these pages have attempted to show, the few thousand Jews living in America in the seventeenth and eighteenth centuries were beset by many difficulties. They had escaped the horrors of the Inquisition and the extreme cruelties inflicted on Jews in various parts of Europe, yet Colonial America was far from a promised land. There was discrimination almost everywhere. When they were treated with tolerance it was often out of a desire to try to persuade them to abandon their own religion for another.

For understandable religious, social, and psychological reasons, they felt impelled to cluster together whenever possible. It was the habit of centuries. Almost everywhere they had gone in the Diaspora they had lived in tight-knit Jewish communities, isolated from the non-Jews. In most cases they remained in big-city ghettos because they were ordered to do so. But even if there was no compulsion, they often chose to live this way for self-protection—physical and psychological. In some of the American Colonies virtual ghettos—like Jews' Alley in New Amsterdam—were established by command of officialdom. In other Colonies the Jews clustered together in order to be able to organize a congregation, establish a school, and keep alive their religion.

In Europe a Jewish community was often a chartered corporation legally recognized by the state. In Colonial America the congregation formed by Jewish settlers had few if any legal rights. However, by organizing, the Jewish settlers were able to meet together in prayer, obtain land for a burial ground, establish a *sedaca* (charity fund), have their meat and fowl killed in the kosher manner, employ a *hazzan*, and in many other ways follow the precepts of Judaism.

A Religion Without Compulsion

In those days, as today in most Jewish communities in America, there were no theological tests to becoming a member of the congregation. Confessions of faith were not required. There were no cast-iron rules to destroy individualism. A man could interpret the Mosaic law as he pleased. There was no strict policing of morals. However, synagogue boards did use their authority to punish with fines, and the denial of synagogue privileges, anyone who violated rules of decorum, observance of the Sabbath, and practice of the dietary laws. While the Jewish community in general believed from the start that every Jew in the area should be affiliated with the local congregation, there was little compulsion or intimidation, except that those who did not affiliate were often denied the right of burial in the Jewish cemetery. One reason for urging affiliation on scattered Jews who had drifted away from their religion was that in many small Jewish communities it often happened that every available male adult was needed in order to have a *minyan*, otherwise there could be no public prayers.

If the Jews were forbidden by some Colonial authorities to hold public religious meetings, they gathered week after week in private homes for prayers. If lack of funds made it impossible to build a synagogue in those Colonies where it was permitted, they rented a building—in one Colony a grist mill, in another the house of a shoemaker. They sent abroad for religious ceremonial articles to beautify their services. Although dwelling among people who in general had no understanding of or sympathy for the beliefs, practices, and customs of Judaism, they nevertheless managed to live by their ancient religion. Some Jewish businessmen were devout enough and daring enough to refuse to engage in any sort of trade on their own Sabbath. In their attempt to lead good Jewish lives, despite their weakness in number, they insisted, wherever and whenever possible, on the circumcision of their male children, the slaughtering of animals and fowl in the ritualistic manner, and the establishment of Jewish cemeteries so they could be buried together. They were also pioneers in matters educational.

They had crossed a vast ocean in search of the right to live as Jews in a free society. By the time of the American Revolution most of them knew they had made no mistake. They had *begun* to realize the dream. Few Jewish immigrants to America ever returned whence they had come.

6

CONTRIBUTIONS TO A REVOLUTION

WHEN the Revolutionary War broke out there were only about two thousand Jews in America. They formed less than one-tenth of one percent of the population. It has been estimated that one-third of all the Colonists—at least in the beginning—were loyal to England, and there were some Jews among these Tories or Loyalists, as they were called, but a vast majority of the American Jews were Patriots. There were many reasons for this. The Revolution's principle of equality had always been one of the fundamentals of Judaism, yet until now the Jewish Colonists in their extensive wanderings had found little respect for equality, either in theory or in practice. This new American concept of all men being created equal, and being equally endowed with certain God-given rights, dovetailed perfectly with the religious ideas by which Jews were taught to live. The freedoms that the evolution sought to secure for New World people were essential for the Jews, if they were to exist and prosper here—or anywhere. Then there was the fact that the Jews of America had no sense of belonging to any other nation, least of all to the nations from which they had so recently fled because of persecution and Inquisition. There was no question of dual loyalty, as with some of the non-Jewish Colonists. In America the Jews could look forward to becoming loyal citizens of a nation founded on principles that were already fundamentals of their own religion.

For all those reasons, most of the several thousand Jews in America in 1775 eagerly supported the Revolution. In whatever capacity they served, they contributed to the cause out of all proportion to their paucity.

Wanted: Traders and Financiers

In each one of the Colonies there were Jewish traders who had had long experience as importers and who also had been trading with the Indians for years. Suddenly they were in great demand by a new government that had to find clothing, food, animals, wagons, and equipment for a civilian army. Another need was for men who knew something about financial matters, for the new government had to have money to pay troops and conduct the war. It was to the credit of the Jews that they volunteered to advance the cash needed in return for IOUs that might or might not someday have value. No better proof of faith in the Revolution could possibly have been asked.

Some Jewish merchants—outstanding among them the Gratz brothers of Philadelphia—signed pledges not to purchase British goods. Some Jewish traders—among them Isaac Moses and Aaron Lopez—armed their vessels with cannon and sent them to prey on British shipping. Many enemy vessels were thus captured, representing a great loss to the British.

Some Emigrated to Fight for Freedom

Jews fought on every battlefield, as officers and privates. Some European Jews even emigrated to America for the express purpose of helping to fight a war for freedom, and then remained as American citizens, to enjoy the benefits of what they had helped win. One such was Benjamin Nones, a French Jew, who left a prospering wine business in Bordeaux to come to Philadelphia and enlist in the Continental Army. Soon after joining up he asked to be relieved of military duties on the Jewish Sabbath. His commander was so impressed with the young man's religious convictions and sincerity that he issued an order granting the request.

Nones fought so gallantly in so many battles—especially in the siege of Savannah—that he was promoted to the rank of major. The battalion of four hundred men he commanded was called "the Jews' Company" because so many of the soldiers were Jews.

After the war Nones ran for public office and during his campaign was "accused of being a Jew, a Republican and poor." In a letter answering the charge he admitted being all three, but stated that in his opinion all three made him more worthy than his rival of election.

In New York Solomon Simson supplied cannon and lead for making bullets to the Colonial troops.

One of the most prominent Jews in Newport at this time was Aaron Lopez, known as the "merchant prince of New England." He owned, entirely or in part, thirty transatlantic ships and more than a hundred coastal vessels that carried fish, lumber, rum, whale oil, and manufactured goods all over the world. He supported the American cause from the beginning, donating much of his wealth. During the war most of his vessels fell into British hands and when the British occupied Newport he lost what was left of his fortune. Many Newport Jews followed him to Leicester, Massachusetts, where they formed the first Jewish settlement in that state and where Lopez became the first Jew naturalized in Massachusetts.

Salomon, a Real Revolutionary

Haym Salomon, who in 1772 had fled from his native Poland to America, played a leading role in the Revolution. He brought with him a talent for languages and a passion for freedom. He was the first Polish Jew in America, as far as the records show. As trade between America and Europe increased, he prospered. In Poland he had known the young revolutionaries Kosciusko and Pulaski. In America he became one of the early members of a body of revolutionaries, the Sons of Liberty, who met secretly behind locked doors, planning how to prepare for the Revolution by setting up secret arsenals. In 1776, when fire destroyed a great part of New York, the British arrested everyone they suspected of sympathy for the Revolution, Salomon among them. His son later declared Salomon was specifically charged with having received orders from Washington to destroy British warehouses and had been caught in the act of so doing. He was condemned to execution.

While he was being held in the Old Sugar House prison, the British discovered his linguistic talents (he spoke English, Polish, German, French, and Russian equally well) and used him as an interpreter with Hessian soldiers who had come to America as British mercenaries. But instead of passing on in German the messages and instructions the British wished to convey to the Hessians, Salomon suggested that they desert, telling them that the Colonists would surely win and they would either be killed or taken prisoner. If that argument failed, he offered them bribes to desert. Before the British became aware of this one-man campaign of sabotage, Salomon escaped, thanks to a rope thrown over the prison wall by friends. That same night he and his rescuers started for Philadelphia by horse. Poor health made it impossible for him to serve in combat, but he performed a much greater service. First he acted as Paymaster-General for French forces fighting with the Colonials, handling immense sums of money, without charging any commission whatsoever. Then he was appointed Official Broker to the Office of Finance of the Continental Congress.

Freedom's Financier

Although some historians claim that Salomon's personal financial contributions to the revolutionary cause have been exaggerated, he clearly deserved being called "freedom's financier." He was a man of not only great patriotism but also extraordinary generosity. Among his official duties was selling captured enemy merchandise for as much as he could get for it. He also floated loans, endorsed government notes, invested most of his own money in government bonds, equipped entire military units from his personal funds, and gave unstintingly to needy service men.

After the war Salomon was as generous to the new nation with his money and his services as he had been during the conflict. During the long sittings of the Continental Congress in Philadelphia, many delegates found themselves short of funds. Salomon advanced them what they needed from his own accounts and refused to accept interest when (if) they repaid the loans. He actually paid the salaries of many revolutionary leaders when the Treasury ran short, among them Thomas Jefferson, James Madison, and James Monroe. His Judaism-inspired generosity to friends and relatives won him the soubriquet, "The Good Jew."

Helped Build a Synagogue

Haym Salomon's contributions to America were not only those of a Polish immigrant who appreciated what the New World offered him; they were also those of a Jew who was motivated, always, by the precepts of Judaism. He was one of the founding members and a trustee of Congregation Mikveh Israel and not only gave liberally to a fund for the erection of Philadelphia's first synagogue on Cherry Alley, but by his generosity encouraged others to give the balance of the money needed to erect a building of great beauty.

When the synagogue was dedicated in 1783 the highest honor—opening the doors—was given to Salomon, because he had supplied more than one-third of the building fund.

That same year Salomon joined four other Philadelphia Jews in petitioning the Council of Censors of Pennsylvania for repeal of the state's test oath law, which required that everyone elected to the Assembly swear that he believed in both the Old and the New Testament, thus making it impossible for a Jew to hold public office. Salomon did not live to see the requirement lifted, but five years after his death in 1785 the test oath was abolished, partly as a result of the campaign in which he had taken part.

Died of Prison Illness

Salomon died at the age of forty-five as a direct result of his war experience—from a chronic lung ailment he had contracted in the dampness of the Old Sugar House prison. To his widow and four children he left what seemed in those days a great fortune—$350,000, against debts of only $45,000. But examination of his assets revealed that they consisted principally of notes that he had accepted for cash from various branches of the Continental government. Instead of a third of a million dollars they were worth slightly less than the

$45,000 he owed. His widow was left with a minus $560. Salomon was never repaid by the government and his heirs carried on a battle for restitution until 1900.

On the 150th anniversary of the Bill of Rights, a monument was dedicated in Chicago showing George Washington, Robert Morris, and Haym Salomon with joined hands, symbolizing the founding of a nation of freedom.

In New York Mayor Fiorello La Guardia once issued a proclamation calling for the observances of Haym Salomon Day.

Washington and Other Jews

Even before meeting Salomon, George Washington had had passing contact with many other Jews. Hezekiah Levy was a contemporary member of the Fredericksburg (Va.) Lodge of Masons to which Washington belonged. Major Benjamin Nones and Colonel Isaac Franks served on Washington's General Staff. Moses Franks was one of three men entrusted with taking a quarter of a million dollars in cash from Philadelphia to Boston at a critical time in the war so Washington could meet his army's payroll. Phillip Moses Russel was Washington's Surgeon General at Valley Forge. At Washington's first inauguration, the *hazzan* of Shearith Israel in New York (according to some accounts) was one of the fourteen religious leaders taking part in the ceremonies.

On that occasion an attempt was made by a self-appointed Jewish leader in Philadelphia, Manuel Josephson, to get all six American Jewish congregations to send a joint letter of congratulation to the new President. The congregational leaders of Philadelphia, New York, Richmond, and Charleston agreed and did sign such a letter, but separate letters were sent from Savannah and Newport. This may have been because of intercommunity rivalry or the fact that the Savannah and Newport letters were both signed by men who, justly or unjustly, were tainted with the charge of Toryism and so they may have been eager to document their loyalty in as impressive a manner as possible. At any rate, the letters were a good idea, for in expressing his appreciation of them, President Washington took advantage of the opportunity to make clear his attitude toward Jews and Judaism in three separate letters. In one he wrote: "May the children of the Stock of Abraham, who dwell in this land, continue to merit and enjoy the good will of the other inhabitants, while every one shall sit in safety under his own vine and fig-tree and there shall be none to make him afraid."

It is no wonder that the Jews of America regarded Washington almost with reverence. He was helping to create a political climate in which Jews could hope to live completely free of persecution or even discrimination—an atmosphere in which Judaism could thrive, openly and happily.

The First Jewish Elective Officer

In Charleston, South Carolina, Francis Salvador, a member of one of the most prominent Jewish families in the country, played an active role in the patriotic cause. In 1774 he was elected to the General Assembly of South Carolina, thus becoming the first Jew in America —perhaps the first Jew in the modern world—to serve in an important elective office. Although not a lawyer, he helped draft the first State Constitution. When the Indians, instigated by the British, began to harass the Charleston Colonists, burning their fields and destroying their homes, Salvador took up his musket and led a force against them. On the night of July 31–August 1, 1776, he was ambushed, scalped, and killed—the first Jew to die for American independence. On his tombstone were carved these words:

> Born an aristocrat, he became a democrat,
>   An Englishman, he cast his lot with America;
> True to his ancient faith, he gave his life
>   For new hopes of human liberty and understanding.

Most of the adult male Jews of the Charleston community— twenty or thirty—served in the same infantry unit. Because they comprised almost 50 percent of the company, it was called "The Jews' Company."

Many Jews Fled to Connecticut

During the Revolution many New York Jews fled that city, rather than live under British occupation. Some loaded all their material possessions into boats and sailed across Long Island Sound to Connecticut, among them Gershom Mendes Seixas, the *hazzan* of Congregation Shearith Israel, who took with him the Scrolls of the Law, other ceremonial articles and the prayer books. Seixas had the distinction of being the first native-born Jewish religious leader in America. Born in New York, he had been graduated from the congregational school established by Shearith Israel. He had rabbinical ambitions, but there was no rabbinical seminary in the country. There was not even a rabbi who might have given the young man instruction. (It was not until the early 1840s that a rabbi who had been trained in Europe was engaged by a synagogue in America.) However, he had been brought up in a religious home, was faithful in his attendance at the synagogue and maintained close contact with the *hazzan*, Joseph Jesserum Pinto, under whose guidance he studied. In 1768, shortly after his twenty-second birthday, the congregation appointed him their religious leader and agreed to pay him £80, plus firewood and the use of a small house, the modest recompense being excused on the ground that he was not a learned rabbi, his knowledge of Hebrew was slight, and he was young and unmarried. Sometimes he was called "the rabbi," but always in quotation marks, or "the Jewish clergyman," or "the minister of Shearith Israel" or "the religious director," or "the *hazzan*-preacher." Because the Jewish community was so small and closely knit, Seixas was related in one way or another to most of the families in the congregation. His father, who had converted to Christianity in Portugal, but re-entered the Judaic faith after arriving in America, had married the daughter of Moses Levy, leader of Shearith Israel Congregation.

In the years that followed the appointment of the young spiritual leader, the New York congregation acquired such a heavy load of charitable expenses that it repeatedly had to deny his appeals for a salary increase until, finally he resigned, hoping thus to force them to give him the additional recompense he felt he deserved. They did.

Always a Minyan

Although there was no synagogue in Connecticut at this time—
and there would be none for another half century or more—so many
New York Jews fled across the border to escape living under the
British that no one had trouble finding a *minyan*.

By 1779, however, so many of those who had gone to Connecticut
had drifted down to Philadelphia that they invited Seixas to join
them, which he did. There he injected new life into Congregation
Mikveh Israel and led the Philadelphia Jewish community in its
fight for civil liberties. Until the Revolution members of the Philadelphia congregation had worshiped in private homes or in rented
rooms. But with the influx of Jewish refugees from those American
cities now occupied by the British, and under the guidance of Seixas,
who was now called "the Patriot rabbi of New York," they decided
to buy land and raise money for the construction of a synagogue,
which was dedicated in 1782, while the war was still in progress—the
second synagogue in America.

In 1783, with the war over and many of Congregation Shearith
Israel's members now back in New York, an invitation was extended
to Seixas to return, but he at first refused, on three grounds: he
was not well enough versed in Spanish or Portuguese, the languages
which members of Shearith Israel wished used in their synagogue;
he had heard that the congregation was being torn by serious internal
disputes in which he did not wish to become involved; and, now being married and having children, he could not possibly exist on his
former salary. In fact, he added, he was considering abandoning the
religious life for a business career in order to provide adequately for
his family. After some weeks of negotiation, he was finally persuaded
to return, for an annual salary of £200. When members of the
Philadelphia congregation heard they were going to lose him, they
vehemently protested, but Seixas left anyway. One of the boldest
steps Seixas took after returning to New York was to deliver a
sermon in English instead of Spanish. Many of the Sephardim in the
congregation objected, but Seixas succeeded in riding out the storm.
In fact, he served a total of forty-eight years as their spiritual leader.

Jews Under Suspicion in Rhode Island

In Rhode Island during the early days of the war the Assembly passed laws requiring all suspected Tories to take a loyalty oath. Among the seventy-seven Newporters under suspicion were four prominent Jews. Their religion as well as their patriotism was at issue. Isaac Touro, *hazzan* of Congregation Joshuat Israel, refused to take the oath, claiming that he was still a Dutch subject. He also stated that such an oath was against his religious principles. Isaac Hart, a distinguished merchant and one of the chief supporters of the synagogue, refused because it was not demanded of everyone— only suspects. Meyer Pollack refused on the ground that such an oath was "contrary to the custom of the Jews." All three definitely were Loyalists. The fourth man, Moses Michael Hays, said he was a Patriot and could have proved it, but he resented his loyalty being questioned. In refusing to sign the oath he demanded that he be permitted to face his accusers, insisting that it was an unjust reflection on his loyalty to be required to take an oath. He also objected as a Jew to being denied the rights and opportunities of citizenship, while being required to shoulder the responsibilities. When Hart's property was seized and he was ordered out of Newport, he fled to Long Island, but instead of finding safe refuge there he was shot, bayoneted, and then clubbed to death by Continentals. Touro, who had been nicknamed "the Jew priest," fled to Jamaica, where he died a few years later.

But these men were exceptions. A majority of the Jews of Newport supported the Revolution and their loyalty was never questioned. After the people of Newport set fire to a British ship that had been sent to collect a tax that the Colonists felt unjust, eight thousand British troops laid siege to the charming seaside city and destroyed much of it. But by this time most of Newport's Jews had already fled, many of them never to return. This brought to a swift close the great days of the Touro Synagogue. Even after the war Newport did not regain its importance as a seaport and commercial center. When the British evacuated Newport, they left most of the public buildings so damaged that the Rhode Island General

Assembly was forced to use the synagogue as its meeting place. Later a Town Meeting was held there. Then the building fell into complete disuse. A contemporary historian rang down the curtain on the stately synagogue: "The building was left to the bats and moles, and to the occasional invasion, through its porches and windows, of boys who took great pleasure in examining the furniture scattered about." (In 1947 what the bats and moles had left of the Newport Synagogue was dedicated as a national shrine.)

A Georgia Jew Defied the British

In Georgia before the start of the Revolution, Mordecai Sheftall, who had given the ground to the Jewish community of Savannah for a cemetery, had become the Jewish founding member of the Union Society, the first cooperative charity undertaking in America, uniting Jews, Catholics, and Protestants in a common social cause. As soon as the war broke out, Sheftall associated himself immediately with the revolutionaries and was made chairman of the Parochial Committee, organized by the rebels to help run Georgia. It soon became the actual government, in fact, if not in name. In his capacity as chairman Sheftall would stand on the dock at Savannah and inform captains of British ships that they were forbidden to unload and must sail away, quickly, unless they wished to face "dire consequences." The Georgia Tories struck back at him in many ways. Once his estate was raided and some of his slaves kidnaped and sent to Florida. Later he was made Commissary General of Purchases and Issues for the Georgia Militia, charged with supplying the Colony's soldiers with food and arms. The next year he was put in charge of obtaining food and clothing for the Continental troops of both South Carolina and Georgia. He took an active part in the defense of Savannah. When the British took the city he was captured and imprisoned, along with 185 other officers and men. The British commander referred to him as "a very great rebel," which gave Sheftall pleasure. Because he refused to answer his captors' questions about where American supplies had been secretly stored, he was thrown into a prison reserved for Negroes, was denied food, and was ill-treated by intoxicated British soldiers. Weak and ill, he was near death when he was saved—according to one story—by his knowledge of Yiddish. A Hessian soldier, able to understand Sheftall's Yiddish because of its similarity to German, was so delighted to find someone with whom he could converse that he took the Jewish prisoner under his special care. After months on a prison ship he was transferred to Sunbury, Georgia, where two fellow members of the Union Society were also confined. Periodically they held meetings of the society. One day the other two elected him president for the ensuing year. Finally Sheftall was released in exchange for a British prisoner held by the Continentals. Following the war he received a grant of land in recognition of his services to the government, but neither he nor his descendants ever received repayment of a considerable sum he had advanced to the Continental government to help maintain the troops.

Israel Influenced Young America

For the Founding Fathers the exodus of the Children of Israel from Egypt was the precedent for their own revolt against tyranny. They had the biblical injunction, "Proclaim liberty throughout the land unto all the inhabitants thereof," inscribed on their Liberty Bell. The day the Declaration of Independence was adopted, a committee was appointed to propose a design for a great seal for America. Benjamin Franklin, Thomas Jefferson, and John Adams recommended a sketch showing the escape of the Israelites from Egypt. Pharaoh was pictured with a crown on his head, sword in his hand, sitting in an open chariot in pursuit of the Children of Israel, who had already safely passed through the divided waters of the Red Sea. On the far shore stood Moses, his face illuminated by a pillar of fire, his right hand extended as he commanded the sea to overwhelm Pharaoh and his men. Beneath the picture was the motto: "Resistance to tyrants is obedience to God." Although this suggestion for the great seal was not adopted, Jefferson henceforth used the quotation from the Book of Maccabees as his personal motto.

The Puritans used the Old Testament to justify their dislike of absolutism and even found biblical passages to support their desire for separation from England. Jonathan Mayhew called monarchy "unbiblical and unHebraic." On the positive side, those who championed civil liberty in eighteenth century America derived their principles chiefly from the Old Testament.

Jefferson, Good Friend of the Jews

When the American Republic was born there was not a single European country in which church and state were separated. Most nations had official religions which had to be accepted if one wished to escape persecution. In the several slightly more liberal countries that tolerated a minority religion, its followers were discriminated against by being denied the right to vote or hold public office. When "Congress shall make no law respecting an establishment of religion, or prohibiting the free exercise thereof," the United States became the first nation anywhere in which complete religious liberty was guaranteed. For Jews, who had suffered more religious persecution over a longer period of time than any other people on earth, this was of tremendous importance.

Although at this time there were fewer than three thousand Jews in the entire United States, there was one Jewish lad, Simon M. Levy, in the first graduating class of the United States Military Academy at West Point. And in 1789, at Philadelphia, which soon would become the capital of the United States, there was a parade celebrating the new Constitution. At the end of the route of march, tables of refreshments were set up for the participants. One table was loaded exclusively with food that had been prepared strictly according to the dietary laws, for the benefit of those Jews who had taken part in the parade, but could not enjoy refreshments unless they were kosher. There were only several hundred Jews living in Philadelphia, yet here was an indication of how well regarded they were and with what respect they were treated.

At this stage the Jews had a loyal friend in Thomas Jefferson, who, although he suffered many misunderstandings and misapprehensions about the dogmas and practices of Judaism, nevertheless expressed his indignation—publicly and privately—by voice and by the written word—at the social, political, and economic barriers erected in the New World against Jews. At the same time he exhibited a refreshing liberality in his personal relationship with individual Jews.

Virginia's First Congregation

It was not until after the Revolution—in the summer of 1789— that a Jewish congregation was formed in Virginia, the oldest colony and now the most populous state. There were understandable economic, political, and religious reasons for this. Virginia was like some prosperous rural area of England, except that the big estates were worked by slaves. Each estate was a town in itself, containing a carpenter shop, a smithy, a store, a mill, and everything else needed to supply the normal wants of eighteenth-century man. This left no room for outsiders. Also, in Virginia no one was eligible for citizenship or public office who did not profess faith in Christ. A Virginia law of 1805 excluded non-Christians, Catholics, Negroes, and convicts from testifying in any court. Another law passed in Colonial times forbade Jews to employ Christians as servants.

When a group of Virginians decided to establish a Colony in the western part of the state, to be called Georgia (no relation to the other Georgia) they asked in their petition for "unlimited liberty of conscience for the publick profession . . . excepting heathenism, Jews, and papists who are to be utterly disqualified and for ever excluded from holding any office of trust or profit in that province."

Madison on Bondage vs. Freedom

Occasionally—and only occasionally—a liberal voice was heard, such as that of James Madison who, in 1774, by inference criticized his native Virginia in writing to a Pennsylvania friend about his Colony:

"You are happy in dwelling in a land where those inestimable privileges of religious liberty are fully enjoyed; and the public has long felt the good effects of this religious as well as civil liberty. . . .

"Religious bondage shakels and debilitates the mind, and unfits it for every noble enterprise, every expanded prospect."

Nevertheless, a few Jews did go to Virginia, not to become plantation owners, as the British did, but to serve the Colony as doctors, lawyers, surgeons, watchmakers, bankers, silversmiths, chandlers, fur traders, and artisans. Those who were traders bought cotton and tobacco, and sold the plantation owners hardware, planters' tools, and such imported luxury items as fine fabrics, china, tea, wine, and furniture from Europe.

By the time of the Revolution there was a thin sprinkling of Jews in Virginia, among them Isaiah Isaacs, a silversmith from England, who, after a few years, was a partner in one of the largest retail establishments in Richmond and owned the Bird in Hand, one of Virginia's best-known taverns, besides having extensive interests in land, houses, and slaves. It is significant that although he was one of the few Jews in a somewhat hostile Christian community, he retained his strong inherent attachment to Judaism. When Congregation Mikveh Israel in Philadelphia solicited funds to build its synagogue, he made a substantial contribution and in his will asked that his two children, whose mother had already died, be brought up "in good Jewish homes." Whenever he signed his name to important documents he did so in Hebrew script.

During the Revolution a number of Jews served in the Virginia militia, while others helped by supplying the military with essentials. One of the most colorful of the settlers in eighteenth-century Virginia was Joseph Darmstadt, a German Jew who had been a member of a regiment of Hessians hired by the British to fight for the Crown. After the war he decided to settle in Richmond, partly because he found a valley just outside the city that had been settled by German farmers with whom he could converse.

Help for Strangers in Richmond

As Richmond, after the war, grew into an important commercial center, the Jewish community also grew. By 1785 it numbered twelve families. In these days so many immigrants and other travelers were coming to Richmond or passing through the city that an organization called the Amicable Society was formed to help needy strangers. By now Darmstadt was a successful merchant and as such was among the society's founders and officers. In 1789 the twenty-nine Jewish families of Richmond—Darmstadt among them—formed the congregation of Beth Shalom (the House of Peace). Although the Ashkenazim were in the majority, the services of Beth Shalom from the start followed the Sephardic pattern.

In Charleston, South Carolina, nine years after the war ended, Congregation Beth Elohim laid the cornerstone of its synagogue, which was completed two years later at a cost of $20,000. It was consecrated in the presence of the governor and other distinguished citizens, and became the religious headquarters of what some historians say was the leading Jewish community of post-war America.

A generation after the Revolution the total Jewish population of the United States was probably little more than 3000, concentrated in New York, Philadelphia, Savannah, Richmond, and Charleston. They made up only about one-twentieth of one percent of the total population, but by now they had their roots well dug into the soil of this new nation. Each congregation had a synagogue which served as the integrating force of the community. Each had a cemetery of its own. Each had a program of assistance for the poor and needy. Each stressed giving their young a good Jewish education. Thus a pattern was being set which would be followed all over the country when, in a few years, the trickle of Jewish immigration from Europe would turn into a tidal wave.

7

JUDAISM MOVES WESTWARD

Napoleon Bonaparte, despot though he was in many ways, opened windows for the people of Europe, giving them a brief glimpse of what life could be like if the French Revolution fulfilled its tripartite promise of *liberté, egalité, fraternité*. Napoleon personally had mixed feelings about Jews, but his conquests extended to millions of Jews the rights set forth in that vital French document of human liberty called *The Declaration on the Rights of Man*. After Napoleon's armies were defeated at Waterloo, the windows were slammed shut, one by one, and the Old Order tried to regain what it had lost. Without waiting for the ultimate success of underground revolutionary movements, hundreds of thousands of freedom-hungry Europeans packed up and headed for America, the one place in which they were sure they could find what they craved.

Usually husbands went alone, planning to send for their wives and children as soon as they could earn the passage money. (Nearly 90 percent of the immigrants through the port of New York between 1850 and 1900 were single males and married men unaccompanied by their families. This was especially true among Jews.) Sometimes all the inhabitants of a village would go together, leaving behind empty houses and a deserted synagogue as a reminder of the place where uneasy Jews had once lived and worshiped together.

Seek Salvation in America

They came to America in search of full religious liberty, economic freedom, political equality, and personal opportunity, all of which had been denied them, to some extent, in Europe. They listened to such calls as that sounded by Ludwig Kempert, the German poet, who wrote:

"It is to America that our longing goes forth! . . . There is no more peace for us in our fatherland. . . . No help has come for us, we are not saved. Seek help in faraway America. Be farmers, merchants, craftsmen, peddlers or Congressmen, brokers or vice presidents of the United States: be cotton planters or sugar refiners. . . . In your adopted fatherland . . . a man is worth what he is, and he is what he does. Before all else, be free—and go to America."

From Village to Metropolis

They came from Germany, Austria, Hungary, Bohemia, Bavaria, Rumania—a few from such cities as Berlin, Vienna, Budapest, Bucharest, the rest from hundreds of smaller places. (It is interesting sociologically that the *Jewish* immigrants were almost always from the villages. The city dwellers did not leave because their economic position was better. Yet these erstwhile villagers invariably ended up in the American metropolises.) Occasionally local political discrimination or religious persecution accelerated the exodus, such as the limitation imposed by officials in Bavaria on the number of Jewish marriages permitted each year.

Some of the immigrants were so well organized that they brought with them their Scrolls of the Law and such ceremonial objects as *shophars* (ram's horns), *menorahs* (candelabras used during the Hanukkah holidays), and *yads* (silver pointers used in reading the *Torah*). Some groups even brought their own religious officials, the *shohet* (trained ritual slaughterer) and the *mohel* (circumciser).

The Forty-eighters

In 1848, after revolutions in Austria, Hungary, and Bohemia were crushed, a new wave of disillusioned Jews, known as the Forty-eighters, set forth for America. Most of those who came between 1815 (Waterloo) and 1861 (the Civil War) were from German-speaking lands, with a trickle from Eastern Europe—a trickle because passports could be had there only in exceptional cases and because the forces motivating the German Jews to emigrate had not yet penetrated into the Pale, where the Jews were virtually unaware of America until about 1870.

Newspapers in Germany wrote often of "the emigration fever." The Prague correspondent of a New York paper dispatched this report to his editor:

"The second class cabins of the boat that is leaving Bremen on April 15 are completely taken by Jews from Prague. The captain is prepared to supply kosher food if desired. The number of those from Prague alone who are to emigrate to America this year is estimated at about four hundred."

Bewildered, Lonely, Frightened

With few exceptions these new immigrants were Ashkenazim who were soon going to change the complexion of Judaism in America. In the early Colonial days the Sephardim had been in the majority and had established the Sephardic ritual, the Sephardic pronunciation of Hebrew and the Sephardic religious customs as the American way. Although there was a gradual influx of Ashkenazim, until the 1800s they were content with this "American way." There were even cases of predominantly Ashkenazic congregations establishing new synagogues and adopting the Sephardic ritual as their own. But with mass immigration from the Germanic countries, this situation began to change and by 1820 the Ashkenazim-Sephardim balance had shifted.

The nineteenth-century Ashkenazic settlers had no desire to learn new religious practices. There was enough that was new and frightening without that. They were bewildered, lonely. The scenery, the language, and the ways of the people here were strange. Even the clothes. The immigrants had fled from intolerable conditions in Europe, but nevertheless back there had been home. Back there they had understood life, even when it was difficult. In this strange new world they found safety and comfort in staying together—with people from the same village or at least the same part of their native country—people who had the same background and the same Old World memories, and who talked and prayed exactly as they did. That was part of the reason they wanted to establish their own synagogues and follow the *minhag* and the customs of Jewish living that they had always known.

Points of Conflict

Also they were critical of the established American Jews for not keeping the Sabbath more strictly, for being careless in their observance of the dietary laws, for shaving, and for giving up their European manner of dress and their European customs. They even accused them of being ignorant of the Torah, and no wonder, they said, for some congregations did not even have rabbis to teach them. And so, in the large cities along the Atlantic seaboard, instead of joining established synagogues they formed congregations of their own. Often the members were all from the same European town, so they named the congregation after the place from which they had fled. They met for prayers in private homes, or rented basements or vacant stores, until they could raise money to build a synagogue.

The first thoroughly Ashkenazic synagogue in North America was built in Philadelphia by Congregation Rodelph Shalom, which had been founded in 1802. Because there was already a Sephardic synagogue there, Philadelphia was now able to boast that it was the first city in America with two permanent Jewish congregations.

Then in New York a dissident group in 1825 broke away from Shearith Israel and formed an independent Ashkenazic congregation, B'nai Jeshurun, made up principally of English Ashkenazim. In that year there were only five hundred Jews in New York.

The Causes of Proliferation

Even after a congregation was organized and a synagogue was built there was often proliferation. It might result from fundamental religious differences, a proposed change in ritual, disagreement over employing a new cantor, or even so petty a conflict as who should be president of the society. And so, year after year, as a result of the rapid increase in the Jewish population and because of schisms, the number of congregations grew. In New York, in addition to the old Sephardic synagogue, there were soon Russian, German, Polish, Dutch, Bohemian, and British congregations.

By 1850 there were thirty-seven congregations in the country, fourteen in New York, eight in Pennsylvania, and two each in Ohio and South Carolina. In the next ten years the total jumped to seventy-seven, with twenty-seven in New York. By 1870 there were 189 congregations, with Maine having twenty-three, almost half the number of New York.

In other cities besides New York the new immigrants also clung to the style of service and pronunciation of Hebrew they had known in Europe, forming factions and establishing synagogues in which they tried to retain the familiar.

What Cost Individualism

Individualism was typical not only of Jews but of Judaism. It had virtues and advantages, disadvantages and drawbacks. In nineteenth-century America it created a certain amount of ecclesiastical chaos. In most other religions there is some sort of central authority. But in Judaism there is nothing comparable to the Pope, the Vatican, the College of Cardinals, the Episcopal House of Bishops, or the Methodist General Conference. The failure of the attempt in 1789 to get the six Jewish congregations then in existence to join in a letter of congratulation to George Washington had been proof of this extreme individualism. In Europe synagogues had been subject to varying degrees of discipline and regulation by the state. But synagogues in nineteenth-century America were free of any controls, either external or self-imposed. In Europe the typical rabbi, instead of being a preacher, a spiritual adviser, a father-confessor or an administrator, was the ecclesiastical head of the Jewish community and as such had the power to pass judgment in matters of law and ritual. But in America in the early days many synagogues functioned without a rabbi and when they did have one, his authority was seldom clearly defined and he was hired and fired at the will of the congregation.

Anybody Can Be President

Not only did the Germanic Jews organize congregations and build synagogues; they also established cultural organizations, charitable societies, orphanages, social clubs, hospital boards, and welfare bodies which served many diverse purposes. They enabled the members to meet with others like themselves and behave naturally, without worrying about the critical stares or the hurtful taunts of outsiders. These organizations gave even the most obscure immigrant tinsmith or female garment worker or dealer in secondhand furniture a chance to become a person of importance—maybe someday even the President. But most important, they performed useful religious, social, and charitable functions in the community, thus enriching American life. In this way they enabled the members to live up to some of the fundamental principles of Judaism.

Many of these organizations were designed to provide protection against the economic hazards facing immigrants in a new land that had not yet developed a philosophy of governmental responsibility for its citizens when they became victims of sickness, poverty, disaster, or old age. *Gemilut hesed* ("doing kindness") societies were formed to make small loans to members when economic distress overtook them. There were coal societies to provide fuel for those who could not afford it. *Bikur hotlim* societies had the principal function of visiting the sick. *Matzoh* societies provided the poor with the unleavened bread that Jews eat during the eight days of Passover. *Hakhnasat orehim* (entertaining wayfarers) clubs looked after itinerant Jews and newcomers. Jewish hospitals were established so that those who wished to follow dietary laws, even while ill, could have kosher food. Mutual benefit societies not only paid death benefits, like an insurance company, but even provided mourners for the funeral. Loan societies advanced money to members in economic trouble, without charging interest. In the 1850s as many as five out of every one hundred Jews in New York were being assisted financially by some form of Jewish charity. Then there were literary, musical, and cultural societies, so the immigrants could meet socially, dance together, keep up with the latest books, read, listen to good music, and satisfy their hunger for greater knowledge. Except for strictly social clubs, all these activities were derived from biblical commandments (*Mitzvot*).

B'nai B'rith Is Born

Some local groups mushroomed into powerful national organizations. For example, in 1843 in New York twelve recent immigrants from Germany founded a mutual aid society to help members when they were ill or out of work. They also aimed to do something about the animosity and disunity then plaguing American Jewry. They called their society the *Bundes Bruder* (Sons of the Covenant). In time it became the B'nai B'rith, one of the largest Jewish service organizations in the world, taking its new name from two Hebrew words also meaning Sons of the Covenant, with more than a third of a million members in 1950 chapters in thirty-five countries, devoted to youth welfare, education, philanthropy, Americanism, interfaith good will, and the defense of Jewish rights. B'nai B'rith and innumerable other national and local lodges attempted to unite American Jews having different nationality backgrounds, who were also separated by minor religious differences. These societies while not an organizational part of the synagogues, served as the instruments by which Jews put their Judaism into practice—Jews who might not enter a synagogue more often than once a year, on Yom Kippur, as well as those more observant Jews who joined with their neighbors in prayer on every Sabbath, as well as on minor religious holidays, and scrupulously obeyed every one of the religious laws.

The Desire to Belong

At first it might have been said that this banding-together was inspired principally by a self-protective instinct on the part of a small minority in a large and strange land. Yet Jewish organizational life grew, and membership rolls increased, and good works multiplied, all out of proportion to immigration figures. Security did not put an end to philanthropy and generosity. Immigrants of decades ago, now successful, remembered when they themselves had been strangers in the land and gave more help than ever to those who could not look out for themselves. Later when Jews in the larger centers of population began to proliferate, B'nai B'rith and some of the other national organizations hoped to be the means of preserving basic Jewish community unity.

As with all immigrants, in all generations, the Germanic Jews, while clinging to the familiar, at the same time showed an eagerness for Americanization, especially for the sake of their children, who craved to *belong*. What this meant in the field of religion was that demands began to be heard for the use of more English in the synagogue instead of German and Slav dialects, a shortening of some of the services, a modification of the dietary laws, abolition of the curtained women's gallery, the addition of a choir, and sermons in English. More and more congregations wanted rabbis and because there were no seminaries in America, rabbis had to be imported—generally from Germany, the center of Jewish scholarship in Europe.

Jews, Judaism, and the Middle West

The part played by Jewish pioneers in the development of the Middle West has been overlooked by many American historians. In 1834 the twenty-five members of Congregation B'nai Yeshurun (Sons of Yeshurun) in Cincinnati sent a letter to older congregations in the East asking for help in building a synagogue. The letter said in part: "We are scattered through the wilds of America as members of the same family and faith, and we consider it our duty to apply to you for assistance in the creation of a house to worship the God of our forefathers . . . There is not a congregation within five hundred miles of this city . . . for the last four or five years nothing was heard but the howling of wild beasts and the more hideous cry of savage men . . ."

When the Forty-eighters arrived from abroad, the Middle West still consisted of many wide open spaces, with cities hundreds of miles apart. In some areas roads were almost non-existent, communications were primitive, traveling was dangerous. Yet the Jewish immigrants, finding the cities in the East crowded, headed for the fertile green Middle West. Some few settled on farmland in the Ohio Valley. Others went into business, opened factories, entered the professions, learned a craft, became tailors, brewers, watchmakers, carpenters, shoemakers.

How Gimbel's and Macy's Began

Still others, seeing how inaccessible stores of any kind were for millions of farmers and villagers, decided to take the city to the country, so they became peddlers. With a pack or a basket or even a trunk strapped to the back, they trudged from farm to farm, village to village, selling calico, pins, needles, lace, ribbon, watches, stove polish, glue, spices, and even groceries to people living far off the beaten path. In addition to such amenities of life, which they called *Kuttle-Muttle*, the traveling peddlers brought their customers news of their neighbors ten or fifty miles down the road, and contact with the world beyond the horizon. Because most peddlers spoke with the accents of their mother tongue they were looked on as foreigners rather than as Jews. At the start of a trip their packs might weigh as much as 150 pounds. They traveled by foot until they could save enough money to buy a horse and wagon. These mobile merchants were taking the first step up the ladder of commerce, at the top of which some would find great pots of gold. Many graduated from peddler to proprietor of a retail business at a permanent location in town. And some of these small shops eventually grew into great department stores, such as Gimbel's and Macy's, and their owners became men of wealth.

As a footnote to the story of the Forty-eighters and the Middle West, the first brick house in Chicago was built by a Jewish immigrant.

Waiting for a Minyan

Because they were scattered so thinly across the country, it was often necessary for Jews in remote places to wait years until they had a *minyan* and could form a congregation. Yet by 1840 there were congregations in at least five towns west of the Alleghenies. Ten years later there were several congregations on the West Coast.

Some Jews took part in the Gold Rush of '49 in California. They came by boat, by wagon, and even by horseback. After digging all day for gold, if there were enough for a *minyan* they would say Hebrew prayers in the evening in a tent, a shack, or an open field. On the Trans-America Building in San Francisco there is a plaque commemorating the Yom Kippur, 1849, service by forty Jewish pioneers held in a room over a store at that location.

Next, they began spreading across the plains and the prairies. By 1840 it is estimated that the Jewish total had increased from the 2000 of Revolutionary days to 15,000. By 1850 the total was close to 30,000. (All these eighteenth- and nineteenth-century figures are the average of the estimates made by various historians, no two of whom agree exactly on any population figure, for no one bothered to take a census of religious affiliations in those days.)

A Rabbi Prays in Congress

Public officials in America since the time of George Washington had taken cognizance of the existence of Judaism, in speeches, letters, and public statements, and the Bill of Rights clearly guaranteed all Americans freedom of religion, but the first time a Jewish spiritual leader was invited to invoke God's blessing on a legislative body in America was in 1850 when Julius Echman, minister of Beth Shalom in Richmond, was asked to open sessions of the Virginia House of Delegates with a prayer.

Ten years later an even more significant event occurred in the history of American Judaism. On February 1, 1860, a rabbi gave the prayer that opened a session of Congress. The Jewish community took this as the first recognition by American lawmakers of the equal status of Judaism with Christianity as an American faith. In his prayer Dr. Morris J. Raphall, the rabbi of Congregation B'nai Jeshurun in New York, pointed out that the American Commonwealth had been established "after the model of that which Thou, Thyself, didst bestow on the tribes of Israel, in their best and purest days." In high tribute to Congress, he compared it to the Jewish Tabernacle: ". . . the heart of the entire nation, where the wants, the feelings, and wishes of all might become known, to be respected by all, so that union might create strength, and concord keep pace with prosperity." And in conclusion he quoted the Psalm: "How good and how pleasant it is when brethren dwell together in unity."

The First Jewish School

Because Judaism lays so much stress on learning, and because back in Europe young Jewish boys went to *heder* (Hebrew school) as a matter of course, the immigrants from Germanic countries were distressed that many American congregations not only had no rabbis but offered no Hebrew education for the young.

As far back as 1731 Congregation Shearith Israel in New York had opened the first Jewish school in North America. Before the days when a public school system was inaugurated, other congregations also established schools. Some of them, like Shearith Israel, offered in addition to religious subjects, reading, writing, arithmetic, and sometimes a foreign language. The level of instruction in Beth Anabah School in Richmond was so high that Christian as well as Jewish parents enrolled their children. In smaller congregations the *hazzan* might make an attempt to teach the children to read a few sentences from the Torah in Hebrew and to say the important Hebrew prayers. But in many communities education of the youngsters was, perforce, neglected.

The First Bar Mitzvah

In Chicago, one of the Forty-eighters arriving from Europe was Leopold Mayer, who joined Sinai Congregation, which then had only twenty-eight paying members and met for prayers on the third floor of a frame building over an auction house. The congregation had neither a rabbi nor a teacher, so Mayer, knowing Hebrew, posted a notice on the door of the rented rooms announcing the opening of a religious school. Soon he had the honor of teaching the first boy in Chicago to be prepared for *bar mitzvah* (literally Son of Command; the ceremony when a boy completes his thirteenth year and assumes the religious responsibilities of manhood).

By 1860 there were approximately 150,000 Jews scattered across America. They formed less than half of one percent of the total population, but already the threads of Judaism were being woven into the fabric of American life.

8

THE STRUGGLE FOR REFORM

I T was the Golden Age of Charleston, richest city in the South. Her port was one of the busiest in America, her industry thriving, her streets lined with magnificent trees, her magnolia gardens the most beautiful in the world, her eighteenth-century homes stately and well preserved. Charleston in 1820 was also the Jewish capital of America. That year there were only 100 Jews in Savannah, 200 in Richmond, 450 in Philadelphia, and 550 in New York City, yet there were 700 in Charleston. It was not only the largest but the wealthiest community of Jews in the country.

Many of the old Jewish families had lived in Charleston for two, three, or even four generations. They were an accepted part of a city that from the first had been relatively kind to them. Jews of Charleston had voted for the first time more than a hundred years ago. They had fought brilliantly in the Revolution. Now they were participating in every facet of community life. Among the 700 were eminent painters, writers, teachers, a playwright, lawyers, physicians, merchants, engineers, politicians, industrialists, a judge, and a Custom House official. Steam navigation on the Savannah River had been established by Charleston Jews. Two of the community's four newspapers were edited by Jews. Four of the nine founders of the Supreme Council of Scottish Rite Masonry in Charleston had been Jews.

Charleston already had a long tradition of religious liberality. On occasion, for example, the Unitarian minister attended services in the synagogue of Congregation Beth Elohim. And so, it was therefore not surprising that the first attempt to liberalize Judaism in America was made in Charleston.

The Scientific Reform of Judaism

In Europe it had already begun. In 1805 a rabbi in Dessau, Germany, had made history when he delivered a sermon to his congregation in German. In 1819 fifty young Jews in Berlin organized the Society for Culture and the Science of Judaism, with the aim of justifying reforms in Judaism by a scientific study of Jewish ritual and tradition.

Orthodox leaders in Europe were outraged at the religious revolution, contending that the proposed innovations would lead to other reforms that would destroy a religion that had flourished for thousands of years with little change. They questioned whether Judaism could survive if Jews "left their ghettos and ceased to be Jews." When full citizenship rights were about to be given to the Jews of Amsterdam, leaders of the Jewish community called on their followers to renounce such rights and obey "the dictates of their faith."

Not to Overthrow, But to Rebuild

The reform movement in Europe, while initiated by laymen, was being carried on by learned rabbis, professional ecclesiastics, and rabbinical students. But when Reform hit America, it was a spontaneous uprising of laymen alone. In 1824 forty-seven leading members of Congregation Beth Elohim in Charleston petitioned the trustees for revisions in the service, stating that "We wish not to overthrow, but to rebuild; we wish not to destroy, but to reform and revise."

They listed four specific demands: the service should be shortened (it usually ran three hours and would have run five except that it was recited so rapidly); a sermon should be delivered in English (sermons in any language were rare; in traditional synagogues the rabbi preaching only on the sabbaths before Rosh Ha-Shanah and Passover); money offerings during the service should be abolished because they were undignified; Hebrew prayers should be translated into English. About the matter of language, the petitioners said:

"It is not everyone who has the means, and many have not the time, to acquire a knowledge of the Hebrew language, and consequently become enlightened in the principles of Judaism. . . . According to the present method of reading the Bible, it affords to the hearer neither instruction nor entertainment unless he be competent to read as well as comprehend the Hebrew language. But if, like all other ministers, our reader would make a chapter or verse the subject of an English discourse once a week, at the expiration of the year the people would, at all events, know something of that religion which at present they so little regard."

First Reform Prayer Book

When the demands were rejected, twelve of the petitioners organized the Reformed Society of Israelites, adopted a constitution, wrote a new and abbreviated service of their own, and agreed to pray with uncovered heads and use instrumental music during their services. The prayer book printed by the Reformed Society contained a number of original prayers and also many hymns of Christian origin. Within a year the number of Reformers had increased to fifty. Jefferson, in a letter on their first anniversary, wrote that in his opinion "nothing is wiser than that our institutions should keep pace with the advance of time and be improved with the improvement of the human mind."

In 1826 they decided to build a synagogue and appealed for subscriptions. A few years later the society disbanded and returned all donations with interest—$6.68 for every $5 subscribed—which prompted the *Charleston Courier* to comment: "There is a moral beauty in the act, which makes it a subject for grateful contemplation. How rare, how very rare such instances!"

The Demand for an Organ

About half the society's members rejoined Beth Elohim, which in 1838 lost its synagogue by fire. While a new building was under construction, thirty-eight members interested in reform requested the trustees to call a congregational meeting to consider a bold suggestion:

"We, the undersigned members of the Congregation of K. K. Beth Elohim, feeling a deep interest in our religion, and anxious to embrace every laudable and sacred mode by which the rising generation may be made to conform to and attend our holy worship, Respectfully petition Your body to call a General meeting of the congregation at the earliest and most convenient period you may deem proper to discuss the propriety of erecting an organ in the synagogue to assist the vocal part of the service.

"Your petitioners would be among the last to ask for innovation in any respect in relation to the usages and formula of the Service. But your body is aware, that in this petition, there is nothing incompatible with the practice of our brethren where they continue strict conformists. It is a matter of notoriety that farther than a century back, an organ was made part of the service in the city of Prague, the capital of Bohemia, and at a later period, organs have been introduced in other parts of Germany and in the South of France."

The Universal Language of the Soul

The petition had the support of Gustavus Poznanski, a Polish Jew who had lived some years in Hamburg, the cradle of Reform Judaism in Europe, and who had come to Charleston from Shearith Israel in New York. He was so popular with all elements of the congregation that he had been elected their spiritual leader for life. His support of the petition may have influenced the trustees, who called a congregational meeting at which the purchase of an organ was approved by a vote of 46 to 40, on the ground that such instrumental music is "the universal language of the soul . . . felt and cultivated by all nations."

Although the petition quoted examples of the use of an organ abroad, many communities in Europe were divided over this same issue, with rabbinical authorities giving conflicting interpretations of the law. The Hungarian rabbi, Aaron Chorin, said it was not only permissible but obligatory to "hold the service in a language understandable to the worshipper and to accompany it with organ and song," while Rabbi Eliezer Fleckles of Prague, contradicting the Charleston petition, wrote that "playing the organ on the Sabbath is in every way contrary to Jewish law, even if it is done through a non-Jew."

Three-Year Court Battle Begins

The defeated minority left Beth Elohim, organized a new congregation called Shearith Israel, after the Sephardic Congregation in New York, and erected a synagogue of their own a few blocks from Beth Elohim. The victorious Reformers, as they were called, now tried to get congregational approval for more changes in the orthodox ritual. Various compromises were worked out. One provided for using the organ only on alternate Saturdays. Eventually the Reformers took the entire matter to court. The trial lasted three years and involved some of the most brilliant lawyers in the South.

(In Europe, recourse to the secular judiciary would have been unthought-of. Only in Reform Jewry in America could this happen— that the state was willing to intervene and that no rabbinical authority could successfully interpose itself. European court decisions usually only confirmed the right of the Orthodox to impose their rules.)

Laws Are Stationary, Life Is Progressive

The Charleston decision finally went to the Reformers, the court taking the position that ". . . human institutions cannot withstand the agitations of free, active and progressive opinion. Whilst laws are stationary, things are progressive. Any system of laws that should be made without the principle of expansibility, that would in some measure accommodate them to the progression of events, would have within it the seeds of mischief and violence . . . Those who now, in the case before us insist with most earnestness on a severe observance of ancient rules and forms, would hardly recognize or understand the same, as they were practiced by their remote ancestors who founded the Synagogue."

The court gave its opinion that the use of an organ was not a basic and fundamental change in the ritual of the synagogue, but simply a matter of form into which the court had no right to inquire. The court clearly indicated a belief that changes could and should be made in religious forms, thus taking the opposite stand of most European courts in similar cases, which generally ranged themselves on the side of the more traditional groups in religious controversies.

The majority of the judges in the Appeal Court sustained the finding of the lower court in favor of the Reformers and that ended the legal aspects of the case. In the Appeal decision both sides were urged to reach a compromise. Instead, the traditionalists of Beth Elohim withdrew and joined Shearith Israel. But Beth Elohim continued to have internal difficulties, largely over how far reform should be permitted to go. Although Shearith Israel prospered, its members were bitter because the Beth Elohim synagogue was much more magnificent than their own.

At Last—a Compromise

Finally, in 1866, a reunion was effected. The Shearith Israel building was sold for $5000 and the reunited congregation decided to use the Beth Elohim building and follow a moderate Reform liturgy. As with all compromises, there were problems, illustrated by the complaints of the choir directress who was constantly under pressure to use Sephardic music or German music; Orthodox music or Reform music; traditional songs or modern songs. In the last of a series of letters to the trustees she reminded them that she was the directress of the choir and would do as she pleased.

To some the Charleston episode may sound like a tempest in a teapot, but it was the first of what soon would be a nationwide series of intramural conflicts—and even lawsuits—as Reform Judaism began to spread across the United States.

Less than two years after the organ was installed in Beth Elohim, Har Sinai in Baltimore became a Reform congregation under the direction of a rabbi brought over from Germany. Then Emanu-El in New York, in 1845, and the following year Beth El in Albany, New York, and in 1858 Sinai in Chicago, and then many others. The Reform movement was especially strong in the Ohio and Mississippi valleys.

By 1890 there were 217 Reform congregations in the United States, 27 of them in New York, as against 316 Orthodox congregations, 152 of them in New York. (U. S. Census of Religious Bodies) The New York figures, however, are deceiving, for most of the 152 Orthodox synagogues were small and altogether had a seating capacity of only 21,000 persons, whereas the 27 Reform synagogues seated 19,000.

No European Handicaps

In Germany, where it all started, Reformers were handicapped in trying to set up their own synagogues by the existence of central communal boards, recognized by the government, which regulated all aspects of local Jewish life. If the Reformers wanted to secede from an established synagogue, both the communal board and the government would try to prevent it by putting difficulties in their way. But in the United States new synagogues were bursting into existence everywhere, like buds on a burgeoning bush in the springtime.

Sometimes an Orthodox congregation would employ an energetic young rabbi who would encourage a liberal element in the congregation to demand reforms and, if defeated, to secede and form a new congregation. Some congregations like Har Sinai in Baltimore and Emanu-El in New York, made sweeping reforms all at once. Others, like Rodelph Shalom and Keneseth Israel in Philadelphia, instead of radically altering their ways, gradually accommodated themselves to the attitudes of their members.

Organ, Choir, Decorum

Sometimes the issue would be an organ, or a mixed choir, either of men and women or of Jews and non-Jews. Sometimes the demand would be for family pews in which father, mother and children could sit together, instead of the traditional Orthodox seating of

women in a curtained balcony. One of the most persistent demands
was for more "decorum," which was one of the favorite words of
the Reformers. Not only in early America but before that in
Europe, synagogues were known for their noise and confusion. During the long chanting of verses from the Torah, members of the
congregation would wander around, chatting with friends and often
drowning out the *hazzan* with the noise of their talk. During
responsive readings, members of the congregation would read aloud
each at his own pace, rather than in unison. The Reformers also
objected to the undignified commotion often caused at the point in
the service when, by tradition, the honor of removing the Scroll of
the Law from the Ark and reading the blessing was auctioned off to
the highest bidder, the money going for the support of the synagogue,
or into some special fund. There were also demands for a modification
of Sabbath worship. In Europe, in Orthodox synagogues, it was
customary for religious Jews to spend all day Saturday in the
synagogue at prayer. But in America this was difficult if not impossible for many men, because Saturday in early times was a
working day. So Reform congregations experimented with holding
the Shabbat service on Friday evening, early Saturday morning or
even on Sunday.

The Torah—God's Word

Such changes generally could be made only by a majority vote
of the board of trustees, and so rival groups fought for such control,
often going to the civil courts to settle the legality of elections.

The Orthodox position was that the Torah had been given to the
Jews by God on Mount Sinai and that every word therein was
therefore holy. If there was conflict between the so-called "realities
of life" and the Torah, the Torah, being God's word, must be
supreme. The rules regarding the conduct of Jewish life were part
of the Torah. No biblical law must ever be revoked, revised, or
disregarded. Orthodox Jews believed that the Talmud—the sixty-
three books of Judaism's oral law that were put into writing in the
eighth century—must remain, always, the official law, not subject to
either revision or revocation. They called Reform Judaism both dis-

tasteful and shocking, and were convinced that if unopposed it might even bring about the destruction of Judaism itself. They chided the Reformers for trying to establish "an undemanding religion," freed of any ritual inconvenience, housed in elegance, and "invitingly Western in tone and language." They accused them of jettisoning all the laws and customs that Judaism had spent several thousand years acquiring.

There was also Orthodox criticism that Reform Judaism, with its handsome buildings, was a religion of the rich, the cultured, and the learned, rather than of the poor, the ignorant, the masses.

The Reform position was expressed in an article in the *Israelite*, a paper published by Isaac Mayer Wise in Cincinnati which stated that if the synagogue did not adjust to the spirit of the age, "we will have no Jews in this country in less than half a century."

Wanted: Beauty and Dignity

One of the motivations of Reform Judaism was the desire of parents to avoid a religious split between older and younger generations by Americanizing Judaism as quickly as possible. They felt that by modernizing and beautifying their synagogues, and modifying some of the antiquated customs, they could make their own places of worship as solemnly attractive to the eye and as dignified as some Christian churches were, instead of being informal gathering places, where, in addition to praying and studying, men chatted and discussed mundane, secular affairs. To achieve such beauty and dignity, they wanted to add choirs and organ music.

The Reformers held that in order to fulfill its destined role, Judaism must constantly keep pace with the ever-changing times, without being held back by the dead hand of the past.

The Orthodox answer was that Jewish law was sacred and supreme; that in case of conflict, life must adjust to the law, rather than the law to life. To the Traditionalists what was most important was remaining steadfast to Eternal Belief.

The Reformers believed that the basic teachings of Judaism have a universal character which all the world, regardless of creed or race, is destined to recognize, eventually, as the supreme truth.

They held that the very essence of Judaism lies in the moral principles of the Torah and that new, scientific methods of investigating the Bible would help them discover the essential truth, which alone is binding. Judaism's principles, they said, are not abstract; they can and must be expressed in daily practice. The Reformers also held that there is a continuous revelation; that God shows himself to man in all ages and not only as he did at Mt. Sinai.

Fear for the Structure of Judaism

But to the Traditionalists, every attempted change in ritual made them fear for the entire structure of Judaism. Ritual is to Judaism what the stones were to the Temple. Pull down the stones, one by one, and soon the Temple is gone.

There was little cohesion to the Reform Movement in the early days. This was manifest at a rabbinical conference held in Cleveland in 1855, with all shades of American rabbinical opinion represented. There was not only the expected conflict between the Traditionalists and the Reformers, but the latter split into two divergent groups: moderates from the East and a more radical group from the West.

For a time every Reform congregation seemed to represent a different wing of the movement and every Reform rabbi seemed to consider it his duty to produce a prayer book of his own. Reform in its early days had no sense of direction, or guidance, and no central organization. It was individualism unfettered.

9

ONE MAN'S CONQUEST

I N the wilds of America, and entirely amongst Gentiles, you will forget your religion and your God."

That warning was given one day in 1817 to Joseph Jonas, then twenty-five years old, by a venerable friend, Levi Phillips. Before leaving his homeland, England, young Jonas had read everything available about America, and especially the Ohio River Valley. This was the section, he decided, in which he wished to settle. At a distance of thousands of miles he even picked the city—Cincinnati—which sounded exactly to his taste. When he reached New York a relative who met his ship said he knew about Cincinnati and told Jonas it was "a promising place." But during the young man's brief stay in Philadelphia his distinguished friend, Mr. Phillips, tried to dissuade him, saying that it was not a city at all—only a few thousand people. Worse, there was not a single Jew among them.

A New Jewish Resting Place

However, Joseph Jonas was young and fired with the desire not only to see Cincinnati but to dwell there. He cloaked his decision in euphemistic phrases, telling his Philadelphia friend that "the fiat has gone forth that a new resting place for the scattered sons of Israel should be commenced, and that a sanctuary should be erected in the Great West, dedicated to the Lord of Hosts, to resound with praises to the ever-living God." More specifically, he promised Mr. Phillips that he would neither forget his religion nor forsake his God. He departed on January 2, 1817, but got only as far as Pittsburgh, where he learned that the Ohio River had frozen over, stopping all navigation. For weeks, he worked there as a mechanic, not getting to Cincinnati until March 8, 1817.

The first Jew in Ohio was quite a curiosity. A Quaker woman, hearing of his arrival, traveled some distance to gaze upon him. As she did, she asked, in awe:

"Art thou truly a Jew?"

Young Jonas nodded.

"Then thou art one of God's chosen people! Will thou let me examine thee?"

A Jew Alone

Finally, with a tinge of disappointment, she announced:

"Well! Thou art no different to other people!"

Although only twenty-five, Jonas described himself as a mechanic, watchmaker, and silversmith. He had political and literary ambitions, as well as the desire to remain a good Jew and someday to create here in "the wilds of America" a center of Orthodox Judaism. He finally satisfied his political ambition when, at the age of sixty-eight, he was elected to the Ohio State Legislature. He satisfied his literary ambition by frequent contributions to Jewish periodicals. In a series of articles written in a strange third-person style he gave a significant account of frontier religion in America, describing in precise detail the problems encountered in building the first Jewish community west of the Alleghenies. He began his account with his arrival in Cincinnati:

"The city then contained about 6000 inhabitants, but the only Israelite was himself. With the assistance of the God of his ancestors, he soon became established in a lucrative and respectable business, and his constant prayer was that he might be a nucleus around whom this first congregation might be formed, to worship the God of Israel in the great western territory. Solitary and alone he remained for more than two years, and at the solemn festivals of our holy religion, in solitude was he obliged to commune with his Maker."

A Mid-West First

The next year "his heart was delighted" with the arrival of an English family he knew, on their way to Brookville, Indiana. After they left he was lonely again. But six months later, three more Englishmen arrived to stay. Now Joseph Jonas no longer could boast that he was "the only Jew in Ohio," yet he was elated. As the next Jewish religious holidays approached, he summoned his Brookville friend and, although they did not have a *minyan*, they "duly solemnized the *vamin tobim* (holy days)." They were well aware they were making American religious history, for Jonas recorded that this was probably the first time "in the western country" that Jewish religious holidays had been celebrated.

Then came three English and three German families, "and the *yamim tobim* of 1820 were solemnized in due form with the legal number and a *Sepher Torah* (Scroll of the Law)." As more Jews came from England and Barbados "our hearts rejoiced, for the prospects of a permanent congregation were near at hand."

On January 4, 1824, Jonas and nine other men met and passed a resolution calling for the organization of a congregation, which began:

"WHEREAS, It is the duty of every member of the Jewish persuasion, when separated from a congregation, to conform as near as possible to the worship and ceremonies of our holy religion, and as soon as a sufficient number can be assembled, to form ourselves into a congregation for the purpose of glorifying our God, and observing the fundamental principles of our faith, as developed in the law of Moses. . . ."

100 Percent Attendance

Ten days later another meeting was held. The original ten were present plus four others—"a full convention of every male of the Jewish persuasion or nation." They adopted a constitution, elected

Jonas as *parnass*, and passed a resolution that a room should be obtained and fitted up as a temporary place of worship.

From here on the story of this westernmost outpost of Judaism is best told in the quaint words of Jonas himself:

"From the period of the arrival of the first Israelite in Cincinnati, to this date, the Israelites have been much esteemed and highly respected by their fellow citizens, and a great interchange of civilities and friendships has taken place between them. Many persons of the Nazarene faith residing from fifty to a hundred miles from the city, hearing there were Jews living in Cincinnati, came into town for the general purpose of viewing and conversing with some of 'the children of Israel, the holy people of God,' as they termed us.

"From the experience which we have derived by being the first settlers of our nation and religion in a new country, we arrive at the conclusion that the Almighty will give his people favour in the eyes of all nations, if they only conduct themselves as good citizens in a moral and religious point of view, for it is already conceded to us by our neighbours that we have the fewest drunkards, vagrants, or individuals amenable to the laws, of any community, according to our numbers in this city or district. And we also appreciate the respect and esteem those individuals are held in, who duly conform to the principles of our religion, especially by a strict conformity to our holy Sabbath and festivals.

The Sweet Voices of Zion's Daughters

"The original founders of our congregation were principally from Great Britain, and consequently their mode of worship (like many British Jews) was after the manner of Polish and German Jews. But being all young people, they were not so prejudiced in favour of old customs as more elderly people might have been, and especially as several of their wives had been brought up in Portuguese congregations. We therefore introduced considerable chorus singing into our worship, in which we were joined by the sweet voices of the fair daughters of Zion, and our Friday evening service was as well attended for many years as the Sabbath morning.

"At length, however, large emigrations of our German brethren settled amongst us. Again our old customs have conquered, and the sweet voices of our ladies are seldom heard. But we have so far prevailed as to continue to this day the following beautiful melodies, *The Twenty-ninth Psalm* (the Psalm of David), which is chaunted as the procession slowly proceeds to deposit the *Sepher Torah* in the Ark; also the *En Kolohenu Ir Kavonenu* (the song *There Is None Like Our God*), and after the service is concluded none attempt to quit their seats until the beautiful hymn *Adon Olam* is finished, being sung by all the congregation in full chorus.

"For several years we had no *hazzan*, and the service was read and chaunted in rotation by Messrs. David I. Johnson, Morris Moses, and Joseph Jonas. We had purchased a burial ground about three years previous to our organization, and at that time Jonas Levy was our *shohet*. Messrs. Morris Moses and David I. Johnson were elected *parnass* and *gobbai* (treasurer) for the year 5586 (1826), about which time Nicholas Longworth Esq. gave the congregation a piece of land adjoining our burial ground. During this year, a committee of correspondence was appointed to correspond with several congregations for the purpose of procuring aid from our brethren to build a synagogue. Applications at this time were responded to from Charleston, S.C., and a remittance forwarded to us of $100, also $50 from Benjamin Elkin Esq. of Barbados, W.I. . . .

"During the month of July (1829) the congregation purchased a suitable lot of ground on the east side of Broadway below Sixth Street, on which our present synagogue is erected; thus far had the Lord prospered our way. . . ."

Where the Money Came From

Jonas reported in detail how the fund-raising committee collected $5 from this source, $10 from someone else, $20 from a well-wisher in Barbadoes. Then—without comment—except for the underlining of the last word in the sentence—he recorded this proof of how at least some Cincinnati Gentiles felt toward the tiny minority: "Fifty-two gentlemen of the Christian faith, our fellow citizens, gave us toward the building $25 *each*."

The foundation stone was laid on June 11, 1835. During the following year contributions poured in from Philadelphia and Baltimore. Congregation Shearith Israel sent five large brass chandeliers that had originally hung in the old synagogue in New York, with the condition that "in case the congregation in Cincinnati at any future period should decline to use them, then to return them to the trustees of this congregation." To which Jonas added this comment:

"The original donor could have little dreamed at the time that his munificent gift would adorn and enlighten a temple erected to the service of the ever-living God in the far west. . . .

"During the months of May, June and July (1836) we sold seats in our new synagogue to the amount of $4500, which enabled us to finish the interior of the building in a much superior style than we originally intended. The edifice is erected with a handsome Doric front, a flight of stone steps over the basement, with a portico supported by pillars. The building is eighty feet in length by thirty-three in breadth, including a vestibule of twelve feet. It has a very handsome dome in the center, ornamented with panels and carved mouldings in stucco.

"On entering the building from the vestibule, the beholder is attracted by the chaste and beautiful appearance of the Ark, situated at the east end. It is eighteen feet in front, surrounded by a neat low white balustrade, ornamented by four large brass candlesticks; it is ascended by a flight of steps handsomely carpeted. . . .

"The edifice when finished was much admired, and the building committee received a vote of thanks from the congregation for their unremitted attentions in procuring the necessary funds and materials, and for the time and trouble bestowed by them in superintending the erection of the building. The ninth of September, 1836, corresponding to the twenty-seventh of Elul, 5596, was appointed for the consecration.

Christians Flock to a Synagogue

"The day having arrived the crowd of our Christian friends was so great that we could not admit them all. We therefore selected the clergy and the families of those gentlemen who so liberally had given donations toward the building. The members of the congregation assembled in the basement rooms, a procession was formed, with the *sepharim* (scrolls) in front under a handsome canopy. . . . Mr. David I. Johnson officiated on the occasion and chaunted the consecration service. He also led the choir of singers, supported by a band of music. The choir consisted of about twenty of the ladies and gentlemen of the congregation.

"Who did not enjoy supreme delight and heavenly pleasure, when the sweet voices of the daughters of Zion ascended on high in joyful praises to the great Architect of the universe on the glorious occasion of dedicating a temple to his worship and adoration. And what must have been the excited feelings of the founder (Joseph Jonas) of this congregation, at the consecration of this first temple west of the Allegheny Mountains, when on knocking thrice outside the inner door he was addressed by the reader within: 'It is the voice of my beloved that knocketh,' and when he responded: 'Open to me the gates of righteousness, I will go into them, and I will praise the Lord!' . . .

"Having passed this great epoch in our history, and established our congregation on a firm basis, and having returned thanks to the Giver of all good for the protection afforded us, and for the prosperity, with His assistance, to which we have arrived at this period, let us now rest awhile, and view the Jewish horizon around us. Alas, it is a bleak and dreary view. In the whole Mississippi Valley, from the Allegheny Mountains to the city of New Orleans included, excepting Cincinnati, not a single community of Israelites is to be descried. Numerous families and individuals were located in all directions; but not another attempt at union, and the worship of God appeared to be dead in their hearts."

Cleveland, a Thriving Community

The rest of the history of B'nai Israel in Cincinnati is like that of any normal congregation in nineteenth-century America. More land was purchased, additions to the building were constructed, a Hebrew school was established, the cemetery was enlarged, additional seats were installed in the synagogue, and the ladies' gallery was expanded. When the first settlement of Jews was founded at Cleveland, Reporter Jonas described that city as "a very thriving community and is in a very wealthy portion of the state. The congregation was formed by considerable emigrations of our German brothers. Being at a great distance from them, and having little correspondence, we are not able to give their numbers. Travellers inform us they are very numerous."

In the articles he wrote about B'nai Israel Jonas sometimes referred to himself as "the Solitary," or "the founder," or simply as "Mr. Joseph Jonas." His reporting had an objective historical quality until he came to tell about the fight over the Sunday school, which had been established in 1842 by "a number of ladies of the congregation" who chose a young woman, Mrs. Luisa Symonds, as superintendent. When other duties compelled her to resign, the Sunday school teachers unanimously voted for Mr. Jonas as their superintendent. This is how Historian Jonas reported the troubles of Superintendent Jonas:

"There were forty-six children in attendance, and still every appearance of increasing; the field is large, and the harvest has every appearance of being abundant. Considerable proficiency has been made by the children; but a blight appears to be moving over our prospects, from a source little to be expected—the *rabbonim* (the rabbis), who ought to be the promoters, not the disturbers of a plan to forward the principles of the Holy Religion in the minds of youth. But perceiving that good might be done without their interference, the *craft* was in danger! and the school must be put down. It was consequently anathematized by them for being held on *Sunday*, the Christian Sabbath! In consequence, the school is not increasing, and through their influence most of the German, and some English children, are prevented attending. The leader amongst these bigoted mischief-makers is Rabbi _____ _____, a talmid or scholar, and the Rev. Mr. R_____ of B_____.

"I am well convinced that righteousness and true religion must prevail, and that the evil spirit of bigotry will be overwhelmed. We have endeavoured to reason and compromise with them, but to no purpose. Still, whilst there are ten children in attendance, their teachers will not weary in superintending, knowing the benefits already done. We feel warm in the cause of the rising generation, and hope this publication . . . may have some influence on their future conduct."

The Solitary Castigates His Fellows

In concluding the series of articles on the religious life of pioneer Cincinnati, Chronicler Jonas wrote: "The congregations in this city are continually increasing. (A second congregation, Benai Yeshurun, had been founded in 1841.) Their character stands high for morality, honesty and sobriety. Sorry am I to say that I cannot state the same for many of them in a religious point of view. If only a *few* of the most able and respectable would commence *sincerely* keeping their Sabbaths and festivals, it would have considerable influence on the minds of the erring brethren. But 'the Solitary' (I, Joseph Jonas) is still thankful to the God of Israel, that he has been made the humble instrument in collecting near 2000 brethren of Israel, to worship the Lord of Hosts in this beautiful metropolis of the Great West."

By 1850 there were some 2500 Jews in Cincinnati. Ten years later that number had nearly quadrupled. By 1860 there were at least four congregations and two rabbis who would have a major impact on the practice of Judaism in America. Jews had predominant influence in the retail trades in Cincinnati, especially in the field of ready-to-wear clothing.

The Origin of Kuhn, Loeb

One of the numerous Jewish shirt manufacturers in the 1840s was Solomon Kuhn, who would bring teenage boys from Germany, employ them as stock clerks until they had learned enough English, and then stake them to a pack and a wagon. Traveling over a wide area, they were able to sell several wagonloads of shirts a year, turning a neat profit. But they were wary of putting their earnings in Christian banks, because the experiences they had had in Europe—or had heard about—had made them distrust all non-Jews, so they brought their money back to Cincinnati and gave it for safekeeping to Kuhn, who finally accumulated such a large sum from his army of traveling salesmen that he went into the banking business. In this field he also succeeded so well that he moved his base of operations to New York and founded the banking house of Kuhn, which later amalgamated with the Loeb Company to form Kuhn, Loeb & Co., the American Rothschilds.

IO

THE WISE-LEESER FEUD

I SAAC MAYER WISE, the organizing genius and ideological guide of Reform Judaism, was born in a small town in what is now Czechoslovakia. He was educated in Prague, was ordained as a rabbi at the age of twenty-three, and emigrated to America when he was twenty-seven. One hot day in July of 1846, with his wife and child, he arrived in New York after sixty-three days at sea, with just two dollars in his pocket, but with a love, already, of this country about which he had read so much in the American newspapers that he had regularly purchased in a Prague bookshop. His first post was as rabbi of a small Orthodox synagogue—Beth El—in Albany, New York, salary $250 a year. There, to improve his forensic ability, he went each Sunday to two Christian churches and listened to the sermons of the city's two most eloquent preachers. To improve his English, he spent two hours a day reading American classics.

$50 for a Singing Teacher

Gradually the young rabbi began introducing reforms in the Albany synagogue. His congregants made no objection when he stopped the weekly auctioning of the right to read from the Torah. When he sought to beautify the service by introducing a choir of mixed voices, they voted him $50 to pay a singing teacher. He eliminated from the liturgy all prayers that he considered turgid and spiritless, and also those calling for restoration of the throne of David, the coming of a personal Messiah, re-establishment of Temple sacrifices, and a return of the Kingdom of Israel to Palestine. He began preaching in German and English on such subjects as desecration of the Sabbath, the evil of habitual card-playing, and the iniquity of saloons.

Only a few months after Wise arrived in Albany, the rabbi of three Orthodox synagogues in New York, Max Lilienthal, suggested the convening of an authoritative synagogical body to be called a *Beth Din* (Court of Law), which would consist of learned men who would decide questions about fundamental ritual and other religious matters, and would seek to supplant the confusion and chaos of the times in Jewish religious circles with some sort of ecclesiastical cooperation and order. He invited Wise to start work on a *Minhag America*—a modification of the liturgy, suitable for use in the United States. The young rabbi eagerly accepted the assignment and with vigor and ambition went to work on it at once. In six months he completed an outline.

A Recipe for Survival

The boldest of his proposals dealt with what language should be used in the synagogue. He himself was an immigrant and still spoke English with a very European accent. Also, he knew that two-thirds of all American Jews did not yet speak English and that their manner of prayer was as varied as the sections of Europe from which they had emigrated. Yet he was adamant that, to survive in America, Judaism must take on an endemic character and make use of English, as well as German.

Wise was hurt but not surprised when his all-American liturgy was vehemently attacked in the *Occident*, the only Jewish publication in the country, which said in part: "We most emphatically object to any such form of prayer, which, as proposed by Dr. Wise, should exclude the petitions for the rebuilding of the Temple, and the re-establishment of the sacrifices. We believe, in common with all Orthodox Jews, in the literal fulfillment of Scriptures."

The paper also attacked Wise's proposal that the length of the Sabbath service be cut so that it would not run for more than two and a half to three hours.

The *Occident* was owned and edited by Isaac Leeser, who was often called the leader of "moderate Orthodoxy." He was twelve years the senior of the young Albany rabbi and a native of Germany. For the next quarter century these two men would frequently cross swords, one representing the Traditionalists, the other the Reformers. Both were brilliant-minded and sharp-tongued. Both were energetic and tireless in their religious and intellectual labors. Each in his own way affected the future of Judaism in America.

Self-Educated But Brilliant

Leeser was born in the province of Westphalia in Prussia in 1806. He studied the Talmud under celebrated Hebrew scholars in Münster, came to America at the age of seventeen, and went to school briefly in Richmond, but he was generally labeled a "self-educated man." For five years, while working in an uncle's mercantile establishment in Richmond as a clerk, he taught in the local Hebrew school on Saturdays and Sundays. The course of his life was changed when he read a series of articles in a British magazine ridiculing Judaism. He became so incensed that he composed an equal number of articles defending both Jews and Judaism. They were printed in a local paper, the *Richmond Whig*, and attracted such attention that young Leeser was invited the next year to become *hazzan* of Congregation Mikveh in Philadelphia. There he moved quickly from the cantor's desk to the pulpit, although not an ordained rabbi. In 1843 he founded the *Occident*, which he edited until his death twenty-five years later. In this monthly magazine he gave his readers local, national, and international Jewish news. He traveled widely delivering sermons, dedicating new synagogues and addressing conventions and conferences, while trying to encourage American Jews to work together in harmony. In the *Occident* he reported his observations.

Editor, Teacher, Publisher, Professor

Leeser's life was many-faceted. He realized that American Jewry needed more Jewish schools, more synagogues, more books, and more publications, and he tried to do something about each of these matters. He argued that American Jewry should no longer depend on Europe for its rabbis and scholars, but should establish its own rabbinical schools. Putting his own preaching into practice, he helped found and was president of Maimonides College, the first seminary in the country for the training of rabbis. He hoped it would become a national institution supported by Jews of all shades of belief. He not only recruited a faculty of scholars but taught in the college himself. However, this was one of Leeser's dreams that was never fully realized, for after six years the college went out of existence, due to lack of funds. In those six years it had graduated only one student. But the idea of thoroughly American seminaries did not die. Before long others were founded, which are still in existence.

Leeser wrote textbooks for Jewish school children, helped establish Jewish hospitals, organized the Board of Delegates of American Israelites, the first union of Jewish congregations in the country, and founded the Jewish Publication Society to produce books on strictly Jewish subjects. His own translation of the Bible into English was for years the only one that American Jews could use—until the Jewish Publication Society in 1917 issued its authoritative translation.

A Blighted Love Affair

Among the members of Leeser's Mikveh Israel congregation was Michael Gratz, affluent merchant and shipowner, whose daughter, Rebecca, was one of the great beauties of the day. Whoever came to call at the Gratz house on Chestnut Street in Philadelphia—men of government, finance, or letters—went away impressed by the girl's beauty, charm, and intelligence. Thomas Scully, a leading artist of the day, did her portrait. Sir Walter Scott was so impressed by the description of her given him by Washington Irving that he patterned the Rebecca in his novel *Ivanhoe* on her and her unhappy romance. Or so the legend goes. She and Samuel Ewing, son of the provost of the University of Pennsylvania, had been deeply in love, but they finally agreed that they should not marry, because of their religious differences. He married someone else, while she remained a spinster all her life. Her love, however, found an outlet in helping others.

She was a charter member of the Philadelphia Asylum, and helped found one of the oldest Jewish charitable institutions in America, the Female Hebrew Benevolent Society. Realizing how greatly the Jewish children of Philadelphia needed religious instruction, she organized—with the help of Isaac Leeser—the first Jewish Sunday school in the United States and acted as its supervisor and president for twenty-six years.

A School for Everyone

Leeser used his magazine to propagate the idea of Jewish day schools, which he insisted should not be connected with any one congregation but should serve the entire Jewish community. Then he organized the Hebrew Education Society. This school, known later as Talmud Torah, was open to any Jewish children in Philadelphia, but it began with a class of only twenty-two pupils. One hundred and twenty years later, however, Leeser's idea had won such universal acceptance that there were well over half a million children enrolled in hundreds of Jewish schools of various types scattered across America.

Leeser was a consistent conservative. He was certain that the reforms advocated by Wise would neither last long nor spread far, and that Orthodoxy would prevail, as it always had down through the centuries. He was a man of high principles and boldness in expressing them. Although in those days it was customary for German Jews in America to mingle socially with German non-Jews, Leeser, at a banquet of the German-Hebrew Benevolent Society in New York, annoyed at an extravagant toast proposed to "the German fatherland," bluntly pointed out that Germany still had not granted equal civil rights to Jews. The year was 1853.

Consistent Radical

Wise was a consistent radical, although his radicalism was limited to ritual matters and did not extend to social causes. His "cause" was union, for which he was to compromise many principles. He was certain that unless something drastic was done to revive, revise, and reform American Judaism, it would not be strong enough to live out the nineteenth century. He, too, was a man of high principles and he, too, was bold in expressing them. A perfect example of this high-principled boldness is the story of his public condemnation of the Governor of Ohio just two years after moving to Cincinnati. At a banquet of the Zion Collegiate Association Wise was introduced to the chief speaker, Salmon P. Chase, then serving his first term as Governor. During a warm and exceedingly friendly conversation, Chase advised the young rabbi to attach himself to the Republican party, which he claimed was the party of reform and progress. Wise said he would seriously consider the advice. That autumn Chase's Thanksgiving Proclamation began: "In conformity with a custom sanctioned by Legislative Resolves, commended by the practice of my predecessors in the executive office, and in itself highly becoming a Christian people, I, Salmon P. Chase . . ."

Unrepublican and Inconsistent

In print Wise countered: "The Governor addresses himself to a Christian people, but he ought to know that the people of Ohio are neither Christian nor Jewish; they are a free and independent people.

"Next, the Governor desires us to thank God 'for the mercies of redemption and the hopes of immortality.' Fall on your knees, Jews, deists, infidels, and atheists, and thank God that Jesus of Nazareth died on the cross to redeem the people of Ohio, as His Excellency, the Governor, decrees. On the whole, we do not see by what right the Governor assumed the prerogative of exercising a religious authority. This is, to say the least, unrepublican and inconsistent with the constitution of the State. . . ."

Leeser and Wise often fenced with each other in speeches, sermons, magazine articles, and books. At times they were almost insulting, one to the other. When Wise arrived in America, Leeser in print called him "a young schoolmaster who also preaches and is said to possess some Hebrew learning." After his first meeting with Leeser, Wise wrote that Leeser "lacked practically all Jewish or Hebrew learning."

Yet a short time later Leeser asked the younger man to write for the *Occident* and Wise accepted the invitation, contributing articles which Leeser printed—then answered in the same or the next issue. After that they often clashed, personally and ideologically, yet one of Wise's biographers wrote that the Reform leader had "a sneaking affection for Leeser."

Turmoil On Rosh Ha-Shanah

As Wise attempted to introduce more and more radical changes in the religious life of Beth-El, members of the congregation began to rebel. Criticism turned to ill will as he introduced family pews, confirmation for both girls and boys, and the right of women to be included in a *minyan*. The opposition was led by the president of the congregation, Louis Spanier. Just before Rosh Ha-Shanah, 1850, six serious charges were filed against Wise by Spanier, all apparently manufactured out of thin air. The document said that because he stood for Reform, "he can be a Jew no longer." Feelings among members of the congregation rose to the boiling point, with everyone intensely "for" or "against." The synagogue was packed the morning of Rosh Ha-Shanah when Wise entered to find his usual seat on the pulpit occupied by a friend of Spanier, who had been instructed to pre-empt it before the service began. Accordingly Wise took a seat in the body of the hall among members of his congregation as the choir sang *En Komocho*. What then happened is told most graphically in the rabbi's own words:

"Excitement ruled the hour. . . . At the conclusion of the song I step before the Ark in order to take out the scrolls of the law as usual, and to offer prayer. Spanier steps in my way, and, without saying a word, smites me with his fist so that my cap falls from my head. This was the terrible signal for an uproar the like of which I have never experienced. The people acted like furies. It was as though the synagogue had suddenly burst forth into a flaming conflagration. The Poles and Hungarians, who thought only of me, struck out like wild men. The young people jumped down from the choir-gallery to protect me, and had to fight their way through the

surging crowd. Within two minutes the whole assembly was a struggling mass. The sheriff and his posse, who were summoned, were
belabored and forced out until finally the whole assembly surged
out of the house into Herkimer Street. . . . I finally reached home,
bowed with pain and inexpressible grief. The constable came and
arrested me as the ringleader of a rebellious mob at a public service.
Naturally, all this had been arranged beforehand; for this constable
who arrested me was the gruffest and roughest in the city. He
seized me by the coat, and thus led me to the police station through
the streets of Albany. Upon our arrival there, the whole rabble was
present in order to feast their eyes on the sight of their rabbi ap-
pearing before court on New Year's Day; but their hopes were
disappointed, for the police judge went into an adjoining room and
received me there. My friends had informed him of what had taken
place, and he dismissed me on my word of honor. . . . Who can
describe that terrible day? Not I! It was agonizing, hellish torture.
This victory of Orthodoxy proved its grave wherein it was buried."

A Slap Heard Round the World

Overnight Wise became a martyr and a national figure. Echoes of
the slap were heard in every corner of the country. Jews all over
America discussed who had been in the right.

Many lawsuits grew out of the incident. In one a jury awarded
Wise $1000 damages, which he never attempted to collect from
Spanier. For months Leeser kept the controversy alive in the columns
of the *Occident*, contending that the trouble originated when Wise,
at a public gathering some weeks earlier, had declared that he did
not believe in "the glorious doctrine of the coming of the Messiah
and the resurrection of the dead."

Of more importance to the future of Reform Judaism in America,
a new congregation was formed in Albany, which Wise himself
named *Anshe Emeth* (Men of Truth). For the next four years the
young rabbi was free to carry on his Reform experiments. Then,
in 1854, he went to Cincinnati, where members of Congregation
B'nai Yeshurun elected him their rabbi for life and where he served
forty-six years until his death.

Cincinnati was then called the "Queen City of the West" (*sic!*) and contained the third or fourth largest Jewish community in the United States.

A Man of Many Facets

In Cincinnati Wise established not only an English-language magazine, the *American Israelite,* to compete with Leeser's *Occident* (today it is the oldest Anglo-Jewish periodical in the country), but also a German-language weekly, *Die Deborah,* for German was still the language of a majority of American Jews. Besides writing most of the contents of the two periodicals, and carrying on his duties as rabbi of a thriving congregation, and continuing with his modernization of the liturgy, and serving as the pioneer of Reform Judaism, he somehow found time to write many books, including several novels which he used in serial form to pad out the columns of the *American Israelite.* The year he arrived in Cincinnati he also put out the first volume of a *History of the Israelitish Nation from Abraham to the Present Time.* That same year he and a brother-in-law founded the Bloch Publishing Company, which published Jewish books, Jewish periodicals, and, some years later, Wise's *Minhag America,* which contained prayers in Hebrew, German, and English. Leeser and other Traditionalists were outraged by the new prayer book, predicting in their writings and sermons that it would soon be "dead and forgotten."

The two antagonists, Leeser and Wise, joined forces in 1855 to call a conference at Cleveland in the hope that moderates in both the Orthodox and Reform groups could find some common ground on which they could present a united front. Both were interested in a national religious organization of American Jews. What divided them was Orthodoxy's stand that the Talmud should be the basis of authority in American Jewish life. The Reformers wanted to be completely free of such authority, but a compromise was finally worked out: the Talmud would be accepted in principle. The Reformers felt that this did not shut the door on change. The Traditionalists felt that any changes would now come slowly and in moderation. But when the compromise was announced to the public, a storm broke. Extreme Orthodox leaders denounced the idea of any change at all, even if moderate and gradual. Extreme Reformers said that any enslavement by the Talmud would prevent necessary changes. When this attempt at unity failed—and it has often been called "the last attempt of American Jewry to unite"—Wise turned his attention to bringing direction to the Reform movement itself. He wrote for, spoke for, and traveled in the interest of Reform the rest of his life.

Samuel Hirsch, Radical

In 1869 a volatile new figure appeared on Reform platforms. Samuel Hirsch, who had been chief rabbi of Luxemburg, arrived in the United States at the age of fifty to become rabbi of Congregation Keneseth Israel in Philadelphia. In that city four years later he presided at a meeting of eastern Reform rabbis and presented his own radical views. The conference issued a declaration stating that the messianic aim of Israel is not the restoration of the old Jewish state but "the union of all the children of God." The resolution also declared that the destruction of the ancient Jewish state had not been punishment for the sinfulness of Israel, but a result of the divine purpose of dispersing the Jews "to all parts of the world for the realization of their highly priestly mission, to lead the nations to the true knowledge and worship of God." It is not surprising to discover that this statement was issued in German.

Year by year, as more Reform congregations were formed, Wise became increasingly impatient for the establishment of a college to train American rabbis. But first, he knew, they needed a united organization of Reform congregations to support such a seminary. Finally, in 1873, delegates from thirty-four congregations met in Cincinnati and established the Union of American Hebrew Congregations. Two years later, with the UAHC as its parent body, the Hebrew Union College was created at Cincinnati, "to preserve Judaism intact." It was the first successful rabbinical seminary in America, Leeser's Maimonides College having already closed its doors. Rabbi Wise became not only the president but one-third of the faculty, for there were only two other members. For exactly a quarter of a century, until the very day of his death at the age of eighty, he taught classes.

Now new rabbis could be trained in the new theology, to head new congregations that would be formed all over the country, as new waves of immigrants poured in from Eastern Europe.

The Pittsburgh Conference

At a conference of the entire Reform movement held in Pittsburgh in 1885, the delegates agreed on eight basic principles of Reform Judaism:

1. Every religion is an attempt to grasp the Infinite. Judaism presents the highest conception of the God-idea.
2. The Bible is the record of the consecration of the Jewish people to its mission. Modern discoveries in the domain of nature and history are not antagonistic to the doctrines of Judaism, for the Bible respects the primitive ideas of its own age.
3. The Mosaic laws were binding in ancient times in Palestine, but today only the moral laws are binding. Ceremonies that elevate and sanctify our lives should be accepted, but others that are not adapted to the views and habits of modern civilization may be rejected.
4. All Mosaic and rabbinical laws that regulate diet, priestly purity and dress originated in past ages and under the influence of ideas foreign to our present mental and spiritual state. Their observance in our days is apt rather to obstruct than to further modern spiritual elevation.
5. The modern age heralds the approach of Israel's Messianic hope for the establishment of the kingdom of truth, justice and peace among all men. We consider ourselves no longer a nation, but a religious community, and therefore expect neither a return to Palestine, nor the restoration of sacrificial worship under the sons of Aaron, nor the restoration of any of the laws concerning the Jewish state.

6. Judaism is a progressive religion, ever striving to be in accord with the postulates of reason. Christianity and Islam, as sister religions, are aiding in spreading monotheistic and moral truth. We extend the hand of fellowship to all who cooperate with us in the establishment of the reign of truth and righteousness among men.

7. The soul is immortal. We reject as ideas not rooted in Judaism the beliefs both in bodily resurrection and in Gehenna and Eden (Hell and Paradise) as abodes of everlasting punishment and reward.

8. In full accordance with the spirit of Mosaic legislation, which strives to regulate the relations between rich and poor, we deem it our duty to participate in the great task of modern times, to solve on the basis of justice and righteousness the problems presented by the contrasts and evils of the present organization of society.

The Significance

These basic principles acknowledged the existence of other monotheistic religions besides Judaism and called for cooperation with them. They declared the Bible to have been written by men and, therefore, it did not need to be taken literally. Dietary laws did not have to be obeyed. Judaism is not a nationality. Return to sacrificial worship is not to be expected. Instead, Jews should work for a better social order. Reform Judaism also made it clear at Pittsburgh that it did not seek authority over its adherents; that every congregation was free and independent. For the next half century this eight-point platform remained the generally accepted position of Reform Jewry.

One historian (Jacob Rader Marcus) says that Wise "may well have been the most important Jew who lived in the United States during the latter half of the Nineteenth Century."

He was an educator in the best sense of the word, for he wanted to improve the world and the lot of its inhabitants. He was convinced that man could better himself and the conditions of life. And, as a Jew, he felt it should all begin with his people.

Religious Universalism

Wise often talked and wrote of universalism, by which he meant that the monotheistic people—Christians, Jews, and Moslems—should associate as intellectual and cultural equals. He believed that Judaism, once liberalized, might be able to spread the idea of religious universalism, at least through all of Europe and America. He believed in the theory of inevitable progress and the improvability of mankind.

Some of the ideas Wise expressed in his voluminous writings were:

"It is not our duty to reform the Orthodox, nor is it the duty of the Orthodox to reclaim the Reformers. Let each worship as he thinks proper, and build up Judaism."

"Dogmas have no place in our system. . . . The existence of One God is no dogma; it is a thesis demonstrated by every department of nature."

"All religions go back to Judaism, and it goes back to Moses. He alone was a prophet in the proper sense of the term."

"Judaism is the religion revealed on Mt. Sinai. . . . If God did not command us to be, do and believe so, we are the worst blunder in history."

"If we are right in regard to the religious education of woman . . . then it is highly necessary that she should have a female academy, where the daughters of Israel would be offered an opportunity to finish their education and have the benefit of a thorough and enlightened religious instruction."

Judaism and Political Liberty

"Judaism is most capable of revealing its full charm under conditions of political liberty."

"Orthodoxy, in the form it assumed in Europe, is not necessarily based on fundamental Jewish doctrine, but is itself an outgrowth of the conditions that for centuries hemmed in the Jews in their medieval ghettoes."

"Judaism is by its very nature an evolutionary religion; growth and continuous adjustment are an integral part of its being."

"Judaism, its ceremonial part excepted, is not alone the religion of Jews, but of all intelligent men in the world who have the moral courage to make themselves independent of inherited superstitions and early impressions. But the religious victory which the intelligent of all nations achieve after much struggle, we Jews learn in the days of early childhood, and therefore we have a considerable advantage."

". . . it is the Orthodox principle that religion must be in conflict with reason. This is as true of Christianity as of Orthodox Judaism. It places religion in conflict with the understanding and consciousness of the Nineteenth Century, to the prolific increase of infidelity."

A New Love of an Old Religion

"What the Reform party proposes, it proposes for the welfare of future generations. It wishes to prevent the endless desertions and splits. It wishes to banish the hideous indifference which has taken hold of a large portion of the Jewish community. It wishes to inspire the Jews with a new love for their religion."

"The Orthodox Jew may look upon it as a violation of his conscience to enter a synagogue bareheaded, but the liberal Jew certainly does not consider it a sin to keep the head covered. . . . If Reform does not teach its followers common-sense, toleration and good manners in all things appertaining to religion, there is not much use of its existence."

II

CHALLENGES OF THE NINETEENTH CENTURY

AMERICAN Jews in the mid-nineteenth century were a relatively free people, living in a relatively free society. As pioneers in the West they were building cities, laying roads, helping to conquer the wilderness. As city people they were lawyers, teamsters, writers, vintners, actors, merchants, doctors, jewelers, auctioneers, plumbers, carpenters, cigar makers, tailors, and teachers—in fact, they were sprinkled through the entire fabric of American life. No matter how few of them there were, they were already beginning to make an imprint on community and national life, as they put their religion into everyday practice.

Jacob Rader Marcus, professor of Jewish History in Hebrew Union College and director of the American Jewish Archives, has compiled and published three volumes of excerpts from the memoirs of fifty Jews who were prominent in the years immediately preceding the Civil War. Each of the fifty had a good claim to fame. The following sketches are of but five men who made contributions to their country in five quite different ways. What all five had in common was that they were Jews, that they represented the best precepts of Judaism, and that they were the human instruments through which Judaism was acting on America.

A Proud Jew

Isaac Touro, the first *hazzan* of the first synagogue in Newport and the man after whom the building eventually was named, took his two sons with him to Jamaica when he fled, as the British were occupying Newport. Both boys were later brought back to Boston, where they grew up. The older, Abraham, after amassing a fortune as a merchant, built his own shipyards and soon had vessels on most of the seven seas. Before long he was widely recognized as one of Massachusetts' leading citizens. While others tried now and then to disguise their Jewishness, Abraham Touro took bold steps to proclaim that he was a Jew, as evidenced by this entry in the town records of Boston for the year 1861: "Mr. Abraham Touro applied to the Town Clerk & requested that his religious profession might be recorded on the Town's books—& that he belonged to a Synagogue of Jews."

When the Newport synagogue was reopened in 1850, it was Abraham Touro who gave $1500 to make sure that "the synagogue, the street on which it is situated, as also the burying grounds, are kept in elegant order. . . ."

A State-Protected Synagogue

In his will he left another $10,000 to the Legislature of the State of Rhode Island to support what he called "the Jewish synagogue in that state," and when the state accepted the bequest it became the first governmental unit in the country—perhaps in the world—to have the distinction of serving as the protector and guardian of a synagogue. To make sure that the terms of the bequest were honored, a law was passed providing that no one, not even the officials of Newport, should "interfere with or restrain the full free exercise of the Jewish religion in said synagogue."

The younger Touro brother, Judah, fell in love with a cousin, Catherine Hays, and when her father forbade the marriage, left Boston for New Orleans, which was then a forbidding place for a Jew. It still belonged to the French, who under their Code Noir made it illegal for Jews to engage in any gainful occupation. Somehow twenty-seven-year-old Judah Touro circumvented the law (two years later New Orleans came under jurisdiction of the United States following the Louisiana Purchase) and opened a retail shop, buying Yankee goods in New England and having them shipped south by water. His honesty and intelligence won him the respect of his customers and soon he was on the road to financial success.

Brotherhood on the Battlefield

When the British attacked New Orleans during the War of 1812, Touro was among the many volunteers who were wounded. His life was saved by a Christian comrade-in-arms who stumbled over his unconscious body on the battlefield and carried him to a first-aid station. This incident had a profound effect on young Touro, strengthening his belief in his own religion, while at the same time making him acutely aware of the need for people of different faiths to work together for the great common good. In those days in New Orleans all who could afford slaves had them, but Touro decided it was wrong to buy and sell human beings, so he not only freed his own slave, but sent him to school and after his graduation gave him money enough to start his own business.

After the war Touro branched out into importing, exporting, operating fleets of ships, and dealing in real estate. And his fortune grew.

Patriarch and Prophet

Judah Touro combined with his deep feeling about his religion a great patriotic love of America. In 1825, just fifty years after the Battle of Bunker Hill, a memorial had been started to commemorate that Revolutionary exploit, but available funds were insufficient to complete it and even the impassioned oratory of Daniel Webster failed to raise additional money. Twenty thousand dollars more was needed. At last, in 1839, a Boston blueblood, Amos Laurence, gave $10,000 on condition that a like amount would be raised at once. Soon the committee received a check for the entire $10,000—from New Orleans, of all places. The donor asked that he be permitted to remain anonymous. But the secret leaked out on June 17, 1843, the day the monument was dedicated. With Daniel Webster, Governor Morton, and John Tyler, President of the United States, on the platform, these lines from the pen of Oliver Wendell Holmes were read:

> Amos and Judah—venerated names,
>   Patriarch and Prophet press their equal claims.
> Like generous coursers running neck and neck
>   Each aids the work by giving it a check.
> Christian and Jew, they carry out one plan,
>   For though of different faiths, each in his heart a man.

Two footnotes to the story: Touro had been born just a few hours before the start of the Battle of Bunker Hill, and, this was the first public memorial in America.

As Touro's wealth increased, so did his generosity to worthwhile causes. He gave money for hospitals, built a sailors' home, financed an infirmary, and founded the New Orleans Free Public Library, which today claims to be the oldest free public library in the world. He seldom turned down an appeal for a contribution. Soon he was being called "the Great Jewish Philanthropist." When he heard that Jews living in Jerusalem were in need of help, he sent them large contributions. When he was informed that a newly discovered colony of Jews in China needed Hebrew books, he not only sent them a sizable financial contribution but also wrote them into his will.

Charity for Congregationalists

His generosity extended to Catholic and Protestant causes. In 1823 this article appeared in a weekly newspaper:

A JEW!

A Congregational church was lately sold by auction at New Orleans to pay off the debts of the trustees and was purchased for $20,000 by Mr. Judah Touro, a native of New England and a Jew, that it might not be converted to any other use than that for which it was intended, and the society still worships in it.

For many years thereafter Touro permitted the Congregationalists to use the building, rent-free.

Four years before his death Touro not only built a synagogue for the Jews of New Orleans, but even provided for the payment each year of the rabbi's salary from a fund he established.

The one tragedy of his life had been his blighted love affair. Although he and the cousin he had wanted to marry were both of the same religion, the outcome was similar to the Rebecca story in that Touro, like Rebecca Gratz, never fell in love again, remaining single all his life. When he died he left his entire estate of nearly half a million dollars to be divided almost equally between Jewish and Christian charities, with Rezin Davis Shepherd, the man who had saved his life on the battlefield, as executor. Shepherd likewise had no family, so he added his property to his friend's and in this ecumenical manner repaid in kind his Jewish friend's generosity to Christian institutions.

Never Before in History—

Not only was this amount of half a million dollars a great fortune in those days, but never before in American history—and perhaps never in the history of any other country—had anyone distributed such a large estate in this manner. There were bequests for an almhouse, for an "Asylum for the Relief of Destitute Females and Children," for a Catholic boys' school, a firemen's association, a seaman's home, a Hebrew hospital. Every synagogue then in existence in America received a gift of $2000 to $5000. There were bequests for Jewish philanthropies all over America, and $50,000 for Moses Montefiore's work in Palestine, which went to build the Jewish Hospital in Jerusalem.

On Touro's tombstone were chiseled these words:

By righteousness and integrity he collected his wealth;
In charity and for salvation he dispensed it.
The last of his name, he inscribed it in the book of
    philanthropy,
To be remembered forever.

Maryland: A Study in Contradictions

Religious liberty did not come to all the people of all the various geographical units of the United States with the passage of the Bill of Rights. It was 1965 before the State of New Hampshire lifted its prohibition against Jews holding public office. Maryland was nearly as backward. It is one of the ironies of American history that Maryland, founded as a haven from religious persecution—for Catholics—maintained a religious ban against Jews holding public office for almost two hundred years after receiving her charter. There are several other ironies to the story of the man who fought a good part of his adult life to persuade Maryland to grant religious liberty to Jews.

Solomon Etting was a member of a distinguished pioneer family of Baltimore. In 1797 he first petitioned the Maryland General Assembly to give Jews the same right to hold public office that all other Marylanders had. Members of the legislative committee appointed to investigate the situation indicated to Etting that they were in sympathy with his plea, but that it was too late in the legislative session to take action. The paradox of the situation became apparent when President Jefferson appointed Etting's brother, Reuben, as United States Marshal for Maryland. Because it was a federal appointment, there was nothing Maryland could do to prevent *this* Jew holding *this* office.

Defeat After Defeat

Etting made it one of his life ambitions to obtain repeal of the Maryland prohibition and so in each legislative session he would see that a new bill was introduced. He worked without respite as a lobbyist, enlisting the support of influential citizens, cornering key members of the Assembly, arguing, pleading. He pointed out the role Maryland's fifteen Jewish families had played in the American Revolution, and reminded the legislators that Jacob Hart, a Baltimore merchant, had raised $10,000 for Lafayette's soldiers. Yet each year the bill was defeated. Then Etting won the assistance of a Scotch Presbyterian, Thomas Kennedy, who came not from Baltimore, where 150 Jews then resided (by 1967 the Jewish population of Baltimore had reached 85,000), but from the western part of the state. Kennedy boldly made this public statement:

"There are scarcely any Jews in the country from which I came and I have but the barest acquaintance with any Jews in the world. There are a few Jews in the United States; there are a few in Maryland. But if there were only one, to that one we ought to do justice. A religious test can never be productive of any good effect. It may prevent the honest and conscientious from accepting an office, but the wicked and ambitious will not be stopped by so feeble a barrier."

And Then, Final Victory

The bill to make Jews full citizens had been proposed as an amendment to the State Constitution. An amendment had to pass two sessions of the Legislature. This bill, entitled *An Act for the Relief of the Jews of Maryland*, passed in 1822 for the first time. But in the next election the fight was carried to Kennedy's home county and he was defeated for re-election and the bill died. But in 1826 Kennedy, re-elected, introduced the bill again and proudly saw it carried for a second time. In gratitude the Jews of Maryland erected a monument in his honor at Hagerstown.

For Etting it was the culmination of a thirty-year fight. The year the bill was passed a second time in the Legislature the voters of Baltimore elected a Jew to their City Council. The Jew was Solomon Etting, who was thus honored for his tenacity in fighting for religious liberty for all men.

Making the Cat-o'-Nine-Tails Obsolete

Uriah Phillips Levy is known to historians as the first Jew to choose the Navy as a career, the first Jewish officer to reach the

highest possible rank in the Navy, and the man who made the cat-o'-
nine-tails and other cruel naval punishments obsolete. Little is recorded about his long fight against anti-Jewish sentiment in the
service, which is the reason he is included in this collection of profiles.

A fourth-generation or fifth-generation American, the son of a
Philadelphia merchant, Levy ran away from home and went to sea
as a cabin boy in 1802 at the age of ten. Before he was twenty he
was master and part owner of a sailing vessel, the *George Washington.*
When he was twenty-one his crew mutinied, seized the vessel, and
left him penniless and stranded on a remote island. It was the first of
a whole lifetime of adventures. When the War of 1812 broke out,
young Levy joined the United States Navy. In an early engagement
he was captured and imprisoned for more than a year by the British.
After the war he remained in the Navy, chasing pirates and slave
traders, and becoming hard-bitten, independent, sensitive, vain, and
easily aroused to anger. Once he fought a duel and killed his opponent. On another occasion, in Paris, hearing a French officer hiss
the name of President Jackson, he challenged the man and thus
extracted an apology to the United States of America, to President
Andrew Jackson, and to Captain Uriah Phillips Levy.

Prejudice, Annapolis Style

Because he had worked his way from cabin boy up through the
ranks, Annapolis graduates resented him and threw all the obstacles
they could in his path. Because he was a Jew he was often snubbed
or ignored by the other officers in the wardroom. Between the years
1818 and 1857 he was court-martialed or faced Courts of Inquiry
eight times. Most of the court-martials resulted in Levy being down-
graded. After one such humiliating experience he happened to be
in Brazil, where the Emperor himself offered him a high post in the
Brazilian Navy, but Levy proudly declined, declaring that the
humblest position in his own country's service was preferable to any
post that any Emperor anywhere in the world could bestow on him.
In 1855 he and dozens of other officers were dropped by the Navy,

without ceremony. Levy was positive that the reviewing board had been motivated in his case by anti-Semitism. Whether this was the sole reason was never conclusively determined, but Levy was able to prove beyond much doubt that at least some of the Board of Fifteen who sat in judgment on him were prejudiced against him because of his Jewishness.

Homage to Jefferson

After being dropped by the Navy, Levy proved his ingenuity and his capabilities by becoming so successful in business that he was thereafter described as "a man of great wealth." He used part of his newly acquired fortune to pay homage to his lifetime hero, Thomas Jefferson, by buying and restoring Monticello, Jefferson's Virginia homestead. His wealth only made his enemies attack him the more. It did, however, enable him to employ the best possible counsel to fight his case for reinstatement in the Navy before a second Court of Inquiry in 1857. In his testimony this time Levy said:

"My parents were Israelites, and I was nurtured in the faith of my ancestors. In deciding to adhere to it, I have but exercised a right guaranteed to me by the Constitution of my native state, and of the United States, a right given to all men by their Maker, a right more precious to each of us than life itself. But, while claiming and exercising this freedom of conscience, I have never failed to acknowledge and respect the like freedom in others. I might safely defy the citation of a single act, in the whole course of my official career, injurious to the religious rights of any other person. . . .

"At an early day, and especially from the time when it became known to the officers of my grade and age that I aspired to a lieutenancy, and still more after I had gained it, I was forced to encounter a large share of the prejudice and hostility by which, for so many ages, the Jew has been pursued."

A Brilliant Appeal

In winding up his appeal to the court, Levy made this statement:

"My case is the case of every Israelite in the Union. I need not speak to you of their number, but I may speak of the fact that they are unsurpassed by any other portion of our people in loyalty to the Constitution and to the Union, by their quiet support of our laws and Constitution, by the cheerfulness with which they contribute their share to the public burthens, and by the liberal donations many of them have made to promote the general interests of education and charity, and in some instances along with these, of which the name of Judah Touro will remind you, of charities controlled by Christians and, sometimes, exclusively devoted to the benefit of Christians. Again, how rarely does one of my brethren, either of foreign birth or American descent, become a charge on your state or municipal treasuries! How largely do they all contribute to the activities of trade, to the interests of commerce, to the stock of public wealth! . . .

"Are the thousands of Israel and the ten thousands of Judah, in their dispersion throughout the earth, who look to America as a land bright with promise, are they now to learn, to their sorrow and dismay, that we too have sunk into the mire of religious intolerance and bigotry? And are American Christians now to begin the persecution of the Jews, of the Jew who stands among them the representative of the patriarch and prophets to whom were committed the oracles of God; the Jew from whom they received these oracles, and who is the living witness of their truth. . . .

Where Will It End?

"And think not, if you once enter on this career, that it can be limited to the Jew. What is my case today, if you yield to this injustice, may tomorrow be that of the Roman Catholic or the Unitarian, the Presbyterian or the Methodist, the Episcopalian or the

Baptist. There is but one safeguard: that is to be found in an honest, wholehearted, inflexible support of the wise, the just, the impartial guarantee of the Constitution. I have the fullest confidence that you will faithfully adhere to this guarantee, and therefore, with like confidence I leave my destiny in your hands."

Complete Vindication

In 1860 a special Commission of Inquiry appointed by Congress completely vindicated Levy of the charges his enemies had concocted and he was named Flag Officer in charge of the Mediterranean Squadron, with the rank of Commodore—the highest rank in the United States Navy at that time.

The Navy in those days expected its men to endure great privations and to submit to heartless cruelties. They fell from icy riggings into the ocean. They often lived for months, while at sea, in small, cramped, and almost airless forecastles. And the universal punishment for even slight violations of Navy discipline was the barbarous practice of flogging with the many-thonged lash called the cat-o'-nine-tails. Commodore Levy's campaign against this system finally resulted in passage of a law abolishing forever corporal punishment in the Navy. In his will Levy asked that this inscription be carved on his tombstone:

FATHER OF THE LAW FOR ABOLITION OF THE
BARBAROUS PRACTICE OF CORPORAL PUNISHMENT
IN THE UNITED STATES NAVY.

The tombstone-makers might well have added:

AND RESOLUTE FIGHTER FOR THE RIGHTS OF HIS PEOPLE

Less than a hundred years after his death—in 1943—the U.S.S. *Levy*, a destroyer-escort vessel named in his honor, was launched at Port Newark, New Jersey.

The obvious conclusion to be drawn from the story of Uriah Phillips Levy is that Jews in those days encountered both prejudice and discrimination in the American armed forces. But equally important is the fact, borne out by the record, that several Presidents, many members of Congress and *some* of Levy's superior officers were animated by an American sense of fair play in dealing with his case and that the end result was the complete rout of the forces of bigotry.

Founder of a Great Hospital

The first Jewish hospital in the United States is known today as Mount Sinai, but when it was established in 1852 "for benevolent, charitable and scientific purposes" it was called simply the Jews' Hospital. In that year a four-story brick building was erected at 138 West 28th Street, between Seventh and Eighth avenues, in Manhattan, on what had been an excellent tomato patch, causing some New Yorkers to complain that good garden land should not be taken for such a purpose. The hospital, with forty-five beds at the start, admitted its first patient on June 3, 1855.

The man responsible was Sampson Simson, an extremely observant Jew who baked his own matzah in his home, and on his graduation from Columbia University delivered an address in Hebrew entitled: *One Hundred and Fifty Years of Jewish History in America.* He studied law while working for Vice-President Aaron Burr as a confidential clerk. He was still a young man of thirty-three when he was beaten up one night by a gang of hoodlums on Manhattan. After that he lived as a country gentleman on his estate in suburban Yonkers. He was one of the first Americans to make sizable contributions to Jerusalem charities. He was seventy-two when, in 1852, he conceived the idea of the Jews' Hospital.

And Money Did Pour In

Many of the Jewish immigrants pouring in from Europe in those days were forced to live in overcrowded, unhealthy flats in the slums of New York. They were often ill and were without adequate hospital facilities. The Jewish community of New York had long discussed the idea of a Jewish hospital, but it was Simson, motivated by both religious and humanitarian considerations, who finally presented a scheme that won instant favor. Members of a hospital association would be enrolled at five dollars a year and would elect trustees who would start planning a hospital. He himself would give the land for the building. A group of young people would organize a ball and raise a thousand dollars. Money would pour in from many other sources. The Jewish community accepted the plan and elected Simson president of the association. And money did pour in—from subscribers as far away as New Orleans. In little over a year the cornerstone was laid.

At first the Jews' Hospital accepted non-Jews only in case of accident or emergency, although the original staff was made up mostly of Gentiles. It was caring for the wounded in the Civil War, regardless of religion, that prompted the idea of changing it to a non-sectarian hospital. To emphasize that it was going to serve the entire community henceforth—without thought of creed, color, or race—the name was changed in 1866 to Mount Sinai. It moved first to 66th Street and Lexington Avenue, and then to 100th Street and Fifth Avenue, where today it has twenty-six buildings covering four city blocks, a staff of 1300 doctors, some of the best facilities in the hospital world, and a reputation second to none—all the outcome of the dream of a religious Jew who read his Torah daily and constantly sought ways to put his Judaism into constructive practice.

A Man of Many Talents

The final profile in this portfolio is of Mordecai Manuel Noah, a character in every sense of that word. He was journalist, politician, playwright, diplomat, author, philanthropist, sheriff, surveyor of the Port of New York, lawyer, judge—many of them at one and the same time. His friends described him as flamboyant, restless, ambitious, versatile, a man of fine presence and real eloquence, a dreamer, a visionary, an enthusiast, a likable near-genius. His enemies said he was overly theatrical, often ridiculous, pompous and con-

ceited, a charlatan. Everyone had a decided opinion about him—
even those who, a hundred and fifty years later, wrote about him.

Mordecai Manuel Noah was born in Philadelphia, the son of a
Revolutionary soldier who somehow became so friendly with
George Washington that the commander in chief attended his wed-
ding. The son worked as a reporter, first in Harrisburg, Pennsyl-
vania, then in Charleston, South Carolina, and finally in New York
City. There he became editor of one newspaper after another: the
New York *Enquirer*, the *Evening Star*, and the *Union*. He also assisted James Gordon Bennett in founding the New York *Herald*.
Then he entered politics, rising to the exalted position of Grand
Sachem of Tammany Hall. By the time he was twenty-three he had
published a play. In that and later dramatic works his theme somehow generally involved American freedom, justice, and liberty, although his greatest enthusiasm was for the history of the Jewish
people.

When the Democrats of New York nominated Noah for sheriff,
a curious politico-theological question was raised by his opponents:
Would it be proper to put a Jew into an office that might give him
the opportunity to hang a Christian? Noah's supporters answered by
asking: What kind of a Christian is it that deserves to be hanged?
At any rate, Noah was elected.

An Appointment Declined

During the War of 1812 Noah declined appointment as American
consul to Riga and thereby became the first Jew to *reject* an important post in the American diplomatic service. But a short time
later he accepted appointment as American consul to the Kingdom
and City of Tunis and thus became the first Jew to *hold* a high
post in the American diplomatic service. He may have accepted
the Tunis appointment because it was far from a routine assignment.
At that time Barbary pirates were constantly creating international
problems as they preyed on American vessels. In fact, Noah's first
diplomatic task was to try, surreptitiously, to free some American
sailors who had been imprisoned in Algeria, while at the same time
placating the Bey of Tunis. He was successful in both missions, but

he was soon recalled because of his religion and because of confusion in his accounts. (The Secretary of State made the political error of putting both charges in writing, over his own signature.) Noah reacted as might have been expected of such a man. In his memoirs he wrote:

"I thought I was a citizen of the United States, protected by the Constitution in my religious, as well as in my civil, rights. My religion was known to the government at the time of my appointment, and it constituted one of the prominent causes why I was sent to Barbary. . . .

"What injury could my religion create? I lived like other consuls; the flag of the United States was displayed on Sundays and Christian holidays. The Catholic priest, who came into my house to sprinkle holy water and pray, was received with deference and freely allowed to perform his pious purpose. The bare-footed Franciscan, who came to beg, received alms in the name of Jesus Christ. The Greek bishop, who sent to me a decorated branch of palm on Palm Sunday, received, in return, a customary donation. The poor Christian slaves, when they wanted a favour, came to me. The Jews alone asked nothing from me. Why then am I to be persecuted for my religion? Although no religious principles are known to the Constitution, no peculiar worship connected with the government, yet I did not forget that I was representing a Christian nation."

In another passage he wrote: "If we once establish distinctions of religion in the appointment of our officers abroad, we shall not dare to send a Catholic to England, a Protestant to France, or a Jew to Spain."

A Refuge for the Jews of the World

Of more interest than Noah's difficulties with the State Department and the White House was his attempt to establish *A City of Refuge for the Jews*, as he himself called it. While in Tunis he saw the conditions under which his own people lived—the poverty, oppression, degradation—and he was both shocked and outraged. Then he began to dream of some way to help these co-religionists establish a land of their own, where they could live decently, as free men.

Palestine at that time was in firm control of the Ottoman Empire and Noah did not have the imagination that Theodor Herzl would show a century later when he tried to lease, beg, or buy from the Sultan in Constantinople enough land in Palestine for a national home for Jews. Instead, the now-retired American Consul to Tunis decided that return of the ancient homeland would have to await the coming of the Messiah. His own task, he thought, was to try to install all the Jews of the world in some comfortable, happy spot where they could live like other human beings as they awaited the millennium. Accordingly, after his return to America he purchased —or negotiated for the purchase—of 17,000 acres on Grand Island in the Niagara River near Buffalo as the site for an immense Jewish settlement.

Ararat-on-the-Niagara

Some of Noah's scheme was sensible and almost practical; some was ultravisionary; some was so eccentric as to seem the vaporings of a diseased mind. He gave himself the title of *Governor and Judge of Israel* and issued a manifesto to Jews all over the world, calling upon them to come and settle immediately in the new colony, which he named Ararat, after the place in Turkey where the ark of the biblical Noah came to rest after the flood. He set September 15, 1825, as the day for dedication of the colony.

Noah was a Zionist before the term was even devised. He anticipated Zionism by almost a century. But in *his* republic-within-a-republic, the persecuted of all countries and all faiths were to be welcome. Gentiles as well as Jews, if they wished, would enjoy political and religious freedom when their arks came to rest at Ararat-on-the-Niagara.

The Jewish population of the world at that time was in the millions. How Noah proposed to house and sustain even a small percentage of that many people on his island was—and is—a mystery, for it is only five miles wide by not more than thirteen miles long.

A Day to Remember

Elaborate preparations were made for the dedication ceremonies. But for some reason never quite clear it was impossible to use Grand Island that day, so Noah transferred the festivities to the nearest available place, the small settlement of Buffalo, population 2500. He may have chosen this frontier village on the edge of Indian territory because he had a good friend there, the Reverend Addison Searle, rector of the Episcopal Church, who was induced to turn over his church for the dedication.

On the appointed day—a day that Noah was certain would go down in Jewish history, if not in world history—he apparently was unbothered by the fact that not a single Jew put in an appearance. One thing that was not lacking was color. It was years—perhaps decades—before Buffalo saw again such a parade as Mordecai Manuel Noah put on that day. First came the Grand Marshal on horseback—an Army colonel friend of Noah. Then a brass band—rented for the occasion. Then a military unit, followed by a delegation of Buffalo citizens—all non-Jews. Then the town officials, looking very important, followed by a contingent of U. S. Army officers in full dress uniforms. Then the Officers of the Corporation. Then a large delegation of Masons, Royal Arch Masons and Knight Templars, in their brilliant costumes. In the midst of them rode their fellow Mason, Mordecai Manuel Noah. There was no mistaking him. The program described him thus:

The Judge of Israel
In black, wearing the judicial robes of crimson silk,
Trimmed with ermine and with a richly-embossed
Golden medal suspended from the neck.

Even the Cornerstone

As the Episcopal organist played the Grand March from *Judas Maccabeus*, the crowd jostled for places in the small church. On the altar, so prominently displayed that no one could possibly miss it, was a piece of sandstone that had been quarried at Cleveland and carved with these words:

Hear, O Israel, the Lord is Our God.
The Lord is One.
ARARAT,
A city of Refuge for the Jews.
Founded by Mordecai Manuel Noah
In the month Tizri, 5586, Sept. 1825 & in the
50th Year of American Independence.

After the lengthy Episcopal service of morning prayer had been read by the Reverend Mr. Searle, Noah, still attired in his flamboyant robes, delivered an address in which he described the Utopia he envisioned as "a land of milk and honey, where Israel may repose in peace under his vine and fig tree and where our people may so familiarize themselves with the science of government and the lights of learning and civilization as may qualify them for that grand and final restoration to their ancient heritage, which the times so powerfully indicate."

Jewish Declaration of Independence

It was a long address. Those who heard it—or read it later— described it as "a sort of Jewish Declaration of Independence." Noah discussed the theory that the American Indians are direct descendants of the Ten Lost Tribes. He demanded the abolition of polygamy among the Jews of Africa. He called on all Christians present to show toleration, good will, and a spirit of liberality toward the Jews who lived among them—if any. The address was a strange mixture of idealism, patriotism, politics, history, religion, and what one critic called "theatrical nonsense."

Then, for the first time in history, a cornerstone of a Jewish national home was formally "laid" on an Episcopal altar with full Masonic ritual.

Back in New York City the next day, Noah issued a Proclamation to the Jews, announcing that Ararat had been established and that their arrival was awaited:

"I, Mordecai Manuel Noah, Citizen of the United States of America, late Consul of said States for the City and Kingdom of Tunis, High Sheriff of New York, Counsellor at Law, and, by the grace of God, Governor and Judge of Israel, have issued this my proclamation, announcing to the Jews throughout the World, that an asylum is prepared and hereby offered to them, where they can enjoy that peace, comfort and happiness, which has been denied them, through the intolerance and misgovernment of former ages.

"In His name do I revive, renew and re-establish the Government of the Jewish Nation, under the auspices and protection of the Constitution and laws of the United States of America, confirming and perpetuating all our rights and privileges, our name, our rank, and our power among the nations of the earth as they existed and were recognized under the government of the Judges. And I hereby enjoin it upon all our pious and venerable Rabbis, our presidents and Elders of Synagogues, Chiefs of Colleges, and Brethren in authority throughout the world, to circulate and make known this my proclamation, and give it full publicity, credence and effect."

Tax Collectors Appointed

After reprinting most of the dedicatory address, the proclamation then called for a census of all the Jews of the world and the imposition of a head tax of three silver shekels a year, to pay for the cost of organizing the government of Ararat and to aid emigrants from all over the world in getting to the land that this modern Noah promised them. Then he appointed "commissioners" who were to carry out the terms of the proclamation—and, presumably, were to collect the funds. Among those listed were most of the distinguished Jewish leaders of Europe.

Nothing whatsoever came of the grandiose scheme. The Jewish leaders ignored their appointment. The Jewish masses ignored the invitation to settle on an island in the middle of an American river on the edge of Indian territory. Not a single building was ever erected at Ararat. The sandstone cornerstone for years stood in the rear of the Episcopal church, leaning against a wall. Now it rests in a glass case of the Buffalo Historical Society. Today magnificent bridges and highways cross Grand Island. The dream of a playwright-politician was soon forgotten. But on one wall of the American Jewish Historical Society there hangs today a painting of Mordecai Manuel Noah which depicts him more as a sincere visionary than an eccentric, and Tina Levitan's book, *The Firsts of American Jewish History*, lists him as "The First American Zionist."

But They Were All Jews

Judah Touro, the great American-Jewish philanthropist; Solomon Etting, who waged a thirty-year fight against religious discrimination; Uriah Phillips Levy, who fought the injustices of mankind in the Navy; Sampson Simson, who helped build a great hospital to care for the sick of the city in which hoodlums had once beaten him almost to death, and the quixotic Mordecai Manuel Noah, who wanted the Jews of the world to come to America and here to wait in peace and freedom for the coming of the Messiah and the re-establishment of Israel—five nineteenth-century men, as different as their occupations, their backgrounds, and their ambitions. Yet all were Jews, who were contributing to America as they kept their Judaism alive.

12

THE STATE DIVIDES; THE JEWS DIVIDE

W<small>HEN</small> Confederate troops attacked Fort Sumter in April of 1861 and the long-brewing war between North and South finally began, there were approximately 150,000 Jews in the United States. A majority lived in the cities. This was partly because in Europe for centuries they had been denied the right to own land and therefore knew best how to dwell urbanly. Also—it could have been cause or effect—being grouped together this way, they were able to practice their religion.

The largest as well as the oldest Jewish community was in New York, where there were nearly 12,000 Jews, organized into fifteen congregations and served by thirty-five charitable organizations. Philadelphia, Baltimore, Cincinnati, and Louisville had also become well settled. Chicago, Detroit, Boston, Cleveland, St. Louis, San Francisco, New Orleans, Milwaukee, and Newark by 1861 boasted of growing Jewish communities. About 50,000 American Jews lived in smaller places.

A Case in Point: Zanesville

The Jews of America at this time were united in their desire to have the same freedoms that Christians were enjoying, but they were divided on most other matters. There was no national organization that could speak for all of them on either religious or secular matters. They had almost as many ways of practicing their Judaism as they had congregations. This resulted in tensions and dissensions,

as in Zanesville, Ohio, where members of the Jewish community for
years were unable to organize a congregation because of disagreement among four groups, each wanting to use the chants and follow
the religious customs that had been familiar to them all their lives in
the places from which they had emigrated.

Although over the years a small percentage of American Jews
had intermarried with Christians and had become converted, most of
the immigrant Jews clung to the religion of their forefathers. Their
synagogues were becoming communal centers as well as places of
worship. Already the stress was on education and philanthropy. The
traditional European rabbi, who devoted his time to prayer and
scholarship, was being replaced by a thoroughly American-type
cleric, who was earnestly trying to adapt Judaism to the conditions of
the new world.

A Testing Time for Judaism

For all the sad consequences that the Civil War would have, it
made better Americans of most immigrants, at the same time strengthening their religion. But American Jews and Judaism went through
many crises and were put to many tests during the four long years of
fighting.

At least ten thousand Jews served in the Union and Confederate
armies—almost 7 percent of the estimated 150,000 Jews in the
country—a slightly higher percentage than for the population at
large. Before the war ended there were four Jewish companies on
active duty: on the Union side, one from Chicago and one from
Syracuse; on the Confederate side, two companies from Georgia.
Four breveted generals in the Union Army were of the Jewish faith
and in both armies there were many hundreds of other Jewish
officers of high rank. Also, innumerable Jewish civilians played important, even vital roles in the cataclysmic affairs of the era.

More than ever before, the war was illuminating how great was
Jewish individualism. There were Southern Jews who were almost
fanatical supporters of the Confederacy, but there were others who
were so much in disagreement with the system that they freed their
own slaves. There were Northern Jews who sacrificed far beyond

the call of duty for the Union cause, yet there were other Northerners, such as Isaac Mayer Wise, who were bitter in their denunciation of the Abolitionists.

Biblical Slaveholders

The rabbinate was as divided as the laymen. In 1861 Dr. Morris J. Raphall, celebrated rabbinical orator, tried to line up Judaism firmly against abolition in a sermon in which he singled out Henry Ward Beecher and asked him, rhetorically: "How dare you . . . denounce slaveholding as a sin? When you remember that Abraham, Isaac, Jacob, Job—the men with whom the Almighty conversed, with whose names he emphatically connects his own most holy name—that all these men were slaveholders, does it not strike you that you are guilty of something very little short of blasphemy?"

Never had an American rabbi fomented such a tempest. The sermon was reprinted in newspapers, pamphlets, and books. It was both praised and denounced by editorial writers, and was quoted on the floors of State Legislatures. Jews—and in some cases other rabbis—eager to demonstrate that Dr. Raphall did not speak for all adherents of Judaism, were quick with rebuttals. They accused him of mistranslating, misinterpreting, and misrepresenting the Bible. Dr. Moses Mielziner, who was to become the rabbi of Congregation Anshi Chesed in New York, wrote that the slavery of the Israelites had ceased with the destruction of the First Temple. Gustav Gottheil, later to become rabbi of Emanu-El in New York, preached two sermons in England in which he contended that there was no justification for slavery in either the Bible or anywhere in Jewish history. Rabbi David Einhorn of Har Sinai Temple, Baltimore, suggested that Jews should be concerned with the spirit and not the literal wording of the Bible, which, in his interpretation, acknowledged the existence of slavery in pre-biblical times, but made it clear that it was an evil to be gradually abolished. The strongest argument advanced by rabbinical authorities was that God himself had made clear the divine attitude toward slavery by emancipating the Hebrew slaves from Egyptian bondage.

Freedom Is Indivisible

In these days, for the first time, Judaism's leaders equated the fundamental rights of the American Negro with the fundamental rights of the Jew, declaring that there could be no real freedom for any one minority without freedom for all. Rabbi Einhorn was just one of many rabbis who took this forthright position. Because Maryland was a border state, it soon became the scene of turmoil. Rioting between Union and Confederate sympathizers broke out. Einhorn, besides being a rabbi, was the founder and editor of a weekly publication, *The Sinai*. Because he used the paper for advancing his abolitionist arguments, a mob destroyed his printing press, and several homes in the neighborhood were set afire. Some of the rabbi's young congregants established a twenty-four-hour guard over his home. The rioting in the neighborhood lasted for four days, after which Baltimore Jews persuaded Einhorn to leave, temporarily, for the North. With the congregation of Har Sinai as split as the country itself, the Board of Trustees of the synagogue then voted to advise Einhorn that it would be desirable, "for your safety as well as out of consideration for members of your congregation," if in the future no comment was made from the pulpit "on the excitable issues of the time." Unwilling to be muzzled in this manner, the rabbi did not return to Baltimore. Instead he accepted an invitation from Congregation Keneseth Israel in Philadelphia, which assured him that there he would be permitted to speak freely.

Many Abolitionist sermons were delivered by Dr. Bernhard Felsenthal of Sinai Temple, Chicago, who, while hesitating to disown Jews who supported slavery, declared that "if anyone, it is the Jew above all others who should have the most burning and irreconcilable hatred for the peculiar institution of the South."

In opposition was Rabbi Wise, who stigmatized the Abolitionists with such words as "demagogues," "fanatics," "red republicans," and "habitual revolutionaries who feed on excitement and delight in civil wars." He called them "visionary philanthropists and wicked preachers" and "demons of hate and destruction." One theory is that

Wise was motivated by his opposition to anything that would con-
trovert his plan for unity among American Jews. He saw the war and
slavery as two such intrusions. Yet, while opposing what he called
the "war mongers of the North" and defending the actions of the
South, Wise nevertheless did not claim biblical justification for
slavery. He was convinced, he often said, that Moses had been
opposed to slavery and had attempted to abolish it.

1. He (Moses) prohibited anyone to enslave a Hebrew, male or
   female, adult or child.
2. He legislated for a people just emerging from bondage and
   slavery.
3. He legislated for an agricultural community in which labor
   was honorable.
4. He legislated not only to humanize the condition of the alien
   laborers, but to render the acquisition and retention of bonds-
   men contrary to their will a matter of impossibility.

In the South the rabbis were less divided. Some, contending that
slavery was not in conflict with Judaism, owned slaves themselves.

Proof They Had Become Americans

The enthusiasm with which almost all 150,000 American Jews
identified with one side or the other in the controversy over
slavery and secession, and the contribution they made during the
Civil War, regardless of which side they supported, were proof of
how thoroughly they had accepted America. This new country, with
all its regional loves and hates, with all its loyalties and obsessions,
was their country, and its loves, hates, loyalties, and obsessions were
now theirs, too. A majority of them were first generation Americans.
Some had been here only a few years. Yet after so short a time they
had become an integral part of America and America of them. In
short, they belonged.

When hostilities finally broke out, Jews gathered in the synagogues
and temples of the North to pray for a Union victory, while men

who also considered themselves "good Jews" assembled in southern houses of worship to pray for a Union defeat. Congregation Shearith Israel held a special service each week throughout the entire four years to beseech God for victory for the North. Rabbi Sabato Morais of Congregation Mikveh Israel, Philadelphia, was not content with such religious conventionalities. He preached against "pernicious politicians," "dishonest army officers," and "greedy businessmen," who, he said, should be exposed before the world and severely punished. His sermons were pro-Union, but he called on America to strip herself of "vice and pride, fraud and rebellion against God" and asked how God's assistance could be solicited by those with "hands polluted with bribery, with minds engrossed in the pursuit of ill-gotten wealth, with hearts of stone that will sacrifice the dearest interests of mankind, aye the lives of myriads, too, in order to obtain some ephemeral power. . . ."

Temporary Censorship

Despite the fact that excerpts from his sermons were printed more often in the daily press than those of any other rabbi—or perhaps because of this fact—his Board of Trustees prohibited him from expressing any more of his personal political ideas from the pulpit. He fought the decision and after many months finally won a reversal of the order. Henceforth he could preach on "normal and religious subjects . . . and on subjects of the day" whenever he chose. To the credit of his congregants, shortly after the end of the war he was elected rabbi of Mikveh Israel for life.

The two stalwarts of the Orthodox or Traditionalist branch of American Judaism during the Civil War were Isaac Leeser, editor of the monthly *Occident,* and Samuel M. Isaacs, editor and publisher of the weekly *Jewish Messenger.*

At the start of his journalistic career Rabbi Isaacs tried to avoid mention of "politics" for fear of antagonizing readers and further dividing a people who, he felt, were already fragmented in so many other ways. But secession seemed to Isaacs no longer "politics" and so the *Messenger* finally proclaimed its loyalty, boldly, to the Union.

Isaacs the Unifier

Whatever unification there was in New York of the various branches of Judaism was largely to Isaacs' credit. He was the one who was responsible for the formation of the first successful, nationwide Jewish organization, the Board of Delegates of American Israelites.

Leeser was broadminded enough to see right on both sides and therefore tried to remain neutral. He praised Jews—Southerners and Northerners alike—who, in the midst of war, tried to live their Judaism. Often in his writings he used the words "conciliation and truth" and "peace and brotherly love" and "moderation and magnanimity." He wrote that Jews, remembering the biblical admonition about being a light unto the nations, had the responsibility of trying to act as peacemakers.

One of the most passionate supporters of the South was Rabbi James K. Gutheim of Nefutzoth Jedudah Congregation in New Orleans, who, during the Union occupation of New Orleans, was ordered out of the city for refusal to take an oath of allegiance. Later he was hired by the congregation of Montgomery, Alabama.

Why No Jewish Chaplains?

One question that especially concerned the rabbinate in those days was whether Jewish soldiers should have the right—or the opportunity—of being served by Jewish rabbis.

Until the Civil War military chaplains had always been Protestant Christians. Then regulations were relaxed and Catholic priests finally obtained the right to serve in that capacity, but rabbis were still not given the privilege, possibly through oversight, possibly through intent. Confederate military regulations concerning chaplains spoke merely of "clergymen" and thus there was no specific legal bar to Jewish chaplains in the South, although in practice there were no Jewish chaplains. In the North a few months after the start of hostilities, Congress passed a national defense act containing a sentence which provided that every army chaplain had to be "a regular ordained minister of a Christian denomination."

Congress Gets a Bill

In 1861 an Ohio Representative, Clement Vallandigham, who was not a Jew and as far as is known was not under any pressure from Jewish constituents, made a motion in Congress which would have permitted a chaplain to be a member of "any religious society." He referred to the "large body of men in this country, and one growing continually, of the Hebrew faith, whose rabbis and priests are men of great learning and piety, and whose adherents are as good citizens and as true patriots as any in this country."

Congressman Vallandigham's motion was defeated. A few months later a YMCA worker discovered that the 65th Regiment of the 5th Pennsylvania Cavalry had a regimental chaplain, Michael Allen, who was a Jew. Although most of the officers and 1200 men of the regiment were Jews, Chaplain Allen considered it his duty to be nondenominational, to the extent that even on Jewish holidays he would preach on such subjects as *Peace and Harmony* or *Friendship and Consideration*, without even mentioning the meaning or significance that the day had for Jews. A friend told how he "taught the word of God with pure unadulterated piety; he breathed into the ears of his hearers no sectarian hatred toward others, but labored zealously for their moral and spiritual welfare."

Broken-Down Reverends

During the controversy a Presbyterian publication carried the charge that "two-thirds of the chaplains in the army are unfit for the place" and one of President Lincoln's private secretaries said that most of the chaplains were "broken down reverends, long since out of the ministry for incompetency or other causes, men who could not induce any respectable church to place itself under their charge."

Lincoln himself was quoted by this secretary as having once said "I do believe that army chaplains, take them as a class, are the worst men we have in the service."

To test the regulations limiting the post to Christians, Rabbi Arnold Fischel of Shearith Israel, New York, sought a commission as a chaplain. The denial of his application was signed by no less a person than Lincoln's Secretary of War. This was a signal for Rabbi Wise, who was always eager to blast the Republican party. Vociferously, he charged that the party was discriminating against American Jewry. He went further, calling the system of government-paid chaplains a violation of the American principle of separation of church and state. Then he pointed out that Jews who vote, pay taxes and get killed in battle like anyone else should be entitled to have religious advisers like anyone else. Leeser, who seldom agreed with Wise on anything, not only supported the Wise position, but went so far as to say that as a result of this bigotry, he was fearful for the future of American democracy.

A Second Class Religion?

The *Jewish Messenger* said government policy was trying to reduce Judaism to a second-class religion. But the *Presbyter*, a Protestant publication, declared that democracy has its limits and asked its readers to imagine the effect of having as chaplains "Jewish rabbis, Mormon debauchers, Chinese priests, and Indian conjurors."

Daily newspapers in New York, Philadelphia, and Baltimore supported Judaism's right to representation. Then a campaign of letters and petitions to Washington was launched. The Board of Delegates of American Israelites, founded two years before the war in an attempt to get unity in Jewish ranks, sent a lobbyist to Washington, who was received at once by Lincoln. The President said he believed the exclusion of Jewish chaplains had been unintentional on the part of Congress and promised that "something will be done about it." Finally a bill was introduced into Congress, but the fight was not easy. Many Reform rabbis and Reform congregations were indifferent. Several Jewish newspapers editorialized against it. Six

prominent rabbis published over their signatures a protest declaring
that the Board of Delegates "represents no particular body of men in
this country or elsewhere." But enough votes finally were mustered
for passage and in July of 1862 a law was put on the federal statute
books which provided that to be appointed a chaplain a man had to
be "an ordained minister of some religious denomination." Nothing
more. No specification of *what* religion. The same act provided for
the appointment of hospital chaplains.

Three Jewish Appointees

Soon after passage of the bill President Lincoln appointed Rabbi
Jacob Frankel of Congregation Rodelph Shalom, Philadelphia, aged
fifty-four, a native of Bavaria, Rabbi B. H. Gotthelf of Louisville,
and Rabbi Ferdinand Sarner, formerly of Brith Kodesh, Rochester,
New York, as chaplains. Some records specify that all three were
hospital chaplains, but other sources say that Sarner became chaplain
for the 54th New York Volunteer Regiment. A Jewish monthly reported that in the Battle of Gettysburg "his horse was killed under
him and he himself received a dangerous wound, from which he
subsequently recovered; this was the result of the very courageous
manner in which he conducted himself during that terrible battle."
A New York Jewish paper said: "Dr. Sarner is probably the first
rabbi who voluntarily took part in a fight since Rabbi Akiba."

Judaism never gave the rabbi the sole privilege of conducting
services. Any layman well acquainted with the services may lead his
fellow Jews in prayer. Services can be held in a field or a cave or a
forest, as well as in a synagogue. Prayer shawls, phylacteries and
even the Scroll of the Law can be dispensed with. This was fortunate
during the Civil War, for even after the chaplain bill was passed in
Congress, there were thousands of Jewish soldiers who throughout
the entire long war never saw a Jewish chaplain. But this does not
mean that they neglected their religion. Writing in the *Jewish Messenger*, one soldier-reporter described how Jewish soldiers on their
own initiative sought out each other and met regularly for religious
purposes. He added that to walk through the forest on the Sabbath

and suddenly hear the sound of Hebrew prayers was to be reminded of Joshua's army, of the Maccabees, and of the Israelite soldiers who fought against Assyria, Babylon, and Egypt.

How to Bury the Dead?

The death of Jewish soldiers posed special problems for their comrades, for Mosaic law and the customs of Judaism contain many strict provisions about burial of the dead. If there were other Jews in the victim's unit, they would try to see that he was given a proper Jewish burial.

Thousands of Confederate soldiers carried prayer cards that had been given to them by M. J. Michelbacher, rabbi of Congregation Beth Ahabah in Richmond. On the card was printed a lengthy prayer composed by the rabbi, who thus tried to encourage Jewish soldiers to communicate with their God, even when they were far from a synagogue and perhaps not even in contact with a single other member of their own faith.

But the War Must Go On!

It was this same Richmond rabbi who each year petitioned the Confederate generals to grant furloughs to Jewish soldiers so they could attend High Holy Day services. To one of the rabbi's appeals General Robert E. Lee himself sent this reply: "It would give me great pleasure to comply with a request so earnestly urged by you, & which I know would be so highly appreciated by that class of our soldiers. But the necessities of war admit of no relaxation. . . . Should any be deprived of the opportunity of offering up their prayers according to the rites of their Church I trust their penitence may nevertheless be accepted by the Most High, & their petitions answered."

But later Lee must have relented, for the diaries of a number of Jewish soldiers tell of attending High Holy Day services in Richmond after Lee himself granted the permission. One of them wrote:

"Before our Jewish New Year, there was an order read out from
General Lee granting a furlough to each Israelite to go to Richmond
for the holidays if he so desired. . . . I did not care to go."

Passover Permits Granted

In the North individual Union commanders often gave religious
furloughs to their Jewish soldiers. Writing in the *Jewish Messenger*
in 1866, a Union soldier named J. A. Joel told how he and twenty
Jewish comrades in the 23rd Ohio Volunteer Regiment stationed at
Fayette, West Virginia, obtained from their commanding officer
permission to be absent for two days from their normal camp duties
in order to celebrate Passover. Although they were in a rural area,
they were determined to hold a proper *Seder*. First they needed
matzah, as a reminder of the bread eaten in the desert by the
followers of Moses. This problem was solved by the camp suter, a
civilian who supplied the regiment with its provisions. He was a
Jew and was going to spend Passover with his family in Cincinnati,
so he promised that as soon as he reached home he would send
them *matzah*. He did. Seven barrels of *matzah* arrived the day
before the start of the holidays. He also sent them Jewish prayer
books.

While some of the men remained in camp constructing a log hut
for the services, the rest went on a foraging trip to see if they
could find what else they needed. The foragers were successful,
returning with two kegs of cider, a lamb, several chickens, and some
eggs. At one point in the *Seder* all present partake of *moror* or bitter
herbs, "which remind us of the bitterness of slavery which our
ancestors were compelled to endure." In modern times horse radish
is often used. Unable to obtain horse radish, the foragers somehow,
somewhere, found a weed that they decided would serve the purpose,
"for its bitterness exceeded anything our forefathers ever 'enjoyed.'"
The *Seder* ritual also calls for eating *karpas*, "a green vegetable used
to remind us that *Pesah* coincides with the arrival of spring and the
gathering of the spring harvest." Parsley is generally used, but the
soldiers were unable to find parsley or any substitute. Then there
was the problem of a roasted shankbone, "which reminds us of the

Pascal lamb, a special animal sacrifice which our ancestors offered on the altar of the Great Temple in Jerusalem on the Passover holidays." From a West Virginia farmer they purchased a lamb. Their ensuing problem was described by Reporter Joel:

"We were still in a great quandry; we were like the men who drew the elephant in the lottery. We had the lamb, but did not know what part was to represent it at the table; but Yankee ingenuity prevailed, and it was decided to cook the whole and put it on the table, then we could dine off it, and be sure we had the right part."

An Indigestible Brick

Another Passover symbol is the *charoses*, a mixture of nuts, apple, and cinnamon, finely chopped and mixed with a little wine, which symbolizes "the mortar with which our forefathers made bricks for the building of Egyptian cities during their bondage." They were unable to get any of these ingredients, so, instead, they obtained a real brick, "which, rather hard to digest, reminded us, just by looking at it, of what purpose it was intended."

And so they had their *Seder*, using symbols to represent symbols. The only conventional items were the *matzah* and the roasted eggs, which symbolize the daily sacrifice that was brought to the Temple in Jerusalem as an offering in biblical times. The role of leader at the *Seder* was taken by the young man who later so graphically reported the entire proceedings for the *Jewish Messenger*. His account of the actual event is too well done and too graphic to be paraphrased or skeletonized:

"The ceremonies were passing off very nicely, until we arrived at the part where the bitter herb was to be taken. We all had a large portion of the herb ready to eat at the moment I said the blessing; each ate his portion, when horrors! what a scene ensued in our little congregation, it is impossible for my pen to describe. The herb was very bitter and very fiery, like Cayenne pepper, and excited our thirst to such a degree, that we forgot the law authorizing us to drink only four cups, and the consequence was we drank up all the cider. Those that drank the more freely became excited and one thought he was Moses, another Aaron, and one had the audacity to call himself a Pharaoh. The consequence was a skirmish, with nobody hurt, only Moses, Aaron, and Pharoah had to be carried to the camp, and there left in the arms of Morpheus."

The others, however, continued with the *Seder* celebration, which Joel summarized in these words: "There in the wild woods of West Virginia, away from home and friends, we consecrated and offered up to the ever-loving God of Israel our prayers and sacrifices . . . there is no occasion in my life that gives me more pleasure and satisfaction than when I remember the celebration of Passover of 1862."

Fasting, Fighting on Yom Kippur

Other soldiers, North and South, celebrated the Jewish holidays as best they could. Some were able to get to the nearest city and attend synagogue services. Hundreds of men in uniform wrote home to their parents describing their experiences on the religious holidays. Some of these letters found their way into print in Jewish publications. In many cities captured by the Union Army, Northern soldiers celebrated the High Holy Days with Southern Jewish families, thus, perhaps, easing some of the tensions of a war in which co-religionists fought each other and brother often killed brother.

Because those who were directing the war were not Jews, some of the most sanguinary battles, by mere coincidence, of course, were fought on Jewish holidays. One soldier wrote home that he had no choice but to fight on Yom Kippur, 1861, but no one could force him to violate the commandment about fasting from sunrise to sunset on Yom Kippur, so he spent the day, as he put it, "both fasting and fighting."

Jews on the Home Front

On the home front, wherever there was a synagogue Jews too young or too old to go to war, cooperated actively, collecting funds, preparing bandages, entertaining the wounded, or visiting men too ill to leave their hospital beds. National fund-raising and relief work in the North was in charge of the United States Sanitary Commission, and so any event held for this purpose had the word *Sanitary* in the name. There were Sanitary Fairs, Sanitary Balls, Sanitary Bazaars, Sanitary This and Sanitary That, and the Jews, true to Judaism's teachings about charity and benevolence, generally contributed far more than their proportionate share.

There was controversy in many cities over whether Jewish participation in these activities should be labeled Jewish. *The Jewish Record* argued that no one talked or wrote about the "pretty Catholics" taking part, or the "smiling Presbyterians," or the "demure Quakers" and so why single out "pretty Jewesses." Rabbi Wise, on the contrary, argued that if every Jewish criminal was identified as such, Jewish philanthropies ought also to be labeled.

Jews' Hospital Treated Anyone

In the ecumenical spirit that the war engendered, the Jews' Hospital in New York decided to offer its facilities to the government. Fifty seriously wounded soldiers were assigned by army medical authorities to the hospital. This meant doubling the bed capacity. During the next three years there were many times when military patients outnumbered civilian patients and of all the soldiers cared for, in the remaining years of the war, only three or four percent happened to be Jewish. Not only did this lead to changing the name of the hospital, but Reform Jews, who had been excluded from membership on the board of directors, were now elected to the board, and several Reform temples began contributing money to the hospital's maintenance.

Rebecca Gratz was far from being a young or even middle-aged woman by the time of the Civil War, but she was still the acknowledged leader of Jewish women's activities in Philadelphia, and as such she did much to maintain Judaism's reputation for philanthropy and good works. Many widows and orphans of soldiers were saved from literal starvation or worse through the activity of her organizations.

Washington's Peculiar Problem

The Jewish community in Washington, D.C., was more sorely pressed than most others, because it was small and not very affluent, while many Jewish soldiers were patients in Washington hospitals and when they died—as many did—it was necessary for someone to provide a Jewish burial. This same situation existed in other communities with a small Jewish population but a large military concentration nearby, such as Knoxville, Tennessee, where a handful of Jews were required to purchase and maintain a cemetery expressly for the burial of Jewish soldiers.

What was probably the first all-denominational funeral in America took place in 1863. It was an especially sad occasion for most of those involved. At that time the Union Army was plagued by a wave of desertions, so the high command decided to try to put an end to it by a dramatic execution. They picked five deserters who had been caught, tried, and convicted, among them George Kuhn, a private from the 118th Pennsylvania Volunteers. When the boy was informed that he was to go before a firing squad, he asked for permission to confer with a rabbi. The army sent for Rabbi Benjamin Szold of Baltimore, who, after talking with Kuhn, decided the young soldier deserved clemency. Abraham Lincoln listened patiently to the rabbi's appeal and then sent him to see the commanding general, who also listened, but was unimpressed by the rabbi's arguments and his biblical quotations, and refused even to consider mercy.

The Execution

At Kuhn's request, Rabbi Szold was with him at the execution. So were 25,000 other people, including all the soldiers of the regiment, for the high command had ordered an "object lesson." Three of the other condemned men were Protestants and were attended by the regimental chaplain, a Protestant. A Catholic priest stood beside the fifth soldier. After the rabbi recited the prayers called *Thillim*, *Yigdal* and *Shema*, he kissed the frightened young Jewish soldier, who clung convulsively to him as long as he could. At exactly 3:00 P.M. the rabbi, the priest, and the minister were asked to leave and the five men were ordered to stand at attention in front of their own open graves. There were thirty-six men in the firing squad. Their rifles crackled in unison. Then the priest, the minister, and the rabbi, standing side by side, read the burial services.

Another rabbi, N. Michelbacher of Richmond, serving as a voluntary chaplain, attempted to save another Jewish soldier from execution. Private Isaac Arnold of Company D of the 8th Alabama Regiment, had been sentenced to death for cowardice and being absent without leave in the presence of the enemy. The rabbi appealed to General Lee, submitting a petition signed by many non-Jews. In his own plea the rabbi said the young immigrant soldier had not realized the seriousness of his offense, and then he added: "From what we have heard, we fear that the fact of being an Israelite and of foreign birth, has had an injurious tendency towards the decision of his deplorable fate—we hope for the sake of the common humanity of our race that this report may be untrue."

The execution was suspended "until the decision of the President shall be known," but the final outcome of the case is not a matter of record.

Invitation to the Unscrupulous

Throughout the war the North and the South were equally short of what the other had. Northern mills were forced to close because of the scarcity of cotton, while the South needed, desperately, medical supplies and factory-made goods. This situation created a new class of smugglers, speculators, adventurers, and unscrupulous traders, willing to violate laws and risk even death for the enormous profits to be had. Big business interests on both sides of the line, prospering as never before, used their influence with political and military leaders to keep the channels of trade open, even though it meant trading with the enemy.

Christian ministers and Jewish rabbis alike denounced the profiteering, using such expressions as "bribery and corruption" and "immoral speculation" to describe what was happening. Army men up to the rank of general and down to corporals and sergeants were involved. Permits for carrying on commercial activities in areas close to the front lines were being issued by the White House, the War Department, and the Treasury, as well as by the army high command and various commanders on the spot. There was confusion and sometimes bedlam.

For Jews Only

Then on December 17, 1862, from the headquarters of General Grant came an order for all Jews—and only Jews—to leave the border areas within twenty-four hours. It read:

General Order No. 11

The Jews, as a class violating every regulation of trade established by the Treasury Department and also department orders, are hereby expelled from the department within twenty-four hours from the receipt of this order.

Post commanders will see that all of this class of people be furnished passes and required to leave, and any one returning after such notification will be arrested and held in confinement until an opportunity occurs of sending them out as prisoners, unless furnished with permit from headquarters.

No passes will be given these people to visit headquarters for the purpose of making personal application for trade permits.

By order of Maj. Gen. U. S. Grant:

Jno. A. Rawlings.

Assistant Adjutant General

American Jewry's Reaction

The news of this document spread not only through the border states, but across the entire country, creating consternation and indignation in Jewish communities everywhere. *The Israelite* echoed the opinion of most when it said:

"In us it is not the Jew but the man and American citizen who feels outraged by such proceedings. As a Jew we feel ourselves in our religious conviction far, far beyond the slanderous jargon of anybody, far beyond the reach of general orders, stump speeches, or other ephemeral pieces of paper. . . . As a man and citizen, however, we feel outraged and demand justice from the hands of the chief magistrate of the country."

Then, like an earthquake that often has more than one tremor, another order from headquarters said: "On account of the scarcity of provisions all cotton speculators, Jews and other vagrants, etc. . . . having no permission from the Commanding General, will leave town within twenty-four hours."

Are We Frogs or Mice?

This time there was no question but that the language was intentionally insulting. Rabbi Wise in his wrath wrote:

"Are we to be slaves of military chieftains? Are we playthings in the hands of presumptuous men to abuse and maltreat us at pleasure? Are we frogs and mice to be trampled under anybody's feet, or are we men who stand by their rights? Is there no law in the land, no authority higher than bayonets? If we stand this, then we are unworthy of being citizens of a free country. If we do stand all this, we must not wonder if one day anybody will treat us as pariahs and outcasts of society. Israelites, citizens of the United States, you have been outraged. Your rights as men and citizens trampled in the dust, your honor disgraced as a class, you have been officially degraded. . . . If the Jews, as a religious community, are handled thus, how will the Catholics, Unitarians, Universalists, or any other religious denomination be treated, if a general or provost officer sees fit to come down on one or the other?"

Mass meetings were held in such places as Cincinnati, Louisville, and Paducah. A resolution was introduced into Congress. Meanwhile, the order was being enforced with callousness and inhumanity. Families were separated. In just one town—Paducah—thirty men and their wives and children were forced to leave. Affidavits signed by "some of the most respectable Union citizens of the city" said that not one of the thirty men had at any time been engaged in trade within the northern lines.

Abraham and the Children of Israel

Animals, vehicles, and other personal property were confiscated. One man who tried to send a telegram to General Grant was clapped into prison. When no reply was received to another courteous but urgent message to President Lincoln, signed by a group of Paducah Jews, one of them, Caesar Kaskel, went to Washington and succeeded in obtaining an audience with the President, who, judging by his astonishment, apparently knew nothing of the order. He expressed his doubt that such an order had actually been issued. But Kaskel had been thoughtful enough to bring proof in the form of documents. After examining them Lincoln said:

"And so the children of Israel were driven from the happy land of Canaan?"

"Yes," replied Kaskel, "and that is why we have come unto Father Abraham's bosom, asking protection."

"And this protection they shall have at once," the President promised.

Lincoln then wrote a note to General in Chief of the Army Henry W. Halleck, directing him to telegraph immediate instructions for cancellation of General Order No. 11 and gave it to Kaskel to deliver personally to the General.

Another Presidential Conference

Rabbis Max Lilienthal and Isaac Wise, and a Paducah layman, not knowing of the Kaskel-Lincoln meeting until they were on their way to Washington, also called on the President. Until this interview Wise had been blind to any of Lincoln's good qualities; so much so that when he learned of Lincoln's election he had written that "the people of the United States have just committed one of the greatest blunders a nation can commit. . . ."

But during the few minutes that the committee of three remained in the Presidential office, Wise was won over. He reported later on Lincoln's "eloquence" during the interview, adding that "he

THE STATE DIVIDES; THE JEWS DIVIDE 171

assured us in every possible form that neither he nor General Halleck believed that Grant issued so absurd an order, until the official document dispelled every doubt. Furthermore that he entertained no prejudice of any kind against any nationality, and especially against Israelites, to whom he manifested a particular attachment. He spoke like a simple, plain-spoken citizen, and tried in various forms to convince us of the sincerity of his words in this matter."

A Medieval Revival

The New York *Times* called Order No. 11 "one of the deepest sensations of the war" and commented:

"It is a humiliating reflection that after the progress of liberal ideas even in the most despotic countries has restored the Jews to civil and social rights, as members of a common humanity, it remained for the freest Government on earth to witness a momentary revival of the spirit of the medieval ages. . . ."

Many other papers lined up on the side of those affected by this ugly discrimination. Leeser in his paper was bitterly sarcastic, declaring the trouble was that the victims of Order No. 11 were "not Christians, not even Negroes, nothing but Jews."

So the order was rescinded, but the damage had been done. Before the war there had been relatively little anti-Semitism in America. But now small sparks of bigotry were fanned into flames of irrationality by a fierce wind that began to sweep across the country. It started in the minds of people under emotional, economic, and political stress. Even after Order No. 11 was revoked, the ugly whispering, the slandering, and the blatant distortion of fact continued, and grew, and spread.

A Few Were Guilty

And what was the truth of the charges on which Order No. 11 had been based? Although such Jewish papers as the *Occident*, in a

spirit of self-criticism, denounced "Jewish adventurers who travel
or glide through the highways and byways of the land in quest of
gain," a report of the Provost Marshal at Memphis disclosed that out
of 198 persons arrested for smuggling in a two-year period, possibly
five—not more—were Jews. A mere 2.5 percent.

But economic envy had been added to the more standard religious
motivation for anti-Semitism. Non-Jewish traders who themselves
were flagrantly violating the law would prosper even more if all
Jewish competition could be eliminated.

In those days if a Jew was accused of a serious crime, or was
arrested, or court-martialed, it was common journalistic practice to
identify him as an "Israelite" or "a Jew" or "a German Jew." But
if a Jew was cited for valor or his name appeared in the casualty
lists, he was never identified in that way.

A Covington, Kentucky, newspaper reporter concluded an article
on the border traffic by asking what more could be expected of
"people whose ancestors smuggled for eighteen centuries yet."

An A.P. Slander

A reporter for the Associated Press, which has always prided itself
on its truthfulness and its objectivity, wrote: "The Jews in New Orleans and all the South ought to be exterminated. They run the blockade, and are always to be found at the bottom of every new villainy."

The Confederate press was just as vitriolic as the press in the North.
In the slave states Jews were held responsible for all the illegal trade
with the enemy, for price inflation, for the shortage of certain
goods, for counterfeiting Confederate money and for avoiding their
military responsibilities. Many of these accusations were, without
doubt, made by non-Jews who stood to benefit by the elimination of
Jewish competition.

The Jews of the South reacted to such attacks with anger, hurt
pride, and bewilderment. They wrote letters to the editor, discussed
the matter in synagogue meetings, and one Jew even challenged a
Richmond editor to a duel.

On the Whole Honorable

Of course there were papers scattered across the country that came to the defense and pointed out the thoughtlessness, the stupidity, and the maliciousness of such attacks. The best articles were in the Jewish press. Leeser in his *Occident* summed it up this way: "No doubt some worthless creatures who were born Jews have done Unworthy things during the war; they may have smuggled on both sides, been spies for everyone who would pay them, and thus disgraced by their shameful conduct the noble name of Israel. But we venture to assert that in all the dealings which the Government has had with Jews, they have acted on the whole as honorably as the same class of other persuasions."

Rabbi Wise put it more positively: "Our sons enlisted in the Army, our daughters sew and knit for the wounded soldiers and their poor families, our capitalists spend freely, our hospitals are thrown open to the sick soldiers of all creeds, our merchants represented at every benevolent association contribute largely to the wealth and prosperity of the cities, give bread and employment to thousands; we keep from politics, gambling houses, public-offices, penitentiaries, and newspaper publications—what else must we do to heal these petty scribblers from their mad prejudice?"

The Warder Cresson Case

But anti-Semitism in America did not begin in 1863. The most notorious case before the Civil War was that of Warder Cresson, U. S. Consul to Jerusalem, who in 1849 went on trial in Philadelphia for insanity, the proof being that he had decided to convert to Judaism, which convinced his family that he must be out of his mind. After two long trials, he was finally set free and was permitted to return to Jerusalem and practice his Judaism.

During the war the word most frequently thrown at Jews in the North was *copperhead* (sympathizer with the South). Ignoring the fact that there were some nine million nominal Christians in the

Confederate states, to a few tens of thousands of Jews, even such respectable publications as the Boston *Transcript* and *Harper's Weekly* singled out Southern Jews and castigated them for their loyalty to the South. Three men were the favorite targets for attack.

The Greatest Mind on the Continent

Judah P. Benjamin was an eminent lawyer from Louisiana, who at different times held three posts in the Confederate cabinet: Secretary of State, Attorney General, and Secretary of War. One of his great admirers, Salomon de Rothschild, of the celebrated French banking firm, called him "perhaps the greatest mind on this continent." And yet the fact that he was a Jew was used by some Northern papers—among them the *Transcript*—as an excuse for denouncing all Jews. Even Confederate supporters attacked him, holding him responsible for all the military and diplomatic defeats that the Confederacy sustained, yet President Jefferson Davis refused to be swayed. Despite great pressure for the elimination of Benjamin from the government, the Confederacy President kept his Jewish friend in a high cabinet post until the very end. During the war the Union offered a considerable reward for his capture, but it was never collected, for Benjamin escaped to England, where he was befriended by Disraeli and Gladstone, and lived the rest of his life as a famous international legal authority.

Ultra-Fire-Eater

David Yulee was a Florida Senator who married a Christian and abandoned Judaism, but he was still a target for the anti-Semites of the North. The *Transcript* pointed out that "his name has been changed from the more appropriate one of Levy" and called him "one of the hottest leaders of the ultra-fire-eaters" (whatever that meant). The paper then added:

"Can it be possible, that this peculiar race—the old Catholics used to call them 'accursed'—having no country of their own, desire that other nations shall be in the same unhappy condition as they are themselves? . . . This stiffnecked generation, by its principal men, takes a lead in attempting to destroy a Constitution which has been to them an Ark of refuge and safety."

Mordecai and Belmont

M. C. Mordecai was a wealthy Charleston businessman and civic leader, who apparently was guilty of no greater sin than contributing $10,000 for the support of the families of Confederate soldiers, but he, too, came in for anti-Semitic vilification.

In the North there was August Belmont, chairman of the Democratic National Committee, who was assailed by Republican orators whenever any other target was lacking. Even though he maintained no affiliation with Jewish organizations, he was often branded in print and from public platforms as "the Jew banker of New York."

August Bondi and John Brown

American Jewry produced many other notables during the Civil War era. All were involved in one way or another with the preservation and progress of Judaism. One of the most picturesque was August Bondi, who, as a boy of fifteen, had fought in the Vienna revolution of 1848. His father was a peddler, a bricklayer, a cigar-maker, and a factory worker. The son was even more versatile, during his long lifetime serving as bartender, grocery clerk, farmer, shopkeeper, cattleman, police judge, printer, schoolteacher, tanner, lawyer, politician, postmaster, life insurance salesman, dealer in real estate, guerrilla soldier, and all-around adventurer. As a young man of eighteen in Texas, Bondi once saw a white hunter deliberately empty a load of buckshot into his slave because the Negro had unwittingly scared away a flock of wild ducks. When Bondi reproached the Texan for his brutality, the local Methodist Episcopal minister, who was in the boat with them, turned on Bondi and berated him with these words, as quoted by Bondi in his autobiography:

"We have no use for Northern Abolitionists and only your age protects you from the punishment you deserve."

The South's Peculiar Institution

A few years later, in Kansas, Bondi met Old John Brown and worked with him and his outlaw band to keep Kansas from becoming a slave state and to help escaping slaves get to Canada. He joined with Brown in the defense of Osawatomie from attack by pro-slavery men and took part in many other curtain-raisers to the Civil War. Bondi's home in Kansas, on the Mosquito branch of Pottawatomie Creek, was a station on the underground railway for Negro fugitives. None of the Jayhawkers, as these underground soldiers were called, was a better shot than Bondi. His friends boasted that he could hit a butterfly at 25 yards with a pistol shot. As much as he loathed what he called "the South's peculiar institution," Bondi was not a fanatical Abolitionist and a rift ultimately occurred between him and Brown because "God's angry man" considered Bondi "much too moderate." During three years of the Civil War Bondi served with distinction in the 5th Kansas Volunteer Cavalry, finally being invalided out because of critical wounds. Late in life, when he was a leading political and civil figure in Salina, Kansas, he wrote his autobiography in a style as robust as the story itself.

Bondi was proud of being a Jew in a day when some others— for whom he had utter contempt—either denied their religion or tried to hide it. His mother had taught him that as a *Jehudi* (a Jew) he had a duty to perform to the country that had given "equal rights to all beliefs"—an admonition he never forgot. In his autobiography he wrote: "I do not regret a single step or instance in my long life, to further and assist the realization of my devout wishes that tyranny and despotism may perish, and bigotry and fanaticism may be wiped from the face of the earth."

Adviser to Presidents

Another Civil War notable was Simon Baruch, the father of Bernard, who would also become celebrated as the "adviser to Presidents." The Baruch family came to America from Posen, Poland

(Mrs. Baruch's family was from Charleston, S.C.). Simon studied medicine in South Carolina and Virginia and early in the Civil War received his degree and became an assistant surgeon to South Carolina troops. In his reminiscences he tells of going without food and sleep for three days and three nights because of the number of wounded men who needed surgical attention, and then banqueting on a peacock which strutted across a meadow near the field hospital and which he and other medical men roasted. Baruch was twice captured by Federal troops. The second time he and 109 other doctors and surgeons and ten chaplains were held as hostages and exchanged for one West Virginia doctor whom the Confederates had sentenced to execution.

The end of the war found Dr. Baruch a full surgeon in charge of a hospital at Thomasville, North Carolina. After the war he became one of the country's outstanding medical men, largely responsible for the laws that made smallpox vaccination compulsory. He was also a pioneer in appendicitis surgery.

Simon Wolf, Jewry's Spokesman

Although there was no religious or political unity among America's 150,000 Jews, those living in the northern states had an unofficial representative at Washington in Simon Wolf, a lawyer who had great influence in Republican circles and correctly boasted of being a personal friend of whomsoever was in the White House. B'nai B'rith used him frequently as its Washington spokesman, as did the Board of Delegates. During his entire lifetime Wolf fought for the civil liberties of American Jews. He also worked through the American government on behalf of Jews in Russia and other eastern European countries. He saved thousands of immigrant American Jews from deportation and worked to keep the gates of America open to Jewish immigration. He was convinced that the best guarantee of religious and civil liberty for all Americans, Jews included, lay in keeping church and state separated. At the age of seventy he wrote a book, *The Presidents I Have Known*, covering his half-century career. Of President Buchanan he said, "He looked upon the Jewish people as a superior class of American citizens."

Filial Love of Duty

In his book Wolf told this story:

"While seated in my office prior to going to my home, I received a telegram from a town in New England asking me to wait for a letter that was coming by express. The letter came, and it stated that a young soldier, American born, of Jewish faith, had been condemned to be shot, and the execution was to take place the next morning. It was in the crucial days of the war when every soldier was needed at the front and when Edwin M. Stanton, Secretary of War, had threatened to resign unless the President would stop pardoning deserters.

"It seemed this soldier could not get a furlough. His mother, who was on her deathbed, had begged for his return, to lay her hands lovingly on his head and give him a parting blessing. The filial love was superior to his duty to the flag, and he went home, was arrested, tried and condemned to be shot. For a moment I was dazed and uncertain as to the course to be pursued. . . .

"It was two o'clock in the morning before we reached the President. The whole scene is as vividly before me as in those early hours of the morning. The President walked up and down with his hands hanging by his side. His face wore that gravity of expression that has been so often described by historians and biographers, and yet he greeted us as if we were his boon companions and were indulging in an interchange of anecdotes, of which he was a past master."

What Would You Have Done?

Wolf then describes how, after he had made his plea for the young soldier, Lincoln told him that it was impossible for him to take any action in the case, because of Stanton. As Wolf was about to leave Lincoln's presence, he suddenly turned back to him and made a final, desperate appeal.

"Mr. President, you will pardon me for a moment. What would

you have done under similar circumstances? If your dying mother had summoned you to her bedside to receive her last message before her soul would be summoned to its Maker, would you have been a deserter to her who gave you birth, rather than a deserter in law but not in fact to the flag to which you had sworn allegiance?" Wolf's narrative continues:

"He stopped, touched the bell. His secretary, John Hay . . . came in. He ordered a telegram to be sent to stop the execution, and that American citizen of Jewish faith led the forlorn hope with the flag of his country in his hands at the battle of Cold Harbor, and was shot to death fighting heroically and patriotically for the country of his birth. When months afterward I told the President what had become of that young soldier, he was visibly moved and with great emotion said: 'I thank God for having done what I did!' It was an impressive scene, one full of pathos and sublime humanity, and is engraved on the tablets of memory as no other incident of my whole life."

An Unjustifiable Slur

On another occasion, when the Associated Press carried a statement by General Benjamin Butler that his troops had captured "150 rebels, 90 mules, 60 contrabands [Negro slaves] and 4 Jews," Wolf again called on the President and told him it was an uncalled-for and unjustifiable slur. Lincoln agreed and gave Wolf a pass to go to Fortress Monroe and protest directly to General Butler, which he did, receiving from the general a personal apology.

On one occasion Wolf was arrested and taken before Colonel Lafayette C. Baker, chief of the Detective Corps of the War Department, who was one of the most powerful men in Washington. Said Baker to Wolf: "You belong to the order of B'nai B'rith, a disloyal organization which has its ramifications in the South, and your organization is helping the traitors." Wolf, in great indignation, replied that B'nai B'rith was educational and philanthropic, and its members in the North, East, and West "are as true to the Union as any other portion of American citizens." Wolf was ultimately released through the intercession of Secretary of War Stanton.

Booth Was His Friend

Wolf not only bore a great resemblance to John Wilkes Booth, but he had played on the amateur stage in Cleveland with the actor-murderer when they were both young. On the morning of Lincoln's assassination Wolf and Booth happened to meet on a street corner in Washington and Booth asked the lawyer to join him for a drink.

"He seemed excited, and rather than decline and incur his enmity I went with him. It was the last time I ever saw Booth. He had just returned from the National Hotel, where he had been calling on the daughter of a Senator. For the third time he had offered his love, and for the third time she had declined. What would have been the consequence had she accepted, it is not for me to conjecture. . . .

"After the tragedy I was compelled to remain in my house until after Booth's capture, for, unfortunately, I resembled him very much in feature. So much so, that Theodore Kaufman, the historical painter, asked me to sit for him for his famous painting of *The Assassination of Abraham Lincoln*."

An Intensity of Malice

Once in a long letter to William Cullen Bryant, the editor-poet of the New York *Evening Post*, Wolf protested unjust attacks made on Jews because of their religion, and then made this observation:

". . . But the war now raging has developed an intensity of malice that borders upon the darkest days of superstition and the Spanish Inquisition. Has the war now raging been inaugurated or fostered by Jews exclusively? Is the late Democratic Party composed entirely of Israelites? Are all the blockade-runners and refugees descendants of Abraham? Are there no native Americans engaged in rebellion? No Christians running the blockade, or meek followers of Christ within the folds of Tammany?

"We have been branded and outraged for four long years, until discretion has ceased to be a virtue, and it is incumbent upon you, the father of the American press, to give us a hearing through the columns of your valuable journal.

"Why, when the authorities arrest a criminal, do they telegraph immediately throughout the Union that a Jew, or another Jew blockader has been caught? Do they, when they catch a James Maloney, say a Methodist or a Presbyterian has been caught? Is it, then, a crime to be born a Jew, which has to be expiated upon the altar of public opinion by a life of suffering and abuse?

"We have no country by inheritance; scattered over the wide world we find a home and refuge wherever tolerance and freedom abide. We become by adoption natives of the soil, and give our toil and devotion to the land and the flag. Local politicians, and even some metropolitan journals, have enunciated the lie that we are cowards; that none of us are in the army, and, if so, on the other side. . . . I can produce the proofs that some of the grandest acts of heroism performed during this war were done by Jews."

The New York *Evening Post* published the letter and also a sympathetic editorial saying that Wolf's "rebukes of a prevalent prejudice" were justified. Commenting on the Wolf letter, President Lincoln said unequivocally that "no class of citizenship in the United States was superior to those of the Jewish faith."

The Greatest American Jew

In the period just before the Civil War, Philip Phillips was often called "the greatest native-born American of Jewish origin." He was a Congressman from Alabama and an anti-Secessionist, but his wife, Eugenia, was so vociferous a pro-Secessionist, that her husband was forced to leave the national capital during the war. Phillips was a religious Jew. In his younger days in Charleston he had served as secretary of the Reformed Society of Israelites, a liberal religious body, and often spoke at synagogue dedications. Once he headed a delegation that asked President Buchanan to correct the injustice to Jews imposed by the American-Swiss Treaty of 1855.

Eugenia Phillips was as exuberant as her husband was sedate. She was so belligerent toward those who disagreed with her politically that she was once described in print as "not without a touch of hysteria." In 1861 she was arrested and imprisoned in Washington for three weeks on charges of espionage. Then she was released and sent to the South. Her husband accompanied her. In New Orleans she crossed the path of Union General Butler, who characterized her in Special Order No. 150 as "an uncommon, bad and dangerous woman, stirring up strife and inciting to riot." He banished her to an island in the Gulf of Mexico. She was as vitriolic with her pen as with her voice, for in her diary, later published as a book, she called Butler "a beast," branded most Yankees as "buffoons," and evened the score, one by one, with those she accused of having persecuted her. The war that Butler waged against this Jewess and other southern ladies put him in top place on the Confederacy's list of "wanted criminals," with a sizable price on his head.

Gratz and Moses

The story of Louis A. Gratz is the account of a German-Jewish immigrant with a strong Orthodox background, who enlisted in the Union Army a few months after arriving in America, and in less than two years rose to the rank of major, serving as Chief of Staff to the commanding officer of the 6th Kentucky Cavalry.

Major Raphael J. Moses was such a southern patriot that until his death he carried a calling card reading *Major Raphael J. Moses, C.S.A.* (Confederate States of America). At one time during the war he was given a severe task: like his illustrious ancestor in the desert of Sinai, he had to feed a multitude—the hundreds of thousands of soldiers serving in Georgia regiments. His title was Confederate Commissary to the State of Georgia, but he called himself "a boarding house keeper in the midst of war." After the war he was elected to the Georgia Legislature. But he failed, because of the successful anti-Semitic campaign of his opponent, to win the nomination for a seat in Congress. He was devoted to Judaism and wanted to go to Washington to fight what he called "race feeling" against Jews. To a man in La Grange, Georgia, who had chided him about being a Jew, he wrote:

"I wanted to go to Congress as a Jew and because I was a Jew, and believed that I might elevate my people by my public course."

In a book of memoirs completed after he was eighty years old, Moses told this story about his Uncle Abraham's wife: "I suppose that I might as well state here that my uncle, Abraham Cohen, fell in love with a Christian girl, a Miss Picken. She went through the usual probation of converts, so as to ascertain whether she was influenced by any other motive than a conviction of the truth of Judaism. She passed through the ordeal without the smell of fire upon her garments, became a Jewess, was married to my uncle, and I remember visiting her at her house in New York in my boyhood when she was scrupulously particular in adhering to all Jewish forms, dieting and others."

The diary then tells how Mrs. Cohen remained a devoted Jew for nearly half a century, until she became seriously ill. Then, while in a coma, she was visited, she later said, by a deceased son who urged her to reconvert to Christianity, which she did, rejoining the Episcopal Church, to which she had belonged in her childhood.

"I mention this incident in my uncle's life," wrote Major Moses, "to show the strong impression made upon the human mind by early religious education. Mrs. Cohen was a strict Jewess for forty or fifty years and died a believing Christian in her eightieth year. . . . so that about half of her life she was a devotee to Christianity, and about equally devoted to Judaism."

Abraham Lincoln and Jews

No account of Judaism and the Civil War is complete without some examples of the good-natured, friendly relationship President Lincoln had with American Jews in general and with some few in particular. All the historical records indicate that he remained above and unaffected by the bigotry of the times. Despite evidence of wrongdoing of individual Jews, Lincoln never once was guilty of generalization. He was sympathetic to Jewish causes and understanding of Jewish problems. A few days after the assassination Rabbi Isaac M. Wise delivered a eulogy in which he said:

"Brethren, the lamented Abraham Lincoln believed himself to be bone from our bone and flesh from our flesh. He supposed himself to be a descendant of Hebrew parentage. He said so in my presence."

Although researchers in the past hundred years have gone over letters, documents, and records with a fine-tooth comb, no one has turned up a single sentence anywhere to indicate that Lincoln ever expressed this thought to anyone else, and there is not a shred of evidence that Lincoln had any Jewish antecedents. But what the researchers do keep finding is more and more evidence of his personal friendship with individual Jews and his complete relaxation whenever he was with one or more Jews. There were no barriers. He seemed perfectly at ease with Jews, almost as if he were a member of the *mishpokhe* (the large family that includes even distant relatives and those related by marriage). Take, for example, his willingness to leave the White House late one night and go to a photographic studio and pose for a considerable length of time just because a Jewish friend asked him to.

Photographer-Philanthropist Solomons

The friend was Adolphus Simeon Solomons, son of an English newspaperman, who, in 1851, had been sent to Europe as a courier by Secretary of State Daniel Webster. A few years later he settled in Washington and for the next half century was a well-known figure in the capital. President Grant offered him the post of Governor of the District of Columbia. He helped establish in Washington the first nurses' training school, a free lodging society, the Associated Charities, and many hospitals. It was in his home that a meeting was held at which it was decided to found the American Red Cross. He possessed the social consciousness that Judaism stresses and throughout his life was an observant Jew, fulfilling the philanthropic principles of his religion. He was active in many Jewish agencies in New York and played a leading role in the founding of the Jewish Theological Seminary there. He was a member of a firm that did contract printing for many government departments and had a photographic studio of its own at 911 Pennsylvania Avenue.

In 1865, just twelve days before the assassination, President Lincoln accepted Solomons' invitation to leave his desk long enough to pose in the Pennsylvania Avenue studio for a portrait photograph.

The war was then rapidly reaching its climax. That very day Confederate troops had given up Petersburg and Richmond, although Lee had not yet surrendered. The President was beset by many problems. His face bore a grave look as he entered the studio and sat facing the camera. Several shots were taken and then Lincoln waited while the negatives were developed. When he was told that the pictures were too grim for any use, the President asked the photographer to come out of his dark room and try again, and to his Jewish friend he said:

"And you, Solomons, tell me one of your funny stories and we will see if I can't do better."

The photograph which was then taken—the last formal, portrait-photograph to be taken before his death—shows how sorely burdened he was with the cares of his offices and how impossible it was for him to smile, even at Solomons' jokes.

A. Lincoln and A. Jonas

Then there is the story of Lincoln and Jonas. They both had been given the name Abraham, one by Christian parents, the other by Jewish parents. Both served as State Representatives, Lincoln in the Illinois Legislature, Jonas in the Kentucky Legislature. Although their backgrounds were as different as Hardin County, Kentucky, and London, England, the localities in which they were born, they had much in common that served as a basis for their deep friendship. When the Whig Party died, both men enlisted in Republican ranks and both served as presidential electors in 1856. Both were popular public orators. After Lincoln's election as President, his friend Jonas wrote to him several times warning him of assassination plots he had uncovered. Jonas never asked a favor of the President. It was a mutual friend who suggested that Lincoln appoint Jonas postmaster of Quincy, Illinois, which was done. Jonas died just a year before Lincoln was murdered. The President, as a final gesture of friendship for his English-born Jewish friend, named his widow to succeed him in the Quincy post office.

Chiropodist Zacharie

Another close friend was Isachar Zacharie, also an immigrant from England, who practiced in Washington as a chiropodist. Secretary of War Stanton was so pleased with how he felt after Zacharie worked on his feet that he suggested similar treatment for the President. Lincoln, in turn, was so pleased that he promptly sat down, after his first treatment, and wrote a testimonial for Dr. Zacharie. That, in turn, led to generals, cabinet members, Congressmen and other high officials in Washington vying with one another for appointments with the Jewish chiropodist.

There is no record of how many times Zacharie treated Lincoln and what they discussed when they were together, but after a few months the President was so impressed with his foot doctor that he gave him an unlimited expense account and sent him to New Orleans on a secret mission. He had three tasks: to assess public opinion, to make a confidential report to the President on how well the military government was functioning in New Orleans, and to help work out a formula for readjusting the exchange rate between Louisiana money and the Union currency. While there Zacharie did all he could to obtain help for Northern Jews who had been caught in New Orleans by the war, and also for those Southern Jews who had been forced to leave the city because they refused to take an oath of allegiance to the Union.

The chiropodist took his assignment with extreme seriousness. Ten days after reporting to Lincoln he was en route back to New Orleans again, with an even more important mission—a mission which Zacharie himself, in a letter to Lincoln, described as "the great responsibility resting on me." Apparently he was entrusted with trying to arrange a negotiated peace between the Union and the Confederacy. This was the spring of 1863. Despite many trips back and forth, the chiropodist failed in his mission, but his deep personal friendship with Lincoln continued. When he was in Washington he often sent baskets of fresh fruit to the White House and he never failed to include "good wishes for Mrs. Lincoln." He always addressed the President as "My Dear Friend." The New York *World* said Zacharie "enjoyed Mr. Lincoln's confidence perhaps more than any other private individual" and added that he was "perhaps the most favored visitor at the White House."

A. Lincoln and A. Kohn

Politics combined with religion led to a strong friendship between Lincoln and still another Abraham—Abraham Kohn—who was president of the K.A.M. Congregation in Chicago and was also Chicago's City Clerk. (K.A.M. stands for Kehillat Anshe Maarav, "Congregation of the People of the West," referring to the German nationality of its founder, as compared to Eastern Europeans.) He worked for the Republican ticket in the 1860 campaign and held many private meetings with Lincoln during which they talked not only of politics but also of religion and the Bible. Just before the inauguration, worried about the mountain of problems facing the President-elect, Kohn decided to send him some message of encouragement, so he painted an American flag and on it lettered six verses from the First Book of Joshua that he thought appropriate. The biblical passage ended with this sentence: "Be strong and of good courage; be not affrighted, neither be thou dismayed, for the Lord thy God is with thee whithersoever thou goest."

The Assassination

At 10:15 P.M. on April 14, 1865, most observant Jews in the United States were on their way to their synagogues or were actually already at worship, for this was the eve of the fifth day of Passover. On this particular Passover they were not only following the ancient tradition and giving thanks for the deliverance of the Israelites from Egyptian slavery, but for deliverance of Americans from the ugliness of a Civil War. In some areas the fighting had not yet stopped, but five days before this Lee had surrendered to Grant at Appomattox and everyone knew that it was almost over.

At 10:15 that night President Lincoln was shot in Ford's Theater in Washington and died the next morning.

Some synagogues were immediately draped in black and Yom Kippur chants were substituted for the more joyful Passover music. Some rabbis in their extemporaneous sermons tried to express the grief that was in the hearts of almost everyone. In Temple Emanu-El, New York Rabbi Samuel Adler began to speak and then was so overcome with his own emotion that he was unable to continue.

As preparations were being made for the funeral, officers of synagogues all over the country, as well as directors of local and national Jewish organizations, met and adopted resolutions in which— often eloquently—they expressed the loss that they felt, both as Jews and as Americans. Many synagogues decided to say the prayers for the dead for the next six weeks for Mr. Lincoln. On June 1, which was set aside by presidential decree as the Day of National Mourning, many rabbis compared this deceased Abraham with his namesake and some recalled that during the war Lincoln had used, almost as a motto, the biblical quotation: "Fear not, Abram, I am thy shield. Thy reward shall be exceeding great."

In New York more than three thousand men representing various Jewish organizations marched in a funeral procession. In smaller cities across the country Jews also participated in the national demonstration of respect and grief. Only one discordant note was sounded. A reader of the *Occident*, in a letter to the editor complained that the *Escava* (memorial prayer) by the rules of Judaism is to be said only for members of the Jewish faith. Editor Leeser gave answer in a sermon a few days later:

"It is, indeed, somewhat unusual to pray for one not of our faith, but by no means in opposition to its spirit, and therefore not inadmissible. We pray for the dead, because we believe the souls of the departed as well as of the living are in the keeping of God . . . The prayers, therefore, offered up this day for the deceased President are in accordance with the spirit of the faith which we have inherited as children of Israel, who recognize in all men created those like them in the image of God, and all entitled to His mercy, grace, and pardon, though they have not yet learned to worship and adore Him as we do who have been especially selected as the bearers of His law. . . ."

After the war ended, Jewish communities all over the country began erecting monuments in honor of their own dead. Some small southern congregations, impoverished by war, issued nationwide appeals for funds for this purpose. As Passover approached that year they also sought contributions of *matzah*. Congregations in New York and Philadelphia shipped two and a half tons of the unleavened bread to Savannah, Georgia, alone. Although Jews in the Union Army and Jews in the Confederate Army had been engaged in trying to kill each other right up to the surrender at Appomattox, as soon as hostilities ceased Jewish publications, including *The Jewish Record*, urged Northern Jews to give organized support to their fellow Jews in the South, and many did.

13

ANTI-SEMITISM LEAVES ITS MARK

I T took years for America even to begin to recover from the disastrous effects of the long Civil War, but by 1877 a new wealthy class was in the making, composed of both Jews and non-Jews. Many men who had started as peddlers by now were merchant princes, with money enough and time enough to be able to enjoy the pleasures of leisure. They were sending their sons to college and taking their wives on expensive holiday trips. A survey of the Jewish population about this time indicated that only one out of every one hundred men was now a peddler. Exactly half the total were in business. Only one-half of one percent were laborers. Many were in the professions. Seventy percent of all Jewish families had servants, ten percent having three or more servants. Most of the 250,000 Jews in America when the survey was taken were affiliated with a synagogue or temple.

That background may have had something to do with an outbreak of anti-Semitism in 1877. Also, the climate of the time was affected by the industrial revolution, the post-war economic recession and the need for America to readjust to a peacetime economy. The post-war influx of Jews from Eastern Europe may also have been partly responsible. Or perhaps the Seligman-Hilton feud was exaggerated out of proportion to its real importance. But what happened is historically significant, for it left a mark on Judaism in America, and affected the relationship between Jews and non-Jews for years to come.

He Clothed the Union Army

Joseph Seligman in those days was often called "the most eminent Jew in America." He had started as a penniless immigrant. With his brothers he opened a clothing store in Lancaster, Pennsylvania, which was so successful that before long they opened other stores in Watertown, New York, Greensboro, Alabama, and San Francisco. Then they established a banking firm. During the Civil War they advanced to the Federal government the credit necessary to purchase more than a million dollars' worth of uniforms and thus they were said to have clothed practically the entire Union Army. Later, in Europe, Seligman sold two hundred million dollars' worth of U. S. Government Bonds to keep the war going, a feat which was described as "scarcely less important than the Battle of Gettysburg."

On the local scene Seligman joined with other private citizens in an attempt to clean up New York City, which then was in the grip of the Tweed Ring, the most corrupt political combine the country had ever known. The Committee of Seventy, as the reformers called themselves, succeeded so well that the Tweed Ring was broken and some of the leaders went to prison.

By the time he was fifty-eight Seligman was financially successful, socially recognized, and politically powerful. It was then that he crossed swords with Henry Hilton.

A Ward Politician

During most of his life Hilton had been a relatively obscure ward politician under the thumb of the Tweed bosses. He obtained a minor place on the bench as the result of a political appointment. But he had a wealthy friend for whom he had once done a political favor, A. T. Stewart, a Scotch Presbyterian who owned New York's leading department store, as well as a wholesale business that supplied drygoods merchants all over the country. Stewart also had a two-million-dollar interest in the Grand Union Hotel in Saratoga, New York, the social capital of America during certain months of the year—a garish, expensive place where people went to see and be seen—to bathe in mineral waters or to gamble. The men spent their days at the Saratoga race track and a good part of the night at the gambling casino. Their wives tried to outdo each other in the number of times a day they changed costumes, and in the quantity of jewels with which they bedecked themselves. Of all the glittering hotels that lined the main streets of Saratoga, the Grand Union was the one patronized by the most socially prominent and by anyone else who could afford it. Seligman over the years had been a frequent visitor at the Grand Union and was well known by the staff.

In 1876 Stewart died, leaving a sizable fortune. He named Judge Hilton as the executor of his estate. In this capacity Hilton took over management of the Grand Union.

No More Israelites

On June 13, 1877, Seligman and his family arrived in Saratoga for a holiday and attempted to check in at the Grand Union.

"I am required to inform you, sir," said the reception clerk, "that Mr. Hilton has given instructions that no Israelites shall be permitted in the future to stop at this hotel."

When Seligman asked him to be more specific, the clerk said Mr. Hilton had decided that a drop in business the previous season was the result of Christians boycotting the hotel because there had been too many Jewish guests. "The nation's outstanding Jew" was indignant. He not only wrote an angry letter to Hilton, but released copies to the press. One New York paper headlined the story: A SENSATION AT SARATOGA.

Indignation meetings were held. There was a threat of action under the New York Civil Rights Law. A boycott was suggested. Hilton defended himself by declaring, in rather peculiar English:

"As the law yet permits a man to use his property as he pleases and I propose exercising that blessed privilege, notwithstanding Moses and all descendants may object."

In another statement he said:

"Personally I have no particular feeling on the subject, except probably I don't like this class as a general thing and don't care whether they like me or not. If they do not wish to trade with our house, I will be perfectly satisfied, nay gratified, as I believe we lose much more than we gain by their custom."

Nationwide Interest

The controversy aroused interest all over the country. Even papers in communities without a single Jewish resident published news articles and editorials.

Just when the Seligman-Hilton controversy was dying down, Austin Corbin, president of both the Long Island Railroad and a real estate company that was working with the Long Island to develop Coney Island into a fashionable resort, made this blunt announcement: "We do not like the Jews as a class. There are some well behaved people among them, but as a rule they make themselves offensive to the kind of people who principally patronize our road and hotel, and I am satisfied we should be better off without than with their custom."

This fanned the flames again. Boycotts were actually organized this time, with the result that the Stewart company's wholesale business was ruined and the retail store was saved only after being taken over by John Wanamaker.

A Hero and a Mosquito

One happy result of the trouble, however, was that the Reverend Henry Ward Beecher, the outstanding Protestant minister of the era, whose sister wrote *Uncle Tom's Cabin*, became from then on an outspoken champion of the Jew and influenced millions of Christians in their attitude. In one statement he spoke of the patrons of the Grand Union as "men who made their money yesterday or a few years ago selling codfish." Then he advised the Jews to ignore the insults: "A hero may be annoyed by a mosquito; but to put on his whole armor and call on his followers to join him in making war on an insect would be beneath his dignity."

Following the Grand Union Hotel controversy, more and more summer resorts brazenly advertised that they were refusing reservations to prospective guests who were Jewish, while private schools in the East began closing their doors to Jewish pupils, and the Union League Club of New York began refusing membership to Jews under any circumstances.

Beecher Prods Cleveland

It was just ten years after the Seligman-Hilton affair that President Grover Cleveland hesistated to appoint a Jew as U. S. Minister to Turkey, until he received a letter from Henry Ward Beecher, which was later released to the press. The letter contained this passage:

"The bitter prejudice against Jews which obtains in many parts of Europe ought not to receive any countenance in America. It is because he is a Jew that I would urge the appointment as a fit recognition of this remarkable people who are becoming large contributors to American prosperity and whose intelligence, morality, and large liberality in all public measures for the welfare of society, should receive from the hands of our Government some such recognition.

"Is it not, also, a duty to set forth in this quiet, but effectual method, the genius of American government? Which has under its fostering care people of all civilized nations, which treats them without regard to civil, religious, or race peculiarities as common citizens? . . . Why should we not make a crowning testimony to the genius of our people by sending a Hebrew to Turkey? The ignorance and superstition of medieval Europe may account for the prejudices of that dark age. But how a Christian in our day can turn from a Jew I cannot imagine. Christianity itself sucked at the bosom of Judaism, our roots are in the Old Testament. We are Jews ourselves gone to blossom and fruit. Christianity is Judaism in Evolution and it would be strange for the seed to turn against the stock on which it was grown."

14

THE BIRTH OF CONSERVATISM

A⊤ the Plum Street Temple in Cincinnati on Wednesday, June 20, 1883, Hebrew Union College held its first graduation. Even before receiving their degrees the students were already in demand. One senior had been elected to a pulpit in Kansas City, another to a pulpit in Fort Wayne, Indiana. This was a proud day for Isaac Mayer Wise and for Reform Judaism—the realization of a deepseated dream.

The graduation exercises were lengthy and impressive. There was a procession, then three or four scholarly addresses, then Rabbi Wise presented the degrees to the four graduates. The valedictory was by David Philipson, who would before long become the rabbi of Har Sinai in Baltimore.

The graduation was followed by a convention of the Union of American Hebrew Congregations, which was celebrating its tenth anniversary. By now there were slightly more than 200 congregations scattered across America, of which well over half—128—were members of the Union. One Reform historian claimed that "almost every synagogue of importance in the country was a member . . ." and rabbis who were later to lead a conservative resistance to Reform still thought of Hebrew Union College as an institution that might serve all American Jewry. (In 1967 the Union of American Hebrew Congregations reported 669 affiliated synagogues with a total of 1,000,000 members.)

The Forbidden Food Banquet

The high point of the Cincinnati celebration was a banquet at a celebrated hilltop restaurant, the Highland House. A Jewish caterer was engaged to serve the dinner. Valedictorian Philipson himself described what happened: "The great banqueting hall was brilliantly lighted, the hundreds of guests were seated at the beautifully arranged tables, the invocation had been spoken by one of the visiting rabbis, when the waiters served the first course. Terrific excitement ensued when two rabbis rose from their seats and rushed from the room. Shrimp (one of the forbidden foods, *terephan*) had been placed before them as the opening course of the elaborate menu. . . . The Highland House dinner came to be known as the *terephan* banquet . . . The Orthodox Eastern press rang the charges on the *terephan* banquet week in and week out."

In his biography of Rabbi Wise, James G. Heller goes further, declaring that oysters and crabs were served, as well as shrimp. As for the aftermath, Rabbi Philipson said the incident culminated in "the establishment of a rabbinical seminary of a conservative bent." Nathan Glazer, professor of sociology at the University of California and author of *American Judaism*, writes that "the reason this incident has not been referred to by historians of the origins of the movement now called Conservatism is that it is embarrassing to trace such great consequences to the serving of shrimp. . . ." Heller concedes that it was "a mistake" that was "seized upon by some veteran opponents, and became a *casus belli*." Everything about Wise and his movement was *terephan*, said his critics.

As minor a matter as it may have seemed to some, it served as a prelude to a divergence of opinion over vastly more fundamental matters.

Einhorn Refuses to Preach in English

About this time a German-born rabbi, David Einhorn, came onto the American scene and quickly became leader of the more intellectual, more radical wing of Reform Judaism. He was so passionately attached to the German language that he refused to preach in English. In fact, he felt that the mission of German Jewry was to bring Reform Judaism to America and that it must be done by spreading German secular, scientific, and religious ideas, and that German was the only possible medium in which to carry on such missionary work. One matter with which Einhorn was vitally concerned was whether Jews are a people or members of a religious group; whether they should be integrated in the countries of their dispersal or try to return, eventually, to the land of their ancestors, Palestine. In Germany the Reformers had eliminated from their ritual all prayers calling on God for a rebirth of Israel. Einhorn was one of the Reform rabbis who met in Philadelphia in 1869 and issued the declaration in German, stating that the destruction of the ancient Jewish state had not been Divine punishment. This, of course, was a direct contradiction of the long-held Orthodox view.

Kaufman Kohler, Radical

Einhorn died in 1879 but his ideas were taken up by a son-in-law, Kaufman Kohler, who had come from a long line of distinguished Orthodox rabbis in Bavaria. His fundamentalism had been such that he literally believed God had conversed with Adam and Eve in the Garden of Eden in Hebrew, the original language of mankind. But then he went to the University of Munich and later to the University of Berlin and studied Arabic, ethnology, and psychology, and he began to look on Judaism with an objectivity that his forebears perhaps had never had. As an example of his radical approach, he wrote:

"In the name of religion, men are not allowed to think, to gain spiritual independence and maturity. That foolish principle has served to transplant crass ignorance and pollution to Jewish soil. . . . Is it not imperative that children be taught nothing in the name of religion which, the next hour, would be contradicted or nullified by the teacher of the natural sciences?"

In 1885 Kohler—who later became president of Hebrew Union
College—called a meeting in Pittsburgh of "all such American rabbis
as advocate reform and progress, and are in favor of united action
in all matters pertaining to the welfare of American Judaism." The
conference lasted three days, with a majority of the delegates agreeing on the eight basic principles outlined in Chapter 10.

Pittsburgh Summarized

These eight principles sought to strip Judaism of much theology
and many practices that had been sanctified by centuries of belief
and familiarity. The Ten Commandments still were to be accepted
and respected, but the 613 biblical commandments compiled by
Maimonides were to be replaced by rule of conduct applicable to
the current nineteenth century and the approaching twentieth century. Reform Jews were not to feel obligated to follow the ancient
dietary laws. Because there were in the world other monotheistic
religions, Judaism ought to acknowledge their existence and cooperate
with them. Instead of hoping and praying for the Messiah to come
and lead the Israelites back to the Promised Land, the Pittsburgh
conferees called on Diaspora Jews to work for the establishment
of truth, justice, and peace in the lands of their present residence,
and to help create a better social order where they lived. Instead
of dreaming of eternal bliss in an afterlife, Reform Jews were
henceforth to use the principles of Judaism to help create a paradise
on earth. At Pittsburgh the delegates emphasized in their speeches
and in their resolutions their belief in man's free will and his latent
power to control his own destiny, unhampered by superstition, and
unbeset by concern for the hereafter. Most of all, they sought to
put Judaism in the forefront of the struggle for social justice.

In these days many Reform temples had already begun to re-
semble Protestant churches much more than they did Orthodox
synagogues. Men and women at worship were no longer separated.
Prayer shawls were no longer used and the men no longer kept their
heads covered. Choirs included men, women, and boys, some of them
not even of the Jewish faith. Organ music was played during

services. Sermons and prayers were in English, with the congregants taking little part in the services except to join in certain responsive readings. A few congregations even held their principal service of the week on Sunday, instead of Friday night or Saturday morning. At weddings the *huppa* (a canopy held by certain members of the wedding party) was no longer being used, and the tradition was abandoned of breaking a glass as a recollection of the destruction of the Temple—an event to be remembered even in moments of great joy. Many minor Jewish holidays were no longer being observed, especially if they were considered to have been national rather than religious holidays.

Mixed Reactions

Those are a few of the outward and visible signs of Reform that were obvious to anyone. Many were delighted with these revisions, feeling that by streamlining Judaism, it had been made more certain of holding its followers. But others deeply resented this "tampering with the fundamentals of the religion." Brought up on traditional Talmudic Judaism and accustomed to the liturgy and customs of the past, they were troubled by all these changes. They especially resented the Pittsburgh statement which shocked them into a realization of what sweeping changes had already been made in American Judaism. They were also worried over the vigor of Reform Judaism and the national strength it was showing.

This was the atmosphere in America that led to the birth of Conservatism. Forty years earlier a man who was often called "the chief founder of Conservatism," Zacharias Frankel, at a rabbinical conference in Frankfort, Germany, used the phrase "positive, historical Judaism." Now, in this country, Sabato Morais, rabbi of Mikveh Israel, the oldest Sephardic synagogue of Philadelphia, came to the fore as the leader of those who found the Pittsburgh Platform unacceptable. He was a fiery young Italian, who had been a member of the underground during the revolution in his native Italy, but had been forced to flee to England, then America, to save his own life. He had the support of eleven congregations, including the three oldest in New York, Rabbi Marcus Jastrow's Ashkenazic synagogue in Philadelphia, and Rabbi Pereira Mendes' Congregation Shearith Israel in New York. They considered themselves Orthodox, but, using Frankel's phrase, they liked to refer to themselves as followers of "historic Judaism." Later their movement came to be called Conservative Judaism.

A Theological Seminary Is Founded

In 1886 they founded, in New York City, the Jewish Theological Seminary. (One complaint against the Reformers was that they had concentrated everything in Cincinnati, a city with a relatively small Jewish population, compared with New York. Sarcastically, the Conservatives called Hebrew Union College "the Cincinnati institution.") There were Sephardim and Ashkenazim among the founders of the seminary. Morais was named president. First classes were held in meeting rooms of Shearith Israel Synagogue in 1887. An attempt to keep the classrooms free of any acrimonious conflict between the Reform and Conservative points of view succeeded so well that the seminary had on its board of trustees men who also served as trustees of Reform temples. But the constitution of the seminary made it clear that the founders were Traditionalists, for it contained this definition of purpose and belief:

"The necessity has been made manifest for associated and organized effort on the part of the Jews of America faithful to Mosaic Law and ancestral traditions, for the purpose of keeping alive the true Judaic spirit; in particular by the establishment of a seminary where the Bible shall be impartially taught and rabbinical literature faithfully expounded, and more especially where youths, desirous of entering the ministry, may be thoroughly grounded in Jewish knowledge and inspired by the precept and example of their instructors with the love of the Hebrew language and a spirit of devotion and fidelity to the Jewish Law."

However, the seminary suffered ten lean years and when Morais died in 1897 there was doubt whether the doors could any longer be kept open. One by one, six of the eleven supporting synagogues had withdrawn their assistance.

But Conservatism did not die in 1897. In a short time a brilliant chapter of its history would be written, as a result of pogroms, massive immigration from Eastern Europe and brilliant new leadership.

15

GIVE ME YOUR TIRED, YOUR POOR . . .

Historians have called 1881 "the Year of the Pogroms." Czar Alexander II was assassinated, and it was decided to place the collective responsibility on the Jews. That year they blamed the Jews for everything that went wrong in Russia, from the weather to a blight that wiped out all the crops in a certain rich river valley. They even blamed them for the poverty of the peasants. That is why it was so easy to organize mobs that went from village to village, killing, plundering, and burning—with Jews, always, the victims.

That year the Jews of Russia were also suffering from the general hard times, which in turn was the result of the breakdown of agrarian feudalism and difficulties attending the birth of industrial capitalism. Fortunately for the Jews of Russia, the gates of America were wide open at that time, and passage on a ship across the Atlantic could be had for a relatively cheap price, especially if one brought his own food. Also, there was free land in the West of America, they said, and plenty of room everywhere for more people.

2,000,000 Jewish Immigrants

And so, in 1881, the great trek began. Before it was over—in a mere forty-four years—two million Jews had arrived in America from Eastern Europe, the bulk from Russia, Poland, and Galicia, then part of Austria, with the rest coming from Hungary and Rumania. These uprooted people were easily absorbed by a rapidly growing America, but they changed the face of Judaism on this continent. Because of them Judaism in the next eighty-seven years would make a much different and a much greater contribution to America than it otherwise might have made.

Those who came in 1881 were goldsmiths, shopkeepers, tailors, cobblers, jewelers, tinsmiths, millers, shoemakers, and followers of a hundred other skilled and unskilled occupations. Some few, when they arrived in this country, were able to continue to practice their old trades, but many had to be trained for new work. Some had friends and relatives here, who helped them readjust to a new life in a place as different from anything they had ever known as a muddy country lane in a village in the Volga Valley is different from the traffic-jammed streets of lower Manhattan.

The Year of the May Laws

Then came 1882, known as the Year of the May Laws. The May Laws were discriminatory edicts that ordered Jews to move out of the villages and small towns in which they and their families had lived for hundreds of years. In the already crowded larger towns and cities to which they were required to move, they were unable to find work of any sort, and housing was so scarce that many were forced to live in the streets. Accordingly, great numbers of them fled across Europe until they reached seaports and there they bargained for passage to America. By now Jewish committees had been set up to help them—at both ends of the trip.

On this side of the ocean the Hebrew Immigrant Aid Society (nicknamed H.I.A.S.) tried to direct them out of teeming New York to the more sparsely settled areas of the country, where both housing and employment could more easily be found for them. Thousands gratefully accepted such assistance, but those who had relatives in the cities along the Eastern Seaboard or who knew anyone in these congested places, wanted to remain there, because there would be no language problem, and there would be synagogues and Hebrew religious schools and kosher butcher shops—and friends. So, gradually, New York became the largest Jewish city in the world, with most of the newcomers packed in the dingy tenements

of the crowded East Side. They slept on cots and folding beds that each night converted thousands of parlors, sitting rooms, and even kitchens into sleeping rooms. Often the beds were used in shifts.

Welcomed, Befriended, Cared For

It was not long after the immigration of the 1880s began that the 200,000 German Jews and the handful of Sephardim in the United States were far outnumbered by the Eastern Europeans. The arrival in this country during such a short period of so many people who were in such great need of help of one kind or another put a strain on the already existing Jewish community. Yet, despite all the differences between the Jews who were arriving from Eastern Europe and those who already had their roots deeply sunk into American soil, the newcomers were welcomed, befriended, cared for, housed, and given jobs by the Jews already here. Many organizations were founded to help them. Money was given generously. Schools and lecture courses were established to enlighten them in the mores of this strange new world. An insight into some of the ways in which the problem was met is seen in the life story of Henrietta Szold, founder of the women's Zionist organization Hadassah, which some decades later built a great hospital on a hilltop in what would someday be re-created Israel. She also later became the prime mover in Youth Aliyah, through which, during World War II, she helped save many thousands of young Jewish lives from the Nazi inferno.

A Jewish Lord Tennyson

Many of the immigrant ships docked at Baltimore, where the well-to-do Jewish community, largely of Western European origin, at first ignored the hundreds of travel-stained people who streamed ashore from each vessel. Instead of using his pen or his voice to attack those guilty of this snobbery, Baltimore's outstanding rabbi, Benjamin Szold, a tenderhearted man who looked like Lord Tennyson and could quote Horace, Homer, and the Talmud with equal facility, each day took his twenty-one-year-old daughter, Henrietta, down to the docks and together they distributed small packages of food, wallets of money, and a friendly welcome to those who came ashore. Henrietta found them drab-looking and unattractive in many ways, but she wrote to her sister:

"I feel very much drawn to these Russian Jews. There is something ideal about them. Or has the suffering through which they have passed idealized them in my eyes? At all events, I have no greater wish than to be able to give them my whole strength, time and ability."

A little later she wrote: "I eat, drink and sleep Russians. . . . In fact, the Russian business so absorbs my thoughts that I have gone back to my early girlish longing to be a man. If I were, I am sure I could mature plans of great benefit to them."

Lessons in English and Democracy

If a younger sister who managed the family's finances had not watched them, the father and older daughter would have ruined the family financially. Rabbi Szold on occasions even gave the coat from his back to a shivering man just off a refugee ship. Henrietta got up at 5:30 each morning and her workday now counted seventeen hours. Soon she was calling them "my Russians" and was lavishing on them the affection a mother gives to her own children.

To help the immigrants Henrietta Szold organized classes in which she taught them English and the principles of democracy. She began with a class of thirty, in a room she rented over a grocery store in a rundown part of town. The number of pupils rapidly increased to fifty, then to a hundred. At midnight, after the last pupil was gone, the slim young woman would ride a horsecar from the slum area to her father's home, often in below-zero weather. Eventually her school attracted such attention that the school superintendent took it over and it became a pattern for similar schools all over the country—the contribution of a single Jewess to American education.

The Transformation of Emma Lazarus

In New York the Young Men's Hebrew Association, which had had its origin in Baltimore twenty-eight years earlier, as an organization to unite Orthodox, Conservative, and Reform Jews in a single community activity, opened in downtown Manhattan not far from the Battery the first Jewish neighborhood center for immigrants. One of the teachers was a young poetess, Emma Lazarus, who until now had been a sheltered, well-brought-up young Jewish woman, educated by private tutors, and who had written poetry that Ralph Waldo Emerson described as "rather good." Shortly after the start of the Jewish immigration from Eastern Europe, a friend took Miss Lazarus on a visit to Ward's Island in New York Harbor. This was where the poor, homeless, travel-tired, bedraggled, and friendless immigrants first landed. Miss Lazarus had never seen such people as these before—bearded men in long black coats and wide-brimmed hats, women in shawls and peasant skirts over a dozen petticoats. Until now she had not been a very religious Jew and had seldom identified with her own people. Once she had even said, quite bluntly, that she disliked "Jewish things." Just recently she had turned down the rabbi of her synagogue when he asked for her help in preparing a new edition of the prayer book. Often she had heated arguments with poet friends about Judaism, the others chiding her for her lack of interest in her own religion. One of them, John Burroughs, the naturalist, on one occasion gave her a long lecture on the influence of Judaism on the lives of two great non-Jewish writers, Thomas Carlyle and Walt Whitman.

But now, suddenly, the refugees were stirring within her an interest in religion—her own religion. She not only joined the faculty of the school being run by the YMHA, but also began studying Hebrew, joined the Zionist movement and wrote extensively about the Jewish immigrants, many of whom she helped become acclimated to America. She even relented and offered to help her rabbi translate prayers from Hebrew into English. The experience transformed her entire life. She had learned the tragedy and the grandeur of Jewish existence. Because she now had vital new material, her poems became more profound and more impassioned, many of them containing a plea for Jewish dignity, Jewish courage, Jewish independence.

Just after the visit to Ward's Island she read an article in a popular magazine defending the Russian Czar's persecution of the Jews, to which she promptly wrote a fiery reply.

A Poem for an Auction

Two years later, at the personal request of William M. Evarts, former Secretary of State, she contributed a poem entitled "The New Colossus" to an auction held at a gallery at Fourth Avenue and 23rd Street, New York. The money raised would go into a fund to build the foundation and pedestal on Bedloe's Island in New York Harbor for an immense statue being given by France. Other compositions contributed to the auction were by Longfellow, Mark Twain, Walt Whitman, and Bret Harte. The poem by Miss Lazarus read:

> Not like the brazen giant of Greek fame,
>   With conquering limbs astride from land to land;
> Here at our sea-washed, sunset gates shall stand
>   A mighty woman with a torch, whose flame
> Is the imprisoned lightning, and her name
>   Mother of Exiles. From her beacon-hand
> Glows worldwide welcome, her mild eyes command
>   The air-bridged harbor that twin cities frame.
> "Keep, ancient lands, your storied pomp!" cries she
>   With silent lips. "Give me your tired, your poor,
> Your huddled masses yearning to breathe free,
>   The wretched refuse of your teeming shore.
> Send these, the homeless, tempest-tost to me.
>   I lift my lamp beside the golden door!"

The Highest Bid, $1500

The auction raised many thousands of dollars. The manuscript of "The New Colossus" sold for $1500. In 1903, several years after the death of Miss Lazarus—she died when only thirty-six—"The New

Colossus" was cast in bronze and affixed to the base of the Statue of Liberty.

Fifty years after Henrietta Szold and Emma Lazarus made their contributions by teaching English and civics to classes of immigrants in Baltimore and New York, Mayor Fiorello La Guardia said such Americanization work as theirs had made possible his own election as mayor of the largest city in the United States and had saved America from what he called "a new slavery."

The Eastern European immigrants brought with them a deep attachment for Judaism, and an intense Jewishness. There had been little change in their Jewish way of life since Talmudic times. They still followed the social habits, religious practices, traditions, customs, and ethics laid down by rabbinical authorities in ancient times. This pattern of Talmudic living had been established in order to assure the survival of Jews—and it had.

Shtetls and Ghettos

In Russia they had lived in *shtetls*. A *shtetl* and a ghetto should not be confused. A ghetto was an area within a large city to which Jews were restricted; a *shtetl* was an all-Jewish town and village, out in the countryside, perhaps far removed from any other community, Jewish or non-Jewish. In their *shtetls* they dwelt in far greater isolation than their fellow Jews in the city ghettos. In this situation they preserved without difficulty their Jewish way of life, which was a smooth blend of religion, ethical values, social structure, and individual behavior. Theirs was the world of the Torah and the Talmud. They prayed in Hebrew but they spoke and read Yiddish, a language all their own. Their religion was more important to them than anything else. It governed every act of their lives. They knew the Torah by heart, as did many German Jews, but their knowledge of the Talmud and the vast literature surrounding the Talmud was also extensive and deep. They knew the Hebrew text of all their prayers and how to chant them as well as any *hazzan*. They pursued the study of Jewish law with single-mindedness and when they used the word *education* they meant religious education. When they spoke of The Law, they said the words as if they began with capital letters.

The Law to them meant Jewish religious law. To them The Law was holy, divine, beyond questioning. In almost any group of a hundred men there were at least a dozen or more who could lead the congregation in prayer. Their religion was so strong that few of their number had ever converted. There was little assimilation, and there was no interest in transforming, revising, or modernizing their ritual.

Reform Shocked Them

Most of them were Zionists in spirit, even those who did not happen to be affiliated with any Zionist organization. They prayed daily for a return to Zion, and their dreams were rich with the thought of Israel-reincarnate. They considered themselves a nation as well as a religion, for the two concepts in their minds were bound inseparably together.

It is little wonder that when they reached America and came into contact with Reform Judaism their reaction was a mixture of shock, amazement, critical curiosity, and scorn. They were hurt and angered by the Pittsburgh Platform's attitude toward Eretz Yisroel. They felt that revising or editing the ancient prayers was sacrilege. Reform's other modernizations of Judaism were to them likewise unpardonable. And so they would have nothing to do with Reform Judaism, and because most of its adherents in America were of German origin they would have little to do with German Jews in general. This created a schism that lasted for decades and still has not disappeared entirely. Because those who had come earlier by now assimilated Americans and had become integrated into the community in everything but religion, these newcomers decided to do the precise opposite. So they re-established their *shtetls* on American soil, clinging not only to their Judaism but to their Jewishness and their old ways of life. This, in turn, encouraged the Reformers to move farther in the opposite direction, thus making the cleavage even more distinct.

The newcomers, wanting to pray in Hebrew and follow the *minhag* to which they were accustomed, and wanting neither organ music nor mixed choirs nor expurgated prayers, established their own congregations.

Familiarity Breeds Content

Men from the same village in Russia would rent a vacant store, an unused loft, or an empty cellar, and gather together every day, morning and evening, as well as each Shabbat, so they could continue to say the same prayers they had always said, in the same intonation, and follow the same ritual that had been familiar to them all their lives. There was seldom any problem about a *minyan*. Contrariwise, it was more often a question of whether they could all crowd into so small a place as the rented room. They generally chose their *rebbe* from among their own number. (A rabbi and a rebbe differed in that the latter was a layman, often with charismatic charm, who was democratically chosen as a leader.)

In Eastern Europe either there was no secular education whatsoever for Jewish children, or, when such opportunities were offered, the Jews looked upon them with suspicion, out of fear that the purpose of such generosity was to wean the children away from their Judaism. As a result most Jewish children in Russia attended a *heder* or religious school. In America the immigrants eagerly enrolled their young in the public schools, knowing that they were free in two quite different senses: free of any charge, and free of any ulterior motive. But these Orthodox parents also wanted their children to have a good religious education.

The Neglect of Religious Education

In Eastern Europe religious education had always been thorough and highly organized. It was there that the institution called the *Yeshivah* was developed. (Yeshivah is from the Hebrew word meaning "sitting.") From these rabbinical academies came a steady stream of brilliant Talmudic scholars. For Jews accustomed to severe concentration on Jewish sacred learning, it was a shock to find that those who had been living for some time in America had—by Eastern European standards—been neglecting religious education. Long before the Civil War most of the synagogue schools that had been established had collapsed because of intense competition from public schools. All that remained were the Sabbath schools or Sunday schools, and the new schools set up to educate immigrants, and a few Talmud Torahs, attended by Jewish children each day after finishing their public school instruction. Determined that their own children would get a more thorough and intensive religious education, the Eastern European Jews set up hundreds of *hedarim*—miniature schools, often occupying a single small room, in which children were taught Hebrew, the Bible, and the prayer book. If the congregation was too poor to rent a room the children might assemble, after they left public school in the afternoon, at the home of the *rebbe* for an hour of instruction in how to read and recite the prayers. Or the *rebbe* might make the rounds of the tenements in which his people lived, spending a short time a day with the children of each family separately.

Finally, in 1887, a full-time elementary school, the Etz-Chaim Talmudic Academy, was opened in New York to teach the conventional curriculum of Eastern Europe. Nine years later the first Orthodox school of higher learning in America was founded when a group of Eastern European immigrants established on the East Side in New York City a small *yeshivah* for the study of the Torah and Talmudic literature.

The Case of Rabbi Joseph

As hundreds of congregations were formed, ground was soon being broken for synagogues of varying sizes and degrees of magnificence—or simplicity. By 1888 there were 130 synagogues of Eastern European Jews in New York City alone. By 1890 there were 533 synagogues in America and before the end of the century the total passed the thousand mark.

Under the European organizational system there would have been a chief rabbi in New York and all the synagogues would have been under a central authority, which would have had the right to regulate community matters, much as the government in Washington regulates matters of a federal nature. Many attempts were made to bring the New York congregations into such a European-type community, but only a minority of them ever agreed. Then, in 1888, representatives of fifteen of the principal Orthodox synagogues met to invite Rabbi Jacob Joseph, well-known scholar and preacher of Vilna, Lithuania, to come to New York as their Chief Rabbi. Members of many of the other synagogues were indignant. Long before Rabbi Joseph reached America a battle had begun in the columns of the Jewish press, in public meetings, and in sermons from pulpits.

One Saturday in 1890 Rabbi Joseph's ship docked in Hoboken, New Jersey, but since his religion prohibited him from debarking until sundown, he spent the entire day aboard ship. Across the river in New York City, thousands of members of the fifteen cooperating synagogues, as soon as evening services were over, took the ferry boat to Hoboken and escorted the dignified-looking, black-bearded rabbi to the quarters they had rented for him on Manhattan's Lower East Side. There the crowds became so great that the police had to be called out.

The controversy that had begun before his arrival now became intense. It was proposed to finance the Chief Rabbi's office by a tax on all kosher products. This created a whirlwind of protest. However, the dignified sage from Vilna rode out the storm and retained his office until his death in 1902. His funeral was attended by 20,000 Jewish mourners. But even in death he was a controversial figure, for as his funeral cortege was passing a nut and bolt factory on the East Side, workmen at upper windows joined in a chorus of jeers and then began throwing nuts and bolts onto the heads of the mourners. This precipitated a riot in which many people were severely wounded. (Incidentally, exactly forty years later, Marine Captain Jacob Joseph, namesake and great-grandson of the rabbi, was killed in action in the Solomon Islands, the youngest captain in the entire U. S. Marine Corps.)

Orthodoxy was late in getting organized in America. It was not until 1902 that hundreds of Orthodox rabbis finally united in the Union of Orthodox Rabbis of the United States and Canada. Later other unions were formed, among them the Rabbinical Council of America, whose members are all Orthodox rabbis educated in America.

Religious But Radical

What perplexed the established American Jews the most about
the new immigrants was the apparent inconsistency between their
ultra-Orthodox religious attitude and their radicalism in other fields.
As Nathan Glazer remarked in his book, *American Judaism:* "It is
not uncommon for a Jewish worker to read an anti-religious Yiddish
paper, vote Socialist, join a Socialist union, and yet attend the
synagogue weekly, or even daily."

The effect of America on the Eastern European immigrants and
their effect on America were narrated in fictionalized form by one
of the immigrants himself. Abraham Cahan was a religious but radical
young Lithuanian Jew who came over in the 1882 wave of immigration. He quickly learned English so he could qualify for a
place on the staff of a New York newspaper. After serving with distinction on the paper edited by Lincoln Steffens, he decided that he
wanted to use his talents in helping transform his fellow Jewish
immigrants into modern-minded citizens of the western world. But
to reach them he knew he would have to write for them in Yiddish,
because many of them still refused to learn a word of English. As
editor of *The Jewish Daily Forward*, which soon was the largest
Yiddish daily in the world, Cahan was able to reach hundreds of
thousands of new American Jews. Then he began to write novels
of immigrant Jewish life. *The Rise of David Levinsky* told the story
of a learned, pious young Jewish student who sails from Russia to
America, and on the ship refuses to eat non-kosher food and spends
most of his time in prayer. In New York he locates Jews from his
home town and joins the synagogue that they have established. At
first slowly, then very rapidly, he changes. First he cuts off his ear-
locks. Then he begins to shave. Then he stops going to the synagogue
because the services interfere with the classes he is attending in a night
school. Now he speaks English instead of Yiddish and begins to forget
his Hebrew prayers.

But David Levinsky's heritage was not totally destroyed and Judaism in America did not die.

16

SCHECHTER'S 1,400,000 FOLLOWERS

As the nineteenth century came to an end, established American Jews—meaning those who had arrived in the country before 1880—were deeply concerned about what effect the influx of so many hundreds of thousands of Eastern European Jews would have on them, on their religious life, and on their relationship with their neighbors. Many were troubled by the extent of the newcomers' religious orthodoxy and the extent of their political heterodoxy. Members of some of the traditional synagogues were as much disturbed as were members of most of the Reform temples. It was not the poverty of the immigrants that bothered anyone—the Jewish community responded generously to every call for funds to help them. It was their piety and their politics, both of which were embarrassing to some people.

In the American Jewish Archives there is an entire volume devoted to *The Attitude of the American Jewish Community Toward East European Immigration as Reflected in the Anglo-Jewish Press, 1880–1890*, which discloses that in that decade there were even Jewish suggestions, published in the Jewish press, that United States immigration authorities refuse entry to several hundred Jewish Russian refugees about to arrive on a certain ship. This, of course, was an extreme attitude and few may have shared it. More typical was the idea that the Easterners eventually should be—and could be—won over to an Americanized religious position. With this in mind a group of wealthy New Yorkers decided to give the moribund Jewish Theological Seminary a new lease on life. The man chiefly responsible for the resurrection was Cyrus Adler, who had been a pupil of

Sabato Morais, one of the founders of the seminary. Adler was intimately associated with some of the most prominent Jewish families in the East and had a wide acquaintance with politicians, philanthropists, industrialists, and scholars. He had been in the Department of Semitics at Johns Hopkins University and then became assistant secretary of the Smithsonian Institution. His vision was that the Jewish Theological Seminary might help turn pious young East European Jews into conservative, enlightened English-speaking rabbis, who could provide twentieth-century leadership for their own people—the East Europeans.

Invitation to a Scholar

One of the first to give Adler support was Jacob Schiff, who had come to America from Germany in his youth and had prospered as a partner in the firm of Kuhn, Loeb and Company. Although he was a Reform Jew, he was sympathetic toward the recent immigrants, as was Louis Marshall, president of Emanu-El, the citadel of Reform. They joined with Mayer Sulzberger, Daniel and Simon Guggenheimer, Leonard Lewissohn, and other wealthy New Yorkers in giving half a million dollars—a great deal of money in 1901—for the Jewish Theological Seminary. Even before the pledges were all in, Sulzberger, writing for the seminary, invited one of the greatest living Jewish scholars and philosophers, Solomon Schechter, to serve as president of the theological seminary, certain that he would be acceptable to most factions of American Jewry.

Schechter accepted and the next year arrived to take charge. The importance of this fifty-three-year-old Yeshivah Talmudist, this mystic philosopher, to the history of American Judaism is so considerable that more about him needs to be told.

Son of the Shohet

He was born in the village of Fokszany, Rumania, of Russian parents. His father, who fled to the Balkans to escape serving in the Czar's army, was the *shohet* or ritual slaughterer of the community and so he took Schechter as his family name. He was such an ardent follower of a celebrated Hasidic rabbi, Schneor Zalman, that he gave his son that name. Because there was no good teacher in town, the father undertook to educate young Schneor Zalman, who, at the age of three, knew the Pentateuch and not long thereafter the Prophets, the Talmud, and the Midrash. His thirst for knowledge was so great that at the age of ten he ran away from home to attend a Yeshivah in a nearby town. He was brought back to his parents but fled again, this time remaining away for several years. In the school where he was now studying there were not enough books for all the pupils, so the boy from Fokszany learned sections of the Talmud and other rabbinic works by heart. The memory he thus acquired was one of his most valuable assets the rest of his life.

When he was twelve he happened onto a Hebrew translation of a book by Josephus on Apion, the first century Greek anti-Semite. Nothing he ever read had excited him so much. Here, for the first time, he learned that the disease which afflicted his own country was not especially endemic to Rumania, but was the result of a virus that for at least seventeen centuries had been poisoning the blood stream of men who apparently were otherwise normal. It was a turning point in the boy's life. At the risk of being discovered and severely punished, he secretly read other books in Hebrew that were on the black list of the extremely Orthodox. He even read a newspaper written in the holy language.

By now he was well on the road to becoming a *maskil* (an enlightened, self-educated Jew). He studied in Rumania until he was twenty-four, acquiring a good foundation of Jewish culture and a deep attachment for his own people, as well as some bitter, firsthand insight into the manner in which anti-Semitism can poison the minds of an entire race. When he was seventeen his parents, in the Orthodox tradition, arranged a marriage for him. When he was eighteen this unhappy union was terminated by a *get* or rabbinical divorce.

Austria, Germany, England

For the next six years he lived in Vienna, supporting himself as custodian of one professor's immense private library and teacher in another professor's home, all the while working to systematize his knowledge. Then he went to Berlin. In those days seekers after Jewish knowledge from all over the world flocked to the German capital, which was also the capital of the *Wissenschaft des Judentums* (Science of Judaism). There he matriculated in the university and in the *Hochschule*, the celebrated rabbinical academy. In Berlin he came into close contact with renowned professors, some Jews, some not. He also had the strange experience of studying with a group of anti-Semitic students whose only purpose in combing the Bible, the Talmud, Jewish history, and other religious literature was to find justification for their animosity toward Judaism.

In Berlin he met a young British Jew, Claude G. Montefiore, a student in the Hochschule, who employed him to serve as a tutor. When Montefiore finally left for England he took the young Rumanian with him. It was in England that Schneor Zalman Schechter became Solomon Schechter. There he devoured hundreds, then thousands of books and manuscripts on Jews and Judaism, which he found in the British Museum and in the great libraries of Oxford and Cambridge. There he acquired a good working knowledge of English, although until his death he always spoke the language with a European accent. In England he began writing, brilliantly, not only about Jews, Judaism, and anti-Semitism, but even on such secular subjects as the character of Abraham Lincoln, who was one of his heroes.

Two Dusty Sheets of Parchment

A chance visit by two Christian ladies of his acquaintance proved to be a turning point in his life. They had just returned from Egypt and wanted their friend, now a professor in Cambridge, to see two dusty old sheets of parchment covered with Hebrew characters which they had acquired on a visit to Cairo. Schechter recognized one, immediately, as a fragment of the *Jerusalem Talmud*, while the other seemed to be an imitation of the Book of Proverbs. Just such a work was the apocryphal *Book of Ecclesiasticus* or *The Wisdom of Ben Sirach* (or Sira) written a hundred years before the Maccabees. In the library at Cambridge there was an English translation of the

Greek translation of this book, but the original Hebrew had been the object of search by scholars for centuries. After comparing the fragment that had been brought to him with the English version Schechter was convinced that he held in his hand a rare object—a piece of the original manuscript.

With the excitement and zeal of a scholar, Schechter went to Cairo to search for the rest of the manuscript. He knew that according to Orthodox law no book, no manuscript, no scrap of paper on which someone has written or printed the name of God can be thrown away, ever. It must either be buried or saved. He also knew that as a matter of general practice, instead of searching books and documents before destroying them, to be sure they do not contain the name of God, the custom in extremely religious circles was to bury or save everything written or printed. This is how the *genizah* (Hebrew for "hiding") came to be established. A *genizah* was a storage place in a cellar or attic, or a crypt, into which were thrown old books and papers.

One Chance in 100,000

The *shammash* of Ezra Synagogue in Cairo knew Schechter by name and when the professor asked about the synagogue's *genizah* the *shammash* took him to a walled-in chamber into which for more than a thousand years one generation after another of rabbis, scholars, and synagogue janitors had dumped papers and books for which they no longer had any use. It was necessary to break through one of the walls of the *genizah* to gain entrance. It was a place of darkness and disorder, but not of decay, for the Cairo atmosphere is so dry that neither wood nor cloth nor paper disintegrates. In the crypt were at least 100,000 manuscripts and books.

Before Schechter could start work he had to obtain permission first from the rabbi of Ezra Synagogue, then from the trustees of the Cairo Jewish Community, then from the British Administration.

For weeks the Cambridge professor worked in the *genizah* by the light of a small oil lantern, squinting through a magnifying glass, as he tried to sort out the worthless from the invaluable. The heat was oppressive and everything was covered with thick layers of dust.

Each day Schechter was afraid he would have to abandon his search. Finally, weary and ill, he filled thirty large sacks with manuscripts that seemed of possible value and shipped them to England. Back at Cambridge a special room was assigned to him for his research. After months and months of work on the fragments, the excited young professor announced that he had not only the complete original of the oldest Hebrew book in existence, other than the Bible, but also manuscripts of many other works of importance to Jewish historians, including the great *Geonim* of Babylon, explaining the Talmud, and prayers of some of the greatest men in Jewish history. His discoveries were treated by the press of the world as sensational news, causing as much excitement then as the discovery of the Dead Sea Scrolls would cause half a century later. Not only had the detective work of a relatively unknown Cambridge professor of rabbinical literature given the nineteenth century one more glimpse into the distant past, but as a result a new name was added to the roster of international scholars. In recognition, Cambridge University awarded Schechter a doctorate of laws.

At the New York Seminary Dr. Schechter gathered together a faculty of eminent scholars, some from Germany, some from Eastern Europe, but all with training in German universities. To this faculty he entrusted the task of turning out young rabbis who would be able to speak English and grapple with the problems of twentieth-century American Jewish society. He was well aware that life in America was making totally different demands on the Jewish immigrants than had life in the teeming ghettos and the isolated *shtetls* of Europe. He wanted to bring traditional Judaism into touch with modern life, while retaining all the rich values of the ancient religion. He held that while Judaism could and should change in response to modern conditions, such revision should be controlled, always, by scholarship, which would set definite limits to change.

The Bush That Was Not Consumed

He taught his students that as Conservative Jews they must try to feel themselves part of all the Jewish people and not permit themselves to become alienated from any faction, group, or bloc of Jews.

As a motto for the seminary he chose six words from Exodus 3:2: ". . . and the bush was not consumed."

To those who asked for elucidation, he would smile and explain patiently that it meant Jews and Judaism had survived for thousands of years, despite the many fires through which they had been forced to pass.

By a combination of brilliant wit, irresistible charm, and profound scholarship, Schechter was able to pass on to the theological students his appreciation of the positive values of historic Judaism which he insisted should be retained. Under his leadership the seminary became before long one of the greatest centers of Jewish learning in the world, with a brilliant faculty, a great library, and wide support from even Reform Jews.

Although the student body from the start included some young men with an Eastern European background, initially the seminary had little influence on the Eastern European situation, for the graduates inevitably would be called by congregations made up of Jews who had been in the country for a considerable time and were conservative in their practice of Judaism. But year by year the number of Conservative synagogues grew and in 1913 Schechter formed sixteen of them into an organization called the United Synagogue of America.

Ovations and Suspicions

During his thirteen years in this country Dr. Schechter won a place in the Conservative movement similar to that held by Dr. Isaac Mayer Wise in the Reform movement. He built the seminary from a small and poorly equipped institution into an internationally renowned seat of Jewish learning. He was a liberal in that he believed there was room in Judaism for various schools of religious thought. In 1913, when he attended dedication exercises in Cincinnati for the new Hebrew Union College building, he was given a resounding ovation by leaders of Reform Judaism, among them Dr. Kaufman Kohler, president of the college.

But Dr. Schechter and his seminary were regarded with suspicion by the more traditional American Jews, who, as Schechter himself once sadly put it, "insist that secular education and modern methods in school and college are incompatible with Orthodox principles." They held that however little Judaism might be "watered down," by the Conservatives, it lost some of its richness and its worth in the process.

An Opportunity for Compromise

Despite all the opposition, Conservative Judaism was attracting more and more followers. The appeal was made to those who felt they had outgrown the Orthodoxy that had been imported from abroad, yet who were ill at ease praying in English bareheaded, listening to hymns sung by a non-Jewish choir, and hearing sermons in which Zionism was often condemned. Conservative Judaism offered to such people a religious solution. While Conservative services were kept largely traditional, they were shortened and were conducted with dignity. At prayer the men wore hats or *yarmulkes* (skull caps) and the *tallit* (prayer shawl). At synagogue functions the dietary laws were observed. Marriages and funerals were conducted in the traditional manner. Young people were given an intensive Hebrew education. But the separation of men and women in the synagogue was abolished, a confirmation or *bas mitzvah* service was provided for girls, and some Conservative synagogues even installed organs. Of increasing importance, nearly all Conservative rabbis were intense Zionists. Also contributing to the growth of the movement was the opportunity it offered for compromise. If a Jewish community was not large enough to maintain both an Orthodox synagogue and a Reform temple, the happy solution was often for everyone to support a Conservative synagogue.

Schechter and the graduates of what came to be called (sometimes affectionately, sometimes in scorn) "Schechter's Seminary" were responsible for bringing tens of thousands of American Jews who had broken with Orthodoxy back to a healthy affiliation with their religion.

By 1967 the United Synagogue of American reported that it had 800 affiliated congregations, with 1,400,000 members.

17

NOTHING JEWISH IS ALIEN

There were 270 synagogues in the United States in 1880. A quarter of a century later there were 1769. Synagogues were being built, bought, or rented at the rate of fifty-seven per year. In New York City alone during this period an average of two synagogues were opened each month. Those are the cold statistics of a situation unprecedented in Jewish religious history, on this or any other continent. Some of the synagogues were modest, for Judaism teaches that the elegance of the religious surrounding is of much less importance than the inner ardor of the worshiper. Often it was an empty store, with curtains hanging at the windows to keep idle passers-by from staring at the men, many of them bearded, who wore fringed prayer shawls over their shoulders and hats on their heads, and walked up and down reading from the prayer books they held in their hands. Sometimes a congregation was fortunate enough to find a Christian church that had been abandoned and was for sale at a price they could meet.

The Scarcity of Rabbis

There was still a shortage of locally trained rabbis, and only wealthy congregations could afford to import them from abroad, so a majority of congregations did without. The *hazzanim* received such meager salaries that many served also as teachers and some even worked at sewing machines in garment factories between one Shabbat and the next. Some congregations had to forego the luxury of a *hazzan* except on High Holy Days, when it was essential to have the supplications to God made in the most musical tones the congregation could afford.

No matter how modest the rented quarters, no matter how poor the congregation, there had to be a *shammash*, who often lived with his family in quarters attached to or adjoining the house of worship. His task was not just to keep the place clean and orderly but also to supervise the order of the service. If there was no *hazzan* the *shammash* might augment his income by acting as a teacher of the young.

In Europe the *mohel*, the *shohet*, and the *mashgiah*, the inspector of dietary regulations, were employees of the community, but in most cases in America they were free-lance operators, although they might belong to federations or associations.

There was much about life in America that was confusing for the immigrants, such as the matter of divorce. In Eastern European countries the Jewish community was a self-contained entity. The state recognized its acting as the agency or surrogate, in such matters as divorce. In America, one of the crucial differences and one which did much to undermine rabbinical and communal authority was that the state would not recognize rabbinical divorce—a civil divorce was also necessary. This could and sometimes did result in a Jew who had received a rabbinical divorce in Europe and then had remarried in the United States being charged with bigamy.

The Kishinev Massacre

As the nineteenth century drew to a close and the twentieth began, violence against Jews in Europe grew worse, thereby increasing the rate of Jewish emigration to the United States. There were pogroms in 1870, in 1881, in 1899, and in 1903. What happened in 1903 at Kishinev, Bessarabia, was called a massacre rather than a pogrom. Not many people were killed—just forty-seven—fewer than the Nazis would murder in a few minutes in any one of their extermination factories forty years later. What made Kishinev so frightening was that drunken mobs, incited by high Russian authorities, for two days vented their fury on the helpless Jewish community, destroying, burning, murdering, and looting, and when the police finally did interfere, it was to disarm those Jews who were trying to defend themselves. What made Kishinev significant was that it became a rallying cry for Jews everywhere. Kishinev was a symbol of the need of Jews for a place of refuge. In America Orthodox, Reform, and Conservative Jews forgot their ritualistic differences in their unanimous protest to God and man. In their synagogues and temples they met to pray— and then to form committees and plan action. In quick order they raised a million dollars to help the victims. In New York City one hundred thousand men and women paraded through the streets to demonstrate their feelings.

A Mighty Migration

Kishinev accelerated the flow of Jews to America. In the next decade 1,500,000—one-seventh of the entire Jewish population of Europe—left that continent.

In the forty-four years ending with World War I, two million Jews came to the United States. During World War I another 100,000 drifted in. In the years immediately following the war, another quarter of a million came. Then, in 1924, Congress closed the gates. Not tightly, but enough so that the human flood became a trickle. Other acts of Congress in 1927 and 1930 reduced the trickle to something resembling the drip-drip of a leaking water faucet. But by now the Jewish population of the United States stood at 4,500,000. This was not yet the peak. The total would be increased slightly when the doors would be opened a little— pathetically little—to admit victims of the Nazi attempt at genocide in the 1940s. And it would also increase, of course, due to natural causes. But the plateau had been reached by the late 1920s.

The Court Jew

The Kishinev Massacre brought Simon Wolf into the fore again. He was the man who had been known in Washington, D.C., since

Lincoln's days as "the Court Jew" and "the representative of the Jewish race." When President James A. Garfield appointed him Consul-General to Egypt he could boast that he had "the highest diplomatic post yet held by a professing Jew." His duties were largely ceremonial. His chief value in Cairo was to boost the morale of the large colony of Egyptian Jews who looked on him as another Joseph.

Once as Wolf was having tea on the terrace of his hotel, the British Consul-General rushed to his table and breathlessly announced:

"My dear fellow, I've just been informed there is going to be an uprising tonight and they are going to slaughter all the Christians and Europeans."

Consul-General Wolf calmly sipped his tea and replied:

"How does that concern me? I am neither a European nor a Christian."

When the newly formed state of Rumania began a campaign of terrorism against its large Jewish population, Wolf suggested that the President appoint a Jew, Benjamin Peixotto, as American Consul to Rumania "to give those people a lesson in equality and justice." Peixotto was appointed, although subsequent history casts doubt on whether the Rumanians learned their lesson.

A Precious Petition

When news of what had happened at Kishinev reached Washington, Wolf made frequent calls on President Theodore Roosevelt, who urged Wolf to try to rally world opinion. It was Wolf, on Roosevelt's suggestion, who initiated the Kishinev Petition that was signed by prominent people in all walks of life, Christians and Jews alike. President Roosevelt then arranged to have it transmitted to the Russians, but they refused to accept it. It served its purpose, however, for it did arouse widespread indignation against the anti-Semitism then rampant throughout Eastern Europe. When Secretary of State John Hay accepted the petition on its return from Russia, he declared:

"The archives of our government contain nothing more precious, and the Jews of the world should feel profoundly grateful for this great and enduring record."

Shortly thereafter Russia invoked its 1832 treaty with the United States to justify its refusal to recognize the passports of American Jews. The story really begins in 1866, when an American citizen on a visit to Russia tried to buy a piece of property in Kharkov and was denied the right on the ground that he was a Jew. Some years later another American traveler was ordered to leave St. Petersburg because he was a Jew. Still later it was discovered that Russian consulates in the United States were denying visas to Americans whom they suspected of being Jews. The final blow came in 1907 when the Secretary of State declared that no more passports would be issued to American Jews for travel to Russia if they had once been Russian subjects, because on arrival there they would still be treated as Russian subjects despite their American nationality. This seemed to be an acknowledgment, without protest, of the Czar's right to claim that once a subject of the Czar always a subject of the Czar.

Schiff Speaks Out to the President

The platform on which William Howard Taft ran for the presidency contained a promise that if elected he would see that all American citizens had equal rights of citizenship. But during his first two years in office only mild protests were made to Russia by the United States government. Then, at a conference with a group of Jewish leaders, including Wolf and Louis Marshall, Taft announced that the United States could not abrogate the treaty with Russia, because this would endanger $60,000,000 of American capital invested in Russia and might accelerate the flow of Russian Jews to the United States. Joseph Schiff, philanthropist and one of the committee members present, bluntly turned to Mr. Taft and said:

"Mr. President, you have said that you are not prepared to permit the commercial interests of ninety-eight million of the American people to suffer because two million feel that their rights as American citizens are being infringed upon. My own opinion has always been that it was the privilege of the head of this nation that, if only a single American citizen was made to suffer injury, the entire power of this great government should be exercised to procure redress for such injury; and now you tell us because some special interests who are trading with Russia might suffer if the abrogation of the treaty was carried into effect, you would not do anything to protect two million American citizens in the rights vouchsafed to them under our Constitution and laws. . . .

"Mr. President, you have failed us, and there is nothing left to us now but to put our case before the American people directly, who are certain to do justice. . . . In 1861, a small but in some respects potential minority claimed that it would be better to permit the slave states to get out of the Union instead of risking a Civil War, but public opinion insisted that the slave must be freed and the Union remain supreme at any cost; the war for the right was thereupon fought and won, even with all the sacrifice it necessitated. To this same public opinion, Mr. President, we shall now turn, and we have no fear of the results."

Taft's Capitulation

On leaving the White House, Schiff pledged $25,000 for an educational campaign to bring about abrogation of the treaty. Sermons were preached in synagogues and temples all over the country. Hundreds of thousands of names were obtained on petitions. Mass meetings were held. Every Jewish organization in the country took some part in the fight. Finally, under pressure from both houses of Congress, Taft capitulated and sent notice to Russia late in 1911 that the treaty would be abrogated. It was a moral victory not just for American Jews but for the principle of human rights.

When Wolf died at the age of eighty-seven it was disclosed that he had used his talents and energies on behalf of some over 103,000 Jews who had come before the Bureau of Labor for deportation and that he had fought for the rights of Negroes, Chinese, Catholics, and other minority groups, as well as Jews. Father Walsh of St. Patrick's Church in Washington once said of him: "The best Christian in Washington is Simon Wolf, the Jew."

Louis Marshall, Shtadlan

American reaction to the Kishinev Massacre made everyone realize the need for an organization that could speak with a single voice for American Jewry on any matter on which American Jewry had something approaching a unanimous attitude. The initiative in forming such an organization was taken in 1906 by Louis Marshall, who has been called "the last of the great *shtadlanim* in American Jewish life." (The word comes from the German *Stadt* or city. It really means "city-leader," a person who, because of the autonomous nature of the European Jewish community, was frequently its representative to the secular government.)

Marshall was an American-born legal genius. In those days in New York City it took two years to get through law school. Young Marshall did it in one, taking his first-year classes in the morning and his second-year classes in the afternoon. By his early thirties he was one of the most respected members of the New York bar. A bachelor half his life, he lived with his Orthodox parents and solemnly took part in the ritual of lighting the Shabbat candles, in observing the *seder*, and in all the other religious rites. He was one of a group of prominent German Jews—including Adolph Ochs of the New York *Times*, Cyrus Adler, the Guggenheims, Jacob Schiff, and Oscar Straus—who wanted to apply the idea of social justice, which is such an integral part of Judaism, to the problems of twentieth-century life. He believed that Judaism is a vital force in Jewish survival. Marshall in 1906 took the lead in forming the American Jewish Committee. There were sixty founders, most of them of German stock and most of them prominent in American-Jewish affairs. A minority of the group was from Eastern Europe. The purpose of the committee was "to protect Jewish rights wherever they are threatened." The committee members selected delegates from all over the United States to attend an organizational meeting nine months later.

Passionate Anti-Zionist

Marshall politically was an arch-conservative. He disliked William Jennings Bryan, distrusted Theodore Roosevelt and was suspicious of Woodrow Wilson. He opposed the direct primary and the referendum, being fearful of "the masses." He respected only "the law." He was a passionate anti-Zionist. He envisioned the Committee as a body of like-minded men who would work behind the scenes, rather than resort to publicized mass action. Later in life Marshall became more disposed to Zionism. One of his last major projects was the formation of the Jewish Agency for Palestine, a venture in which he and Chaim Weizman were prime movers. Marshall and the Committee took an active part in the successful fight to abrogate the Russian-American treaty.

The Ku Klux Klan was at the height of its power in these days, having enrolled four million members in its anti-Jewish, anti-Catholic, anti-Negro fanaticism. Marshall did frequent battle with the Klan. On one occasion he declared that even if the Klan would "let up on the Jews and would be only against Negroes or any other part of our population" he would fight it with just as much determination. He championed the cause of American Indians, Japanese-Americans who were being discriminated against, and victims of anti-Bolshevik measures which he thought violated the Constitution. In fighting Oregon school laws, which took from Catholics the right to operate parochial schools, he won the right for any religious group to have its own schools if it wished. He was often called the "watchdog of his people" and always lived up to his own description of himself: "Nothing Jewish is alien to me." He was a Reform Jew, yet he advocated amalgamation of the Conservative and Reform theological seminaries. He often spoke wistfully of the warmth, the poetry, and the psychological appeal of Orthodox Judaism, which he feared some American Jews were losing.

18

J.D.C., WAR BABY

FOR most Americans, until the United States became a belligerent, World War I was just a newspaper story—something to read about objectively—something remote from life and emotions. But not for the majority of American Jews. Especially not for those who had arrived since 1880. The fighting on the Eastern Front took place almost entirely within the Russian Pale, the area in which most of the Jews who had not already fled to the West still lived. Almost everyone had relatives back there.

And then came the Revolution. There was fighting between White Russians and Red Russians, and it was all happening in an area where for decades the populace had been encouraged in anti-Semitic excesses, and so it was no surprise that both sides put upon the Jews, committing the same old crimes in the same old ways—murder, rape, burning, and looting. Yet when it was all over and accusing fingers were pointed, everyone feigned innocence and blamed the other.

The Creation of J.D.C.

These were sad days for Jews, even for those who had escaped to America and were themselves safe, thousands of miles away, in a country whose President, while some of the bloodiest battles of history were being fought, was campaigning for re-election on the slogan, "He kept us out of war!" American Jews, while flocking to their synagogues and temples as never before to pray for an end to this latest torment of their people, took a positive, constructive step by creating the most remarkable relief and rehabilitation agency the world had ever known. Its full name was the Joint Distribution Committee of the American Funds for Jewish War Sufferers, but it was soon shortened to the Joint Distribution Committee, and then to J.D.C., and finally to *The Joint*, or simply *Joint*, a word not especially euphonious and meaning little to those who knew nothing of its aims and its accomplishments. Yet J.D.C. almost immediately began making Jewish history. There is significance to the fact that it came to be nicknamed *The Joint*, because it began as a coordinating body of a number of separate and already established Jewish charities —Orthodox, Conservative, and Reform, as well as secular—and as the war went on and its work became increasingly important, it became the only project on which all American Jews were completely united.

American Jewry Comes of Age

J.D.C. was formed by amalgamating two independent bodies, the American Jewish Relief Committee, which had been created at a conference called by the American Jewish Committee, and the Central Relief Committee, a strictly Orthodox body. Until recently the total population of the American Jewish community had been numbered in six digits and its significance in the world picture had been slight. Not many years before this the Jewish community of Frankfurt, Germany, had raised more money for the relief of Jews in the Balkans than had been contributed for the same emergency by all the Jews of America combined. But now world Jewish leadership began to shift from Europe to America. With the organization of J.D.C., American Jewry began to come of age. From now on American Jews would accept the responsibility of going to the aid of Jews who needed to be fed, clothed, housed, or moved out of the place of their suffering, wherever that might be.

The first J.D.C. chairman was Felix Warburg, New York financier and philanthropist. In its early stages the organization was solely a disbursing agency, allocating the money raised by its cooperating committees to agencies in the receiving countries. In the first year these cooperating committees raised a million and a half dollars—a record figure for so small a group in so short a time. But the need was mounting, as the war spread and as more and more European Jews were engulfed, so J.D.C. started its own fund-raising campaign, devising techniques which soon became standard for all Jewish fund-raising efforts and eventually were widely copied, even by non-Jewish fund raisers. The response of the American Jewish community was so great that a total of $16,500,000 was raised during the war years, and before the United States became a belligerent nearly three-quarters of a million Jews in Poland and the Baltic states were entirely dependent on J.D.C. for their continued existence.

Symbol of Hope

As the years and the decades went by, J.D.C. became one of the most experienced bodies anywhere in the world in dealing with human tragedy. It collected and expended, wisely, larger sums than almost any other philanthropic organization, Jewish or non-Jewish. It picked experienced administrators who in turn surrounded themselves with experienced social workers, who gave up the comforts of a normal life to work under often dangerous conditions with a devotion rare even for social workers. Gradually, as time passed, J.D.C. became a symbol of hope when all other hope failed; a symbol of deliverance when all doors seemed locked and barred.

The end of the war, instead of making possible a gradual tapering off of such aid, necessitated stepped-up operations, for now there were pogroms in more than a hundred Polish towns, and in the Ukraine a civil war which cost a quarter of a million Jewish lives, and anti-Jewish riots in Rumania, Hungary, and Lithuania. Everywhere in Europe there was hunger, and in many places the threat of famine. J.D.C. not only had to continue emergency aid and alleviate the misery in war-ravaged Jewish communities, but also it was called upon to begin reconstruction—the reconstruction of houses, villages, towns, and cities, and the rehabilitation of human lives. In the first two years following the end of hostilities more than $27,000,000 was raised for such purposes.

ORT and OSE

ORT and OSE also played important roles. OSE are the initials of the Jewish Health Society—in Russian. It was founded in Russia before the war, but it was American doctors and nurses, most of them Jews, who revived the society after the war and saved thousands of lives by setting up hospitals, X-ray stations, nurses' training schools, dispensaries, sanitariums, public baths, milk centers, pediatric clinics, and other medical and sanitary institutions.

ORT is the Organization for Rehabilitation through Training, originally a Russian-Jewish organization which provided vocational training for tens of thousands of boys and girls, on the theory that Jews would be more self-reliant and more welcome wherever they might go if they had skills fitting them to work in the modern industrial world. ORT grew into a worldwide organization of great importance, as one world war led to another and as scattered pogroms merged into the greatest pogrom of all—the Final Solution.

When the United States entered World War I there were new problems and additional responsibilities for the Jewish community. President Wilson, well understanding that no one group of American Jews could speak for all, called a conference of Reform, Conservative, and Orthodox leaders, which in turn created the National Jewish Welfare Board, to deal with all matters involving Jews in the armed forces. To serve the great number of Jews in the army and navy, twenty-five rabbis were commissioned as chaplains. The same Jewish committee that approved these appointments also put out a prayer book for servicemen, which included traditional prayers as well as some from the Union prayer book. Jewish recreational centers were established and arrangements were made wherever and whenever possible for Jewish servicemen to celebrate Jewish holidays, including participation in *Seders* on Passover.

After the war, the Jewish Welfare Board, instead of going out of existence, used the organization it had built up to direct the growing community center movement.

Problems of Post-War America

Peace presented almost as many problems for American Jews as war. Not only were there the bloody aftermaths, with which J.D.C. was concerned, but there were now political questions to be decided—questions in which Jews had a special interest, for despite the slaughter there were still some members of their *mishpokhe* left in Europe. But again, American Jews were handicapped by their many-sidedness and by the fact that they had no central organization to speak for them. J.D.C., like the Red Cross and other humanitarian organizations, assiduously avoided becoming politically involved. The Jewish Welfare Board likewise was limited in its field of operations. The American Jewish Committee represented an extremely limited segment of American Jewry—German Jews with non-Zionist leanings.

Efforts to create a democratically elected body that could represent the entire Jewish community at the peace conference were opposed by the American Jewish Committee, although favored by most of those with roots in Eastern Europe and with Zionist sympathies. In 1916 a compromise was reached. The American Jewish Committee agreed to take part in a congress if it would deal only with peace problems and if it would disband as soon as it performed this function. Three thousand people cast ballots for delegates to such a congress, but before the gathering could assemble, the United States entered the war. This postponed the meeting until 1918, when some of the delegates finally did meet and formed the American Jewish Congress, which adopted a statement of principles and appointed a delegation to represent American Jewry at the Versailles Peace Conference.

The fate of millions of Jews was to be decided at the peace table. The principal issue for the Jewish delegates was assimilation versus nationalism. The Balfour Declaration had already been issued. Even within the Zionist movement there were divisions. Could the British be trusted with the mandate over Palestine until the Balfour promise was realized?

There was wrangling of many sorts at Versailles and when it

was all over no single person, no single group, no single nation
was happy with all the decisions, but the American Jewish Congress
delegation left with the satisfaction that it had persuaded the men
at the green baize table to write into the treaties provisions guar-
anteeing the rights of European minorities—*all* minorities.

The Greatest Forgery of All Time

Even before the Treaty of Versailles was drawn and signed, an
extraordinary document made its appearance in Western Europe—
a document that would have an effect on the life of every American
Jew for a long time to come. Some historians call the *Protocols
of the Elders of Zion* the greatest political forgery of all time.
This bizarre literary fabrication—the creation of anti-Semitic Russian
officers and a slightly mad monk, Sergei Nilus—first appeared in
print in 1903 in a Russian newspaper, *Znamia* (*The Banner*), published by a reactionary leader in Kishinev, Paul Krushevan, noted
anti-Semite. The serialized exposé was entitled *A Jewish Program
to Conquer the World*. The nine articles purported to be the actual
wording of a stolen record of twenty-four meetings in Basle, Switzerland, in 1897, the time of the First Zionist Congress. At these
clandestine gatherings, "the chiefs of the twelve tribes of Israel"
allegedly devised plans whereby Jews, liberals, and Freemasons, working together, would overthrow all existing governments and seize
power for themselves. This was to have been done by "the corruption of European women," by the use of "strong liquor to befuddle
the leaders of European opinion," by stirring up economic distress,
and finally by blowing up the various capitals of the world. On
the ruins would then be created a world state run by Jews and
Freemasons.

After serialization of the articles, what purported to be a fuller
text was published by Nilus in 1905, in collaboration with the Russian
Army Staff of the St. Petersburg region. This little book went
through many editions and was translated into French, English, and
German. As World War I drew to a close and revolution flared
in Russia, fleeing White Russian officers took copies of the *Protocols*
with them to Western Europe and used them in an attempt to ex-

plain the cause of the Russian upheaval. The *Morning Post* of London (now defunct) devoted many columns to an analysis of the alleged plot, commenting on the apparent success it was having. In the United States the *Protocols* came to the attention of Henry Ford who ordered them serialized in his own newspaper, the *Dearborn Independent*.

After the revolution, a search of the files of Czar Nicholas II gave the first clues to how and why the forgery had been committed. The Czar, desiring material that would both damn the Jews and tend to justify the Russian pogroms, had ordered a court functionary named Rachkovsky to produce it. Unable to discover any actual evidence that might have satisfied the Czar, Rachkovsky decided to concoct some. He remembered having heard of a literary work by a Dr. de Cyon, a physician, journalist, and financier, who amused himself by digging up old satires, which he would rewrite, adapting them to current situations, and then circulate them among friends. Recently he had written such a satire directed at a personal enemy, Count de Witte, then Minister of Finance of Russia. Dr. de Cyon had done little more than change the names in a novel that had been published in 1864 and had immediately been suppressed by Napoleon III, *Dialogue aux Enfers*. In this earlier work the author, Maurice Joly, a popular satirist, told of a conversation in hell between Machiavelli and Montesquieu, during which a worldwide financial plot was outlined. Rachkovsky, unable to obtain Dr. de Cyon's permission to rewrite his rewritten version of the *Dialogue*, had the manuscript stolen from the doctor's villa and used it as the basis for his own *A Jewish Program to Conquer the World*. There were no Jews in the *Dialogue*. There were no Jews in Dr. de Cyon's novel. But with the help of the monk, Rachkovsky turned the story into an anti-Semitic document. The *Dialogue* had been directed against Napoleon. Dr. de Cyon had substituted Count de Witte for Napoleon. Rachkovsky and Nilus substituted the Jewish race for Count de Witte. And now the story purported to be fact, not fiction.

In 1921 the *Times* of London exposed the *Protocols* as "a cruel and vicious forgery" and told how, why, and by whom they had been fabricated. But that exposé failed to stop their circulation, although it did destroy their credibility in responsible circles. In 1927 Henry Ford finally apologized for having sponsored the *Protocols* in his newspaper, but only after executives of the American Jewish Committee sent him many letters giving him at great length the full story of the forgery. In his letter of retraction, Mr. Ford said:

"I confess that I am deeply mortified that this journal has been made the medium of resurrecting exploded fictions, for giving currency to the so-called *Protocols of the Elders of Zion*, which have been demonstrated to be gross forgeries, and for contending that the Jews have been engaged in a conspiracy to control the capital and the industries of the world, besides laying at their door many offenses against decency, public order and good morals. . . . I deem it my duty as an honorable man to make amends for the wrong done to the Jews as fellow-men and brothers, by asking their forgiveness for the harm that I have unintentionally committed, by retracting so far as lies within my power the offensive charges laid at their door by these publications, and by giving them the unqualified assurance that henceforth they may look to me for friendship and good will."

The Jewish community of America welcomed this retraction, but by the time it came many small minds had already been poisoned.

During World War II, after Hitler's aides had developed the technique of The Big Lie, the *Protocols* were revived and republished in the languages of all the countries the Nazis were trying to subvert. Even in the United States the forgery became, again, the sacred book of anti-Semitic and pro-Nazi literature. In 1942 a committee composed of leading American historians, headed by John C. Curtiss, published *An Appraisal of the Protocols of Zion* in which they agreed that the document had no claim whatsoever to authenticity. For years, perhaps centuries, truth would continue to run after falsehood, never quite catching up. In every generation new men of malice—or merely of stupidity—would whisper, then slyly display a book or a paper, and tell again the story of how the *Protocols of the Elders of Zion* prove that Judaism is a sinister international conspiracy aimed at world domination.

On Being Different

One of the powerful rabbinical figures between the two world wars was Abba Hillel Silver, who came to America from his native

Lithuania as a child and at the age of twenty-four, in Cleveland, became rabbi of one of the largest Reform congregations in America, known simply as "The Temple." Under his guidance it acquired, before many years, a reputation of being "the most liberal Jewish congregation in America." Quickly Rabbi Silver developed into a prophetic orator, a brilliant writer, and a courageous liberal. He helped put the first child labor laws and the first unemployment insurance act onto the Ohio statute books. At various times in the 1930s and the 1940s he was head of the Zionist Organization of America, the United Jewish Appeal, the American Section of the Jewish Agency, the Central Conference of American Rabbis, and the American Zionist Emergency Council. He was one of the principal witnesses at the UN hearings which preceded passage of the 1947 Palestine Partition Plan and when the State of Israel was declared, he was given Visa No. 1 in recognition of what he had done to help bring about the re-creation of the state.

Rabbi Silver's most provocative book was *How Judaism Differed.* In it he wrote that the attempt to gloss over the differences between the world's great religions as a gesture of good will is a superficial act which serves neither the purposes of scholarship nor the realities of the situation. It is far better, he contended, to seek ways of working together on the basis of a forthright recognition of dissimilarities, than to make a fictional assumption of identity. Again and again he stressed that one of the fundamental qualities of the Jew and his religion is "different-ness."

Judaism differs from other religions in that it has never contended that: a) man needs to be saved from some original sin; b) man should not enjoy life; c) men are not equal; d) men are not free; e) death is better than life.

Rabbi Silver's most illuminating chapter is entitled: "On Being Different." In the beginning Judaism gave mankind the sensationally new and different concept of humanity and the vision of universal peace. Other Jewish ideas and ideals such as human brotherhood, unity, freedom, and compassion were fundamentally alien to the ancient world. But from the very beginning the sons of Abraham dared to be different.

19

HE THAT IS GRACIOUS UNTO THE POOR . . .

THERE are no statistics to prove or disprove it, but it is probable that American Jews are the most highly organized people in the world. There are many American cities in which a family may belong to a Reform Temple as well as to a Conservative or Orthodox synagogue, and the young matron of the family is not only invited but pressured to join Haddassah, the Council of Jewish Women, the Temple Sisterhood, the Ladies Auxiliary of the Synagogue, ORT, Pioneer Women, the Women's Auxiliary of the Home for the Aged, and B'nai B'rith Women, among others, while at the same time being called upon to work for such non-denominational organizations as the Red Cross, the P.T.A., the Girl Scouts, the YMCA, the Women's Club, the United Fund, and the local concert series. If she is capable and willing she may be the president of one Jewish organization, the program chairman of another, the head of the membership drive of a third, in charge of the donor luncheon of a fourth, and on committees of several more.

Most of these Jewish organizations were founded in the period between the two world wars and many grew out of the desire of Jewish leaders to do something constructive about the diversity and fragmentation of Jewish life in America.

Shadings of American Judaism

In many cities there were now three definite religious groups: Orthodox, Conservative, and Reform. But they did not all fit into

iron-clad categories. Each group had its shadings. There were Conservative synagogues that followed traditional customs so closely
that a stranger would have thought himself in an Orthodox synagogue, and other Conservative synagogues with services that might
easily have been mistaken for Reform. The Reform ritual was even
more diversified. Rabbi Judah L. Magnes, addressing his Temple
Emanu-El congregation in New York in 1910, declared:

"A prominent Christian lawyer of another city has told me how
he entered this building at the beginning of a service on Sunday
morning and did not discover that he was in a synagogue until a
chance remark of the preacher betrayed it."

There was also the division between Sephardim and Ashkenazim,
each with unique religious customs and with quite different ways of
pronouncing the holy language. The Ashkenazim were further fragmented by being partly of German origin and partly from Eastern
Europe, with all the inherent differences. Then there were Zionists
and anti-Zionists, as well as assimilationists and non-assimilationists.
America was responsible for still other diversities. Southern Jews
and Northern Jews still had their points of conflict, while New
York Jews were acquiring special characteristics that set them apart
from Jews practicing the same religion in exactly the same way but
residing in such places as Charleston, West Virginia, or New Orleans,
or Berkeley, California.

The Evils of Fragmentation

Then there were divergent attitudes toward what should be done
and how it should be done. Those still under European influence
wanted the synagogue to be the core or hub, with all Jewish
activity, even if not of a strictly religious nature, directed from the
synagogue. Others wanted welfare and eleemosynary enterprises
independent of any strictly religious control. Those from Germany
favored outright giving to those in need; those from Eastern Europe
advocated interest-free loans.

All this resulted in confusion, overlapping, annoyance on the part
of those who were solicited so often for funds for the same general
purpose, and inefficiency in the expenditure of the money raised.

Rabbi Magnes was one of the many who were bothered by so much fragmentation. He saw that in New York alone there were many separate Jewish organizations working for the same goals: the relocation of needy Jews, care of the sick, and distribution of food and clothing to those unable to provide for themselves. He felt that what American Jewry needed most of all was centralization—as much centralization as so diverse and individualistic a people as American Jews could tolerate. The American Jewish Committee had had only limited success as a centralizing body, for it was neither democratically elected, nor could it begin to speak for American Jewry as a whole.

The Kehillah and Its Accomplishments

In 1909 Rabbi Magnes, who was later to achieve renown as president of Hebrew University in Jerusalem, persuaded other Jewish leaders to join with him in forming a *Kehillah*. This is a Hebrew word for a community-wide organization such as existed in many European countries where centralization was part of the accepted way of Jewish life. Rabbi Magnes was an idealist in this matter, as he would become later in advocating a bi-national Arab-Jewish state in Palestine. In both cases his arguments were sound and his theories good, but he found in New York that it was impossible to form even a loose organization that would have anything approaching the unanimous support of New York's million or more Jews.

Working with Magnes was Mordecai M. Kaplan as chairman of the Committee on Education. Within a year the *Kehillah* established a Bureau of Education, with Samson Benderley as director. Although the *Kehillah* collapsed, the Bureau continued and before long had these notable accomplishments to its credit: extensive studies were made of Jewish educational problems in New York and elsewhere across the country. A Hebrew Principals' Association and a Jewish Teachers' Association were organized. Conferences were held on the aims and methods of Jewish education. A professional journal, *The Jewish Teacher*, was founded, as well as several magazines for the pupils. A system of licensing teachers was inaugurated. Modern textbooks and teaching aids were published. Classes were organized in

Jewish art, Jewish dramatics, and in the observance of Jewish festivals. Many university-trained young men and women were attracted to the field of Jewish teaching and their work had a profound effect on the entire future of Jewish education in America. Soon at least 25 percent of all Jewish children were receiving some sort of Jewish education. The work of Magnes, Kaplan, and Benderley was responsible for ending a long period of educational disunity and confusion.

Philanthropy and Righteousness

The idea of the *Kehillah* was copied in many smaller communities in the United States and there it proved a success, but the New York Jewish community was too large and shapeless, individuality was too intense, divisions were too great, and allegiances were too divided, so the New York *Kehillah* was doomed from the start. One of the problems was that it was no longer possible to reach many Jews through their synagogues and temples, especially some of those who were financially able to make large contributions to Jewish causes. While still nominally followers of Judaism, many of them had become so obsessed with the materialism of the times and had gone so far in assimilation that they had all but severed their actual religious connections, yet they were willing and often eager to finance Jewish charitable institutions, fight anti-Semitism, and help Israel. And so, more and more organizations were formed that had no direct connection with the established religious bodies, although they might hold their meetings in the synagogue auditorium, recruit most of their members from the synagogue roster, and ask the rabbi to give the invocation.

Nearly all local, national, and international Jewish organizations that were formed between the two wars engaged to some extent in fund-raising. Whatever their function, they needed money to operate. As with most non-Jewish, community-wide charities, the fund solicitors were able to point out that all contributions were deductible on the donor's federal income tax report. But Jewish solicitors asking fellow Jews for contributions to Jewish causes had an advantage.

One of the many Hebrew words for charity is *tzedakah*, meaning not only assistance to the poor but righteousness. Judaism holds philanthropy to be one of the cardinal virtues and down through the ages no virtue has been so assiduously cultivated by religious Jews, who anticipated by many centuries the modern attitude toward social responsibilities. Judaism has always regarded the poor man as a child of God who had been unfairly disinherited from his patrimony. Therefore, he is treated not as an object of pity but as a man who has been denied his just due, which is an adequate living. Accordingly, charity is not compassion but the rectification of a failure of the community, or of the system.

Help for the Needy

It is a theory of Judaism that to lavish money on the synagogue when there are hungry to feed and naked to clothe and orphans to support is a perversion of religion. The Talmud compares those who refuse to make charitable contributions to idolators.

The Jews' attitude toward the less fortunate goes back not centuries but thousands of years. In biblical times a portion of the harvest was always set aside for the poor and Jews who lived in towns or cities were taxed to provide for the needy. Every community had officials who collected such taxes and administered them. Every community also had a *Tamhui* or central depot from which food was distributed to the needy, and a *Kupah* or charity fund from which money was given to the needy to buy food for Shabbat.

In Europe, even in medieval times, every ghetto had its lodging house for indigent strangers, which also served as a hospital in case of need, and the service of a salaried physician was available for everyone—those who could pay and those who could not, alike.

Charity, the Highest Duty

For thousands of years Jews were brought up on the story of how King David was forbidden to build the temple because the gold and silver which he had saved for the purpose should have been used during the three years of famine in his regime to feed the poor and to save lives.

Charity had always been regarded by Jews as not only the highest of all duties, but equal to all the other commandments combined.

The Book of Leviticus set down as law that "if thy brother be waxen poor, and sell some of his possession, then shall his kinsman that is next unto him come, and shall redeem that which his brother hath sold. . . . Thou shalt not give him thy money upon interest, nor give him thy victuals for increase."

One of the Psalms says: "Happy is he that considereth the poor; the Lord will deliver him in the day of evil."—41:2.

Proverbs 19:17 says: "He that is gracious unto the poor lendeth unto the Lord, And his good deed will He repay unto him."

Even Paupers Must Help Others

In ancient times each Jew was expected to devote a tithe or tenth part of his income to philanthropy. Even the pauper who lived on the charity of others was told that he must contribute his mite to those in greater need than himself. But during the second century devout Jews were going to such extremes in their giving that a rabbinical council issued a decree forbidding any Jew to devote more than one-fifth of his wealth to charity.

Josephus wrote that "He who refuses a suppliant the aid which he has the power to give, is accountable to justice."

The Talmud is heavily interspersed with comments, advice, and regulations about the value of charity, its administration, its scope, its application, the form it should take, and even its limitations.

Eurydemos wrote: "Charity equals in importance the whole Temple cult."

Hillel said: "The more charity, the more peace."

Maimonides frequently wrote about charity. On one occasion he said: "Nobody is ever impoverished through the giving of charity."

When and How to Give to the Poor

The Talmud contains many specific instructions about when to give charity, how to give charity, and what not to do when sharing wealth. One passage says: "What you give to charity in health is gold; in sickness, silver, and after death, copper." Those who are reluctant to give are warned: "The door which does not open to the poor will open to the physician." Also: "What you do not give in charity voluntarily, the heathen will take from you forcibly." And then these don'ts:

"Do not humiliate a beggar; God is his right hand."

"Watch not the poor while he eats in your house."

The Talmud Says . . .

Again and again the Talmud urges Jews not to be ostentatious about giving and not to demand credit for giving:

"It is better not to give alms than to give it in public, with embarrassment for the recipient."

"To boast of the help you gave a brother in need is to cancel the good of your deed."

"We must be considerate of the sensibilities of the poor."

Frequently Jews have been told that they must give cheerfully and without hesitation:

"Give graciously, cheerfully and sympathetically." (*Maimonides*)

"He gives twice who gives quickly." (*Rabbi Leon of Modena*)

It was a Talmudic rule that the poor who asked for clothing were to be investigated but never those who asked for food.

Another rule provided that every "public fund" should be collected by no less than two persons and be disbursed by no less than three, because charitable funds were considered a sacred trust that should not be mismanaged or misspent. Collectors for charitable causes "who sometimes exact contributions beyond the giver's means" were liable to punishment.

It was a rule, set down in the Talmud, that Gentiles should not be discriminated against in the giving of charity; that their poor should also be aided, their sick visited, their dead buried, just as if there were no religious differences. However, Baron Maurice Hirsch, German philanthropist, commented:

"In relieving human suffering I never ask whether the cry of need comes from one of my own faith or not; but what is more natural than that I should find my highest purpose in bringing to the followers of Judaism, oppressed for a thousand years and starving in misery, the possibility of physical and moral regeneration . . . and thus furnish humanity with much new and valuable material?"

Defining the peculiarity of Jewish charity, Mendelé, the Russian-Jewish satirist, wrote:

"What nation on earth has customs as strange as ours? Our poor *demand* alms, as if they were collecting a debt, and our benefactors . . . *invite* paupers to their table."

The Rules of Maimonides

Since the twelfth century, the definition of the various degrees of charity expounded by Maimonides has been a guide to Jews everywhere in their charitable activities and is included in a section of the Union prayer book published by the Central Conference of American Rabbis entitled: *Selections from the Bible and Later Jewish Literature, to Be Read on Day of Atonement as Time Will Permit:*

"There are eight degrees or steps in the duty of charity. The first and the lowest degree is to give, but with reluctance or regret. This is the gift of the hand, but not of the heart.

"The second is, to give cheerfully, but not proportionately to the distress of the sufferer.

"The third is, to give cheerfully and proportionately, but not until solicited.

"The fourth is, to give cheerfully, proportionately, and even unsolicited, but to put it in the poor man's hand, thereby exciting in him the painful emotion of shame.

"The fifth is, to give charity in such a way that the distressed may receive the bounty, and know their benefactor, without their being known to him. Such was the conduct of some of our ancestors, who used to tie up money in the corners of their cloaks, so that the poor might take it unperceived.

"The sixth, which rises still higher is to know the objects of our bounty, but remain unknown to them. Such was the conduct of those of our ancestors, who used to convey their charitable gifts into poor people's dwellings; taking care that their own persons and names should remain unknown.

"The seventh is still more meritorious, namely to bestow charity in such a way that the benefactor may not know the relieved persons, nor they the name of their benefactors, as was done by our charitable forefathers during the existence of the Temple. For there was in that holy building a place called the Chamber of the Silent, wherein the good deposited secretly whatever their generous hearts suggested, and from which the poor were maintained with equal secrecy.

"Lastly, the eighth, and the most meritorious of all, is to anticipate charity, by preventing poverty; namely, to assist the reduced fellow-man, either by a considerable gift, or a loan of money, or by teaching him a trade, or by putting him in the way of business; so that he may earn an honest livelihood; and not be forced to the dreadful alternative of holding out his hand for charity. To this Scripture alludes when it says: And if thy brother be waxen poor, and fallen in decay with thee, then thou shalt relieve him; yea, though he be a stranger or a sojourner; that he may live with thee. This is the highest step and the summit of charity's golden ladder."

Jewish Philanthropy Set the Pattern

Zealous to live up to all of Judaism's admonitions about charity, American Jews vied with one another in philanthropic activities, and in so doing often devised methods and set examples which the non-Jewish community years or even decades later would emulate. One example: federated charities. The Community Chest movement in America dates back to 1914, but as early as 1895 the Jews of Boston experimented with a new concept in social welfare work by forming the Boston Federated Jewish Charities, which established a single fund-raising apparatus for five organizations: a free burial society, a children's orphanage, a free employment bureau, a women's sewing circle, and a general relief society. The idea of joint fund-raising spread from Boston to Cincinnati and then to many other cities. In 1900 representatives of thirty-six cities attended the first official national conference on Jewish organized charities. This was many years before formation of the United Community Funds and Councils of America. By the start of World War I, there were twenty-five Jewish federations functioning in the major cities of the country.

In most communities the first charitable organization was called the Hebrew Benevolent Society, with the function of making sure that whatever funds were available in a community for charity were parceled out equitably. Such societies began to appear in the 1840s and 1850s. The first charitable establishments actually constructed were hospitals. In addition to caring for those who were ill and also impoverished, they made it possible for the religious Jew to avoid the twin dangers of being fed forbidden food and being dissected after death. Among the better-known Jewish hospitals were Mt. Sinai, New York; Michael Reese, Chicago: Mt. Zion, San Francisco; Beth Israel, Boston, and the Cedars of Lebanon, Los Angeles.

The History of Orphanages

Then came orphanages, the earliest being established in Philadelphia and Cleveland. Orphanages were important for a double reason: Judaism's well-known concern about the physical welfare of fatherless children, combined with the danger that such children might be made innocent converts to a religion other than Judaism.

Then, starting in 1865, came the construction of homes for the aged. Before the end of the century there were such institutions in the twelve principal American cities. Then there were societies, buildings, or activities on behalf of wayward girls, juvenile delinquents, women deserted by their husbands, husbands deserted by their wives, inmates of prisons, indigent brides, impoverished travelers and, in fact, anyone in trouble or in need.

Judaism's admonition about not discriminating against Gentiles in dispensing charity was heeded by those who changed the name and the admission rules of the Jews' Hospital in New York. It was also heeded by others who established new institutions. But it was best exemplified by a young woman who, like Henrietta Szold and Emma Lazarus, was *shocked* into a life of service.

Lillian Wald, Humanitarian

Brandeis, Einstein, Lehman, and Wise—judge, scientist, statesman, and rabbi—followed four entirely different roads in their pursuit of justice. Lillian Wald found still another, yet she was driven along it by the same deeply implanted Jewish compulsion that drove them: "Pursue justice!"

Lillian Wald was born in Cincinnati of immigrant parents but began her career as a student nurse in New York City. There one day a Jewish Sabbath School asked her to teach a class for young immigrant women and she agreed. It was held on Henry Street, in an East Side neighborhood the like of which the heretofore-sheltered young lady from Cincinnati had never seen. The filth, the deafening noise, and the general squalor overwhelmed her. Garbage that had been thrown from upper windows lay putrefying in the street. Push-cart vendors filled the air with noise as they cried their wares in Yiddish, German, Russian, and broken English. Women, their faces devoid of emotion, sat in their doorways staring into space. For Lillian it was like a scene from a nightmare. Yet most of these slum dwellers were her people—Jews!

That started it. Miss Wald, who was in her early twenties, persuaded a classmate in the nursing school, Mary Brewster, a Christian, to move with her into the slum area, where they began serving people in need. They accepted a small fee from those who could afford it, but most of their clients were unable to pay anything for the advice, medicine, food, clothing, and even money that the two girls dispensed. Their original backing came from Jacob Schiff, the Jewish philanthropist, who helped them finance their combination nursing home, employment agency, community house, and food distribution center.

Henry Street Settlement

That was in 1893. For the next forty years Lillian Wald worked among the poor of the East Side. Henry Street Settlement became better known by more people in New York than Grant's Tomb or the Flatiron Building, and it acquired an international reputation as a social work center. In the days when there was no such thing as a school doctor, Lillian Wald took a boy in the last stage of scarlet fever out of a school room to the office of the head of the City Health Department to prove a point. Eventually she succeeded in having 150 school doctors appointed. She was largely responsible for passage of a bill establishing a Children's Bureau in the federal government. She became involved on the side of her people in many labor-management disputes, to the displeasure of Jacob Schiff and some of her other wealthy backers. She was a suffragette, a pacifist, and a prohibitionist, which won her more enemies. During World War I she was listed by U. S. Military Intelligence as one of sixty-two Americans "active in movements which did not help the United States when the country was fighting." Among her distinguished associates on the list were Charles Beard, the historian, Norman Thomas, and Jane Addams of Hull House. For years she campaigned for appointment of public health nurses. She imported music, drama, handicrafts, and dancing to relieve the squalor of the tenement district. Before long Henry Street Settlement was so well known that its visitors included such people as Governor Alfred E. Smith, Herbert Lehman, Franklin and Eleanor Roosevelt, Ramsay MacDonald, the Gershwins, Senators, Governors, painters, poets, musicians. Some came back as "graduates" of Henry Street, after they had made good in the large outside world.

The House on Henry Street was not restricted to Jews, or to people with white skins, or to members of any human category. Nor was it financed entirely by Jews. Nor was it staffed entirely by Jews. There was no overt connection between the house on Henry Street and Judaism. Yet in that house for forty years a proud Jewess demonstrated one way—her way—of answering the command of the prophets.

20

THE FOUR WHO LED LABOR

In the ancient world, physical work was held in great disdain. The Thracians, the Scyths, the Persians, the ancient Egyptians, and even the Greeks and Romans considered labor degrading and therefore despised it. Aristotle expressed the opinion of most Greek philosophers when he declared that laborers, artisans, and merchants were unfit for citizenship. Cicero spoke for most Roman leaders in saying that no gentleman could ever be a laborer, a mechanic, or a tradesman. In the western world until late in the nineteenth century work was considered at best a necessary evil, to be avoided if possible.

Judaism has always tried to teach the opposite. The Bible again and again extols the value of work and calls that man fortunate who is able to eat the fruit of his own labor:

"Sweet is the sleep of a laboring man, whether he eat little or much; but the satiety of the rich will not suffer him to sleep." Ecclesiastes 5:11.

"Prepare thy work without, And make it fit for thyself in the field; and afterwards build thy house." Proverbs 24:27.

Jeremiah and Malachi both wrote sympathetically about the laborer and critically of employers who exploited their workers.

Under Mosaic law, if a man stole and killed a sheep, he was condemned to pay the original owner four sheep in return, but if he stole an ox, he was required to pay back five oxen, because the ox is a work animal.

Angels and Work

Rabbi Isaac Wise once pointed out: "The genius of the Hebrew language coined the word *malak* for angel, which is identical with *melaka*, for work or labor, so that angel and the working factor are identical."

In modern Hebrew the word *avoda* is used to mean both "to work" and "to worship."

The Talmudic rabbis also had a great deal to say about the sanctity of labor:

"He that defrauds a laborer of his hire is a shedder of blood."

"Only manual work can make you blessed."

"If you have no regular work, find something to do—perhaps in a neglected yard or field."

"A man must work with his two hands before God will bestow blessing upon him."

"Work is a splendid means of warming oneself up."

"Love work."

"Labor ennobles."

"Who works for a living is greater than he who fears God."

"Flay a carcass in the street and earn a wage and say not, 'I am a great man and such work is degrading to me.'"

"Let not a man say, 'I come from a noble and distinguished family and I cannot stoop to work and degrade myself.'"

"Fool, your Creator, God himself, performed work before you were born!"

"Great is labor; it confers honor on the laborer."

Maimonides in a letter to a friend, wrote: "A coin earned by manual labor is worth more than all the revenue the Prince of the Captivity derives from gifts."

Study+Work=Virtue

The great rabbis, being scholars themselves, constantly stressed the value of intellectual pursuits, yet they urged their students to combine study with labor. Most of them followed their own advice, working as tailors, bakers, potters, charcoal burners, blacksmiths, and artisans of many other sorts, even those as celebrated as Hillel and Akiba.

Rabbi Gamaliel III, whose father compiled the Mishna (a systematic digest of the oral law published at the end of the second century) wrote: ". . . all study of the Torah which is not combined with some trade comes to naught in the end and drags sin in its train."

In an age when human exploitation was both cruel and commonplace, Judaism became a pioneer in championing the rights of labor. Judaism insisted that a workman is entitled to a just wage; that he must receive what is due him before sunset of each work day; that he must be given at least one day's holiday in every seven.

Judaism was especially condemnatory of those who exploited labor. Employers were told that they must not presume to control the bodies and souls of their workers. Jeremiah's warning was specific and clear: "Woe unto him that buildeth his house by unrighteousness, and his chambers by injustice; that useth his neighbor's service without wages, and giveth him not his hire."

Again and again Judaism pointed out that the laboring man has dignity, being a human being, and that this dignity must be respected.

New World Exploitation

There was historical coincidence between the arrival in New York of hundreds of thousands of Jews from Eastern Europe, starting in 1881, and the sudden demand in New York about this same time for cheap labor. The coincidence was both fortuitous and cruel. The average Jewish immigrant came with only a few dollars in his possession, which meant that he had to find immediate employment. Few had any technical skills that fitted them for jobs in the American economy, and it was no longer possible to do what earlier Jewish immigrants had done—go off peddling. America was becoming too settled and too economically sophisticated for that. Whether they came from the large cities of Eastern Europe or not, few had either the means or the desire to leave the relative friendliness of New York. In New York alone the Jewish immigrant could be sure of being able to keep kosher and observe the Sabbath, if he wished. Also in New York mutual benefit and charitable agencies were available. So they accepted whatever work was offered, and that is how so many landed in the garment trade—not because of any special ability or experience with the needle, but because this was a way to keep from starving to death in New York.

In those days most of what America wore was being made in and around New York—women's dresses, men's suits, blouses, skirts, corsets, shirts, hats, caps, and undergarments. There were factories, also, in Chicago, Boston, Philadelphia, and in some smaller places, but New York was the capital city of the business. Some of the manufacturers were Jews who had arrived in earlier waves of immigration. Most of the sub-contractors were Jews. The manufacturer would have a small factory in which skilled cutters turned out piles of sleeves, trouser legs, patch pockets, and other units of a garment, which would be given to the sub-contractors for sewing. Most sub-contractors used their own living quarters, in East Side tenements, as workshops. To such places they would carry or haul by bicycle, pushcart, or specially designed four-wheel carts mountain loads of material, cut and ready for sewing.

100-Hour Weeks

In the sub-contractors' flats every square foot of space was occupied by the pieceworkers. Old-timers (those who had been in the country a few weeks or a few months) would show their *landsmen* (people from the same area in Europe) how to take the pieces of material and either by hand or by sewing machine convert them into trouser legs, or sleeves, or patch pockets. The work was easy to learn; the pay was tragically low. Many had to work ten to fifteen hours a day, seven days a week, to earn enough to subsist. Even those with the nimblest fingers and the most experience made no more than $12 a week, working full time—that is, up to 100 hours a week. Often the workers would have to sit around for hours waiting for the sub-contractor to arrive with the work. Then there were slack seasons, when there might be no income for weeks at a stretch, and the corner grocery store would refuse to extend credit, and there was the danger of actual starvation.

Each worker was wedded to his *Katrinka*, the half-affectionate name the immigrants gave their sewing machines. (The sewing machine had been patented in the United States only thirty-five years before the wave of East European immigration began in 1881.) Some sub-contractors owned the sewing machines and charged each worker two dollars per week for the use of a machine. Others required their employees to supply their own machines. It was a common sight in Manhattan in those days to see a bearded Jew, still dressed in the style of the East and with *payos* (side curls) hanging down each cheek, trudging through the streets with his sewing machine strapped across his shoulders. Perhaps he had been fired; perhaps he had quarreled with a sub-contractor and had quit; but whatever the reason, he and his *Katrinka* were moving.

Sewing Machines on Fire Escapes

The crowded tenement workshops were poorly lighted. In summer they were suffocatingly hot; in winter bitterly cold. As many as forty men and women worked in close proximity. There was often little ventilation and sanitary facilities were primitive. So much perspiring humanity crowded together in such quarters created a situation obnoxious for those even slightly sensitive.

The sub-contractor saved money by using electric light bulbs of such low wattage that they gave off nothing more than a feeble yellow glow. Or he used one or two kerosene lamps to light a room full of men and machines. Every room of the tenement was used and in summer sewing machines were even set up on the fire escape. When exhaustion finally set in, a worker would often curl up on the floor beside his *Katrinka*, and sleep until the morning light announced that it was time to commence again. The dream was always of saving enough money to buy enough sewing machines to become a sub-contractor and thus achieve independence and a small measure of security. But before long the most stupid worker realized that he was trapped. If he found ways to speed up the job, in order to increase his day's pay, the piecework rates would be manipulated so that the total return would remain just about what it always had been.

Dinginess, Filth, Squalor

Besides being exploited by their employers, the immigrants were often despised by others in the garment trade, for working for such a pittance. Many were physically weak from malnutrition and overwork, and some contracted tuberculosis because of their working conditions, so at best they were tired and listless. A majority of them were still unable to speak English. They were foreigners in a strange land and it was natural for them to assume that this exploitation was "the system." So they were meek and submissive.

In those days there was little inclination on the part of the government—local, state, or federal—to interfere in the relationship between capital and labor, although one New York inspector did write a report in 1886 in which he gave this succinct description of conditions: "They usually eat and sleep in the same room where the work is carried on, and the dinginess and squalor and filth surrounding them is abominable."

Jews and Trade Unionism

In view of the attitude of Judaism toward labor, it is not surprising that Jews have played a dominant role in trade unionism in America over the past century. It began in 1869 with formation of the Noble and Holy Order of the Knights of Labor, which tried to teach workers that they were wage-earners first, and after that carpenters, shoemakers, bricklayers, Catholics, Jews, Democrats,

Republicans, white, black. It boasted at one time of 700,000 members, but its leaders were educators, proselytizers, and agitators, not labor executives, and so the Knights of Labor died during World War I.

Then in New York, Chicago, Milwaukee, St. Louis, and a few other large cities, all-Jewish organizations called United German Trades were set up, with the self-appointed task of educating newcomers to America in the value of trade unionism, and encouraging them to join the appropriate craft unions. In 1885 a counterpart was formed among Eastern European Jews, the *Yiddischer Arbeiter Verein*, but it soon collapsed. Then in 1888 the United Hebrew Trades was organized. It worked for regulation of child labor, against the sweatshop, for an eight-hour day, against exploitation of labor. Its main function was to educate Jewish immigrants who had become tailors, barbers, printers, garment workers, and practitioners of other trades in the wisdom of joining trade unions. Some labor leaders disapproved of an organization based on religious affiliation, but a majority conceded that only in this way could the immigrant Jews be introduced to trade unionism.

In the early days, the union movement was constantly in a state of tension as its various leaders struggled to make it more political or less political. Many of the Eastern European Jews were socialists and insisted on attacking what they considered the root evils, while others wanted to concern themselves simply with wages, hours, and working conditions.

The situation was further complicated by the fact that some of the intellectual Jews who were most deeply involved in the labor movement were either agnostics or atheists, and were aggressively antireligious. This antagonized many rabbis and alienated many of the Orthodox. In 1890 this group of workers, as an act of defiance, gave a Yom Kippur Ball. On this most sacred of all the religious holidays in the Jewish calendar, Jews who have little contact with their religion at any other time of the year—Jews of every shade of thought and practice, from extreme Orthodox to atheistic—crowd into synagogues and temples. On this day most Jews fast. Orthodox Jews spend the entire day in prayer and refuse to travel in any conveyance, public or private, and do no work of any sort, and concern themselves with repentance. Nothing could have offended the sensitivities of religious Jews quite as much as to have fellow Jews desecrate this solemn holiday by holding a ball.

On the side of management, Edward Albert Filene, Boston department store owner, was unique. Unceasingly he advocated higher wages, shorter hours, and social insurance. Many of his ideas would have been radical even for a representative of labor to propose. He promoted the development of consumer cooperatives and was considered the father of the credit union movement, fighting for passage by the Massachusetts Legislature of a bill legalizing such cooperative savings and loan associations.

Hillquit, Forty Years a Labor Leader

The four Jews whose names have been written the largest in American trade union annals all studied as small boys in Hebrew schools abroad, one in London, one in Lithuania, one in Latvia, and the fourth in Russia.

Morris Hillquit came to America from Latvia in 1887 when he was seventeen. He started life here as a cuff maker in a New York tenement workshop. Even though the flat was small and stuffy, the young immigrant was happy because while his fellow workers sewed and stitched they discussed political, social, and literary topics and often sang revolutionary songs above the whir of their machines.

Six years after arriving in America, with only a feeble smattering of English, young Hillquit was graduated from New York University Law School and was admitted to the bar. He spent the next forty years as a lawyer, labor leader, and politician, running for Congress five times and twice for Mayor of New York. Shocked at conditions under which his fellow Jews were working in New York, Hillquit decided to devote his life to a triple task, which he described as "educating them to a realization of their human rights, organizing them for resistance to their exploiters, and securing for them tolerable conditions of labor and life." He knew no Yiddish, so he set himself the first task of learning the language that was common to most of the people he wanted to reach.

When Hillquit and three other Eastern European Jews decided to form the United Hebrew Trades, there were only two strictly Jewish unions in New York, the Hebrew Typographical Union, whose members were employees of struggling newspapers and job printing plants on New York's East Side, and the Chorus Singers' Union, whose members worked during the day—most of the men as cigar makers and most of the women in the needle trades—and met at night to rehearse or sing in the chorus of the two Yiddish theaters then operating in New York, for which they received between $3 and $4 a week. These two unions had a total membership of forty. But before many years had passed, the United Hebrew Trades, under Hillquit's leadership, could boast of a membership of a million.

The Knee Pants Makers' Union

One of the first groups organized was the Knee Pants Makers' Union. Its members were mostly illiterate Jews who worked under the worst of sweatshop conditions, an average of ten men to each tenement shop. Each man had to provide his own sewing machine, as well as the needles and thread he used, and it was impossible for him to make more than $7 a week, no matter how many hours a day he worked, seven days a week, at top speed. Hillquit and his associates decided to call the knee pants makers out on strike. The problem was that the immigrant workers had so little sense of group action that there was a danger they would give in and return to their sewing machines at the slightest threat or discouragement. To prevent this, Hillquit assembled the entire membership of the Knee Pants Makers' Union in a rented hall and kept them there under his control day and night, permitting them to leave for only eight hours out of every twenty-four, to go home to sleep. While they were in the hall he entertained them with speeches and educated them in how to conduct a meeting according to parliamentary rules and how to transact the business of a union. After one week, the contractors weakened, storming the hall in a body to demand a settlement on the workers' own terms. Hillquit, the United Hebrew Trades and the Knee Pants Makers' Union had all won a significant victory.

Jewish Bakers Finally Organize

Jewish bakery workers who specialized in making Jewish rye bread in dark sub-cellars on the East Side were the most difficult to organize. They were recent immigrants from Galicia, Hungary, and Poland, and worked eighteen hours a day, six days a week, and on the seventh day, Thursday, worked from early morning straight through until noon Friday. They labored naked to the waist in rat-infested shops that had neither ventilation nor hygienic accommodations. The walls and ceilings were wet and moldy. The air was putrid with obnoxious odors. The ovens were primitive. Every operation had to be done entirely by hand. Wages averaged $6 to $7 a week. Most of the workers slept and ate in the bakery cellars, for which privilege they paid back to their employers most of their wages. Hillquit considered these "pale-faced, hollow-chested, listless and brutified men" almost hopeless material for a labor struggle, but he finally organized them and they went on strike for a six-day week, with Saturday as their weekly holiday.

Result, a State Law

The strike led to a New York State investigation, which in turn led to passage of a state law limiting work in bakeries to ten hours a day. Employers fought the case up to the United States Supreme Court, which ruled that "there is no reasonable ground for interfering with the liberty of person or the right of free contract, by determining the hours of labor or in the occupation of a baker . . ." The court then declared the New York law unconstitutional because, said the court, it curtailed "the right of the individual to labor for such time as he may choose" and the right of the employer to purchase labor in such a manner as he pleases.

Hillquit's comment: "I am still wondering why a few theorists, ignorant of the daily struggles and sufferings of the toiling masses, should be allowed to determine industrial relations, social conflicts and human rights, irrevocably and regardless of public sentiment and the enactments of popularly chosen legislative bodies."

During the first eighteen months of its existence, the Jewish Hebrew Trades increased the number of its affiliated bodies to thirty-two, including practically all industries in which Jewish workers were engaged in any substantial number—from soda water workers to musicians. By the end of World War I it had 250,000 members. In New York it became so powerful that at one time it practically controlled several important industries.

Sam Gompers, the Cigar Maker

Samuel Gompers was born in the ghetto of London, one of the six children of a cigar maker of Dutch origin. At the age of six he was sent to a Jewish free day school and also to a night school in which he studied Hebrew and the Bible. When he was ten he went to work as an apprentice shoemaker at wages of six cents per week. He doubled that wage—to twelve cents a week—when he switched to his father's trade, cigar making. When he was thirteen the family moved to New York, where they rented a tenement in the most crowded part of the East Side. There father and son supported the family by making cigars at home. When he gave up this piecework and took a job in a cigar factory young Gompers began to learn from bitter experience about exploitation, about how sporadic employment could be, how wage cuts were put through at the whim of the manager, how unsanitary and repulsive working conditions were. He experienced the hazards of a strike, the danger of being blacklisted for little or no reason, the agony of trying to find another job.

Gompers was twenty-two when he joined Local 144 of the Cigar Makers' Union in 1872. That was when his career really began. Two years later he was president of the local. At the age of thirty-one he was elected vice-president of the Federation of Trades and Labor Unions and in that capacity was the person principally responsible for getting the first Monday of September declared Labor Day, an honor that was dully recognized in 1882 when the day was celebrated in New York for the first time.

Labor's Goal—More!

When the American Federation of Labor was formed at Columbus, Ohio, in 1886, Gompers was elected its first president, at a salary of $1000 a year. Before long he was recognized as an able, fearless, intelligent, and ambitious champion of the rights of the working man—the first great internationally known Jewish labor leader. As a result of his direction, child labor was limited, sweatshop conditions were somewhat cleaned up, industrial planning was encouraged, and the unions established health centers, schools, and vacation resorts. Under his guidance the A.F. of L. campaigned for collective bargaining, for slum clearance, for the abolition of prison labor, and for the adoption of an eight-hour day and later a forty-hour week. For almost forty years—until his death in 1924—Gompers served as president of the A.F. of L. Once he was asked what labor's objectives were and replied, monosyllabically:

"More!"

But "more" to him meant not just more wages. He was intensely interested in more security and above all in more dignity for the working man. When he said "more" it also meant more justice, not just for members of the A.F. of L. but for Americans in general. Gompers admitted—almost boasted—that he was not a "conforming Jew," by which he meant that he had rejected Orthodoxy. He professed an intensive dislike of organized religions in general, claiming that by nature he was a nonconformist. He called himself a "philosophical anarchist." And yet he had never ceased being, as he himself described it, "an immigrant Jew who was once a ghetto kid." Regardless of his attitude toward synagogues and rabbis, he had the traditional Judaic opposition to injustice. His entire approach to labor's problems, as well as his humanity, his intellectual awareness and his idealism, was that of one who had learned the precepts of Judaism as a boy in London.

Sidney Hillman and Amalgamated

Sidney Hillman was born in Lithuania to parents who fully expected that he would become a rabbi, but instead he became a preacher of trade unionism. For several years he attended a rabbinical academy. Then, when he was about eighteen, he became involved in a revolutionary movement against the Czar and was imprisoned. After his release he came to America and when he reached Chicago took a job at $6 a week in a clothing factory. There he led the strike of 1910, when 40,000 garment workers left their shops. The year World War I started in Europe, Hillman, then only twenty-seven, became the first president of the Amalgamated Clothing Workers of America, a position he held the rest of his life—for another thirty-two years. During the early days of the New Deal, President Franklin D. Roosevelt often called Hillman in for advice on industrial-labor matters and offered him several federal posts. After the United States became involved in the war Roosevelt appointed Hillman to the National Advisory Defense Council and the Office of Production Management. Under Hillman's able guidance, the Amalgamated Clothing Workers of America pioneered in constructive labor-management relations and led in developing health, welfare, and unemployment insurance programs. This was in the era before social security had become a matter of government concern. Amalgamated also started two banks and an insurance company. Hillman helped found the Committee for Industrial Organization in 1935. When it became the Congress of Industrial Organizations in 1938 he was chosen as one of the vice-presidents. In 1943 he became chairman of the CIO Political Action Committee. When he died in 1946, he was mourned by organized labor in America, Palestine, Europe, and Latin America, as well as by those connected with management who appreciated what he had done for peaceful cooperation between employers and employees in America. In some of the eulogies mention was made not only of the fact that he was a Jew, but also that he had helped Judaism make a major contribution to America by putting his religion's precepts to work.

David Dubinsky, Master Baker

David Dubinsky was also born in Eastern Europe—in Brest Litovsk
—in 1892, the eighth of nine children, but he grew up in Lodz, the
second largest city in Poland, which then had a population of several
hundred thousand Jews. (In World War II the Nazis exterminated
almost all the Jews of Lodz.) David studied in a Hebrew school
until he was eleven. Then he went to work, following in his father's
footsteps as a baker. His normal work-week totaled eighty hours.
The wages he drew, even after becoming a master baker, were
barely enough for subsistence. Then the Bund came to town. Its full
name was the General Jewish Workers' Union, but everyone called
it simply the Bund. In Lodz it organized a union of bakers. The
members were exclusively Jews—young radicals who talked of trade
unionism and socialism, and, in whispers—of revolution! David became not only a member of the bakers' union—of which he was
elected assistant secretary even before he reached the age of *bar
mitzvah*—but also an ardent Bundist. As a result of a strike the
bakers won a wage increase, but their leaders were arrested, Dubinsky
included. He was then fifteen. He served a prison term, was finally
released, and then was arrested again and sent to Siberia. After two
years he managed to escape. Somehow a brother in New York made
contact with him and sent him a steamship ticket. And that was how
David Dubinsky, on New Year's Day, 1911, arrived in New York
on the S.S. *Lapland,* with some 700 or more other steerage passengers. He was eighteen years old and had just $20 to his name.

No one in New York seemed to want a master baker, so young
Dubinsky entered the garment trade as an apprentice cutter. Within
seven months he was taken into Local 10 of the Cutters' Union, a
subsidiary of the International Garment Workers' Union, which had
been organized about ten years earlier by fewer than a dozen workers, who had had a total capital of less than $30.

THE FOUR WHO LED LABOR

The Great Revolt

Two years before Dubinsky's arrival in America, 2000 young women blouse makers—representing 20,000 members of the ILGWU —had crowded into a union hall and almost hysterically had voted to strike. "The Uprising of the Twenty Thousand," as it came to be called, ended in victory for the workers and this encouraged 60,000 workers in the needle trades to go on strike a few months later. "The Great Revolt" was for higher wages, better working conditions, and a closed shop. It lasted twelve weeks—the greatest walkout of labor America had ever experienced. Management tried to beat the strike by hiring guerrillas, buying judges, and engaging in sundry forms of intimidation, but the ILGWU won the strike, although the settlement was called a compromise. Two Jews were responsible for the "Protocol of Peace" that ended the chaos in the ladies' garment industry—Louis Brandeis, who many years later would become an Associate Justice of the United States Supreme Court, and Louis Marshall. (See Chapter 22)

The strike had many aftereffects. It established a pattern for labor relations in America. It made clear that henceforth the ILGWU was a force not to be ignored. It proved that women could be organized into a union, could take orders from union leaders, and could suffer, if need be, in the interest of justice.

The ILGWU's position was further strengthened within less than a year by a tragedy unequaled in America. On the afternoon of March 25, 1911, fire broke out in the Triangle Waist Company's loft factory in New York. When the employees tried to flee they found that the only fire exit had been locked and sealed in order to keep out union organizers. Flames consumed 146 workers, mostly girls.

From 33,000 to 200,000

That was the background of the union that was soon to be run by the boy from Lodz. By 1918 Dubinsky was a member of Local 10's executive board. By 1921 he was president of the local. By 1929 he was secretary-general of the ILGWU. In 1932 he was elected president. He was just forty. His friends advised him to reject the job. The union was in a bad way. Membership had dropped from 99,000 to 33,000, and half the 33,000 were unemployed or on part-time. There was no money in the treasury and the officials often had to forego their salaries. But Dubinsky saw the situation as a challenge to his intelligence and his ambition, so he accepted the presidency.

David Dubinsky and Franklin D. Roosevelt were elected Presidents the same year. Within two years, partly due to the New Deal's strong pro-labor stand, the ILGWU membership had jumped from 33,000 to 200,000, debts had been paid off, and there was more than three-quarters of a million dollars in the bank.

Dubinsky once said that "labor should be a social pressure group, pushing its views on great social questions, lobbying for progressive legislation, keeping our society in balance." He was against labor taking part in party politics, but he insisted that workers must be concerned with the world in which they labor. This was a Jew talking—a Jew who was putting into practice his religion as he understood it.

The American rabbinate in general has always supported labor in its long fight for recognition. In 1918 the Central Conference of American Rabbis adopted a comprehensive pronouncement on economic justice in America in which the Reform rabbis unequivocally came out for an eight-hour day, one day of rest in every seven, a fixed minimum wage, and collective bargaining. All those rights have since been won, but in 1918 it took courage for a religious body to advocate them.

In 1933 the Rabbinical Assembly of America put the Conservative rabbinate on record as favoring a thirty-hour week. For 1933 that, too, was radical.

21

SOCIAL JUSTICE, THE MAJOR CONTRIBUTION

JUDAISM from its start has had a passion for social justice. It was the cry of the prophets and the law of the Torah. Specific examples of how social justice could be achieved are sprinkled through the Talmud. As people chosen for a special mission in the world, Jews down through the ages have been admonished: "Pursue justice!" And so they have. This has been their principal contribution to America—spotlighting injustices wherever they were found, demanding reforms, proposing improvements, fighting for a better way of life for all men.

In their Bibles Jews read:

"Seek justice, relieve the oppressed." Isaiah 1:17.

"To do righteousness and justice is more acceptable to the Lord than sacrifice." Proverbs 21:3.

"Righteousness and justice are the foundation of thy throne; mercy and truth shall go before thee." Psalms 89:14.

"It hath been told thee, O man, what is good; and what doth the Lord require of thee: only to do justly and to love mercy and to walk humbly with thy God." Micah 6:8.

"Judge the poor and fatherless: do justice to the afflicted and destitute." Psalms 82:3.

Half a Rainbow for Justice

Jewish religious and secular literature, especially in the nineteenth and twentieth centuries, dwells constantly on the obligation of pursuing justice:

"Never forget that you have been the people . . . which brought justice into the world and earn yourself forgiveness for having given a god to men by being forever the soldiers of justice and of human brotherhood." Bernard Lazare.

"Break the rainbow in two, make of one half a bow for Amor, and of the other half a fiery sword for Justice." Oyved Moshé.

"According to Israel's law no man has a right to more than bread, water and wood as long as the poor are not provided with the necessaries of life." Rabbi S. Schechter.

In every Jewish community in America large enough to have a *minyan* there are probably examples of how Jews in humble walks of life, as well as in high places, have sought to live by the divine imperative. A volume with as many pages as *Who's Who* could be filled with the proof. But here are the stories of just nine twentieth-century American Jews who exemplify what Judaism means by "Pursue justice!":

Albert Einstein, Israelite

Albert Einstein was the only Jew in his class at the Catholic school he attended in Munich, Germany. His reaction was to assert his Jewishness on every possible occasion and to feel possessed by a great religious zeal. Later he went through a period of doubt in which he shared Spinoza's ideas about God, yet he never ceased to affirm his Jewish identity. He believed that "only a life lived for others is a life worth living" and often said that Judaism represents democracy in dynamic action. His creed was that social justice is the right of all men; that truth, justice, and liberty for everyone must always remain Jewish goals.

In 1910, when he was offered a professorship at the German University in Prague, he was given a questionnaire to fill out, which required that he state his religion. Although his wife was not Jewish and he might have passed as a non-Jew himself, he wrote in a firm handwriting *Israelite*.

Between the two world wars he was an active campaigner for peace, declaring in 1930:

"If you can get only 2 percent of the population of the world to assert in time of peace that they will not fight, you will have the solution for international troubles. Even so small a proportion as 2 percent will accomplish the desired result, for they could not be put in jail. There are not enough jails in the world to accommodate them."

Einstein's personal philosophy embraced pacifism, Zionism, socialism, and humanism. He rejected a personal and vindictive God— "a God who plays at dice"—but he did believe in a God of the natural order, whose laws are absolute. His most intimate connection with Judaism was his deep yearning for social justice, which linked him directly with the Jewish prophets. Once he remarked that "God may be sophisticated but he is not malicious."

During the fifteen years that Einstein was an American citizen he gave his support—as a Jew and as an American—to many causes that concerned brotherhood, international understanding, social justice, and peace. He was deeply saddened—almost embittered—by the knowledge that his mathematical discoveries had made the production of an atomic bomb possible, and that a letter he was persuaded to write to President Roosevelt had triggered the Manhattan Project, which led directly to Hiroshima and Nagasaki.

A few years before his death he wrote: "The pursuit of knowledge for its own sake, an almost fanatical love of justice, and the desire for personal independence—these are the features of the Jewish tradition which makes me thank my stars that I belong in it. . . . History has given us a difficult row to hoe; but so long as we remain devoted servants of truth, justice and liberty, we shall continue not merely to survive as the oldest of living peoples, but by creative work to bring forth fruits which contribute to the ennoblement of the human race, as heretofore."

Herbert Lehman, Proud Jew

Herbert Lehman was born in New York City, the youngest of eight children. The father was deeply religious. In Montgomery, Alabama, where he first lived after his arrival from Germany, he helped establish an Orthodox synagogue and regularly attended services on Shabbat and the Holy Days. In New York he helped establish what his son called "a warmly Jewish home" in which prayers were said in Hebrew and such rites as the Passover *Seder* were scrupulously observed. The father took an active interest in Jewish philanthropy and Jewish communal affairs. Herbert was greatly influenced in his Jewish thinking by a brother, Irving, who was always militantly proud of being a Jew. At the outbreak of World War I Herbert Lehman helped found J.D.C. During his fourteen years in Albany, first as Lieutenant-Governor under Roosevelt and later as Governor himself, he placed great stress on social service, unemployment relief, workmen's compensation, unemployment insurance, and what he himself called "things that affect the day-to-day life of people." His concern for the mentally ill—there were then 100,000 in state institutions—resulted in the erection of many additional hospital buildings. During his regime New York State enacted what one labor leader called "the greatest code of labor and social legislation ever passed by any state in the nation." During the war, at President Roosevelt's request, he resigned as Governor to become director-general of the United Nations Relief and Rehabilitation Administration, because, as Lehman put it, "he wanted Hitler and the Nazis to know that he was appointing a Jew to bring relief and rehabilitation to the people and areas they had ravaged. My appointment was to be a symbol to the world."

When Reform Judaism chose him as "Jewry's Man of the Century" he delivered an address connecting Jews, Judaism, and justice:

"Our mission is to fight for freedom, human dignity and the rights of free men, not only for ourselves, but for all who are denied their enjoyment and protection, anywhere. Our mission is to be a messenger of peace to all the peoples and to all the nations of the world. Our mission is to advance and defend the cause of justice and brotherhood among the nations, among all peoples, and at home. Our mission is to assist the persecuted and the downtrodden anywhere in the world, wherever they are in need or in danger. . . . On many fronts at home and abroad the forces of repression, fear and ignorance are gaining the upper hand. . . . Conformity and avoidance of controversy are widely hailed and accepted. . . . How do we reinvigorate moral purpose in a frightened, fearful and escapist world? Here is the challenge, if ever there was one, to our faith and to all faiths. Fear has crept in where faith ought to be. Let us resolve to overcome that fear."

More specifically, about himself, Lehman once wrote: "My Jewish heritage has unquestionably affected my political and social thinking. All through my years of public life I have felt strongly the importance of keeping faith with the ethics of Judaism, and its basic concept that 'creed without deed' is meaningless. As a Jew and a human being I have accepted no boundaries except those of justice, righteousness, humility and charity. . . . In a very real sense the aims and ideals of the Jewish religion are identical with the purposes of democracy. . . . In these difficult days of declining liberalism, it is important for us as Americans and Jews to try to regain the moral perspectives first charged by our Jewish heritage. Our mission is to fight against injustice when practiced against any minority, anywhere in the world. We Americans of Jewish heritage have a special obligation consistent with our ancient heritage to be messengers of peace."

Louis Brandeis, Optimist

In the opinion of Stephen Wise, Louis Dembitz Brandeis was "Our greatest Jew!" and the rabbi put the exclamation mark there himself. Yet in some ways Brandeis did not become a real Jew until he was fifty-four years old. He was born in Louisville, Kentucky, to refugees from Bohemia who belonged to no synagogue and who taught their children that "only goodness and truth and conduct that is humane and self-sacrificing toward those who need us can bring God nearer to us." (Those words were written by the mother.)

In Harvard Law School young Louis obtained the highest scholastic marks in the history of that institution. When serious eye strain forced him to have fellow students read to him, he adopted the motto: "Read less; think more." Eleven years after being admitted to the bar he was recognized as one of the most brilliant corporation lawyers in the East. In 1910—fifty-four years old and at the peak of his legal career—he was appointed chairman of the Arbitration Board in the strike of New York's garment workers and for the first time in his life discovered something about the hopes, fears, dreams, and nightmares of the mass of Jewish immigrants in New York. To him they seemed aflame with a typically Jewish pursuit of social justice, and his contact with them fanned the flames of a similar zeal within him.

His several biographers agree that now, for the first time, he began really to feel himself a Jew. He had had no formal religious training and until this time had belonged to no Jewish organizations, never attended religious services, ignored the dietary laws, and identified with the Jewish community in Boston, where he lived, only by making contributions to the Boston Jewish Charities Fund. Some members of his family had gone further and had intermarried. Now, suddenly, he was aware that his own ideas of brotherhood, social justice, and civil liberties were part of his Jewish being—that he owed them to Judaism. Years later he put it this way:

"It is the Jewish tradition and the Jewish law and the Jewish spirit which prepare us for the lessons of life."

As a result of the strike arbitration experience Brandeis decided that only by expressing himself Jewishly could he—and others like him—make their best contribution to America.

"The twentieth-century ideals of America," he said, "have been the ideals of the Jew for more than twenty centuries."

Brandeis found many outlets for his new interest. First, he became a Zionist and spent seven years of his later life working with other Jews here and abroad to try to bring the Jewish dream to reality. He had more to do than history has thus far recorded in bringing about the Balfour Declaration. He directed the approach to the

British through President Wilson, and after luncheon one day at the White House he conferred with Lord Balfour, then British Foreign Minister, about what the British would and should do. The Balfour Declaration followed.

Several years later, when Wilson heard that an attempt was being made to bar Brandeis from membership in the exclusive Cosmos Club of Washington because he was a Jew and a reformer "and would be a disturbing element in a club of gentlemen," the President dispatched a personal note to the admissions committee saying that the rejection of Brandeis would keep out of the club a man he held in the highest esteem. Less than one year later Wilson proposed Brandeis for membership in an even more exclusive club: the United States Supreme Court. The Establishment of those days—including such heavyweights as President A. Lawrence Lowell of Harvard and former President William Howard Taft—began battle. The opposition centered in Boston. This led columnist Walter Lippmann, himself a Jew, to call Brandeis "a rebellious and troublesome member of that most homogeneous, self-centered and self-complacent community in the United States"—Boston.

The fight over whether the Senate should confirm the appointment was long and acrimonious. Brandeis himself took it phlegmatically, writing to his brother: "I suppose eighteen centuries of Jewish persecution must have inured me to such hardships and developed the like of a duck's back."

He was opposed first because he had often defended the interests of the common man against rich and powerful corporations, earning the appellation, "the people's lawyer." During the Senate debate one member put it bluntly:

"The real crime . . . is that he has exposed the iniquities of men in high places in our financial system. He has not stood in awe of the majesty of wealth."

He was opposed, also, because he was a Jew and no Jew had ever sat on the Supreme Court bench. Stories were whispered. Somehow the *Protocols of the Elders of Zion* got into the controversy. Wilson was denounced even more than Brandeis. One friend said to him, "Isn't it a pity that a man as great as Brandeis should be a Jew?", to which Wilson was reported to have replied, "But he would not be Mr. Brandeis if he were not a Jew."

Wilson had made the nomination in January. It was almost five months later that the Senate Judiciary Committee voted 10 to 8 to confirm. A week later the Senate voted 47 to 22 for confirmation. So the first Jew mounted the Supreme Court bench. During his twenty-three years as an Associate Justice Brandeis wrote 528 opinions, 74 of them dissenting opinions, nearly all of which made history, for they were forecasts of the America of the future. Brandeis was now more than ever a crusader *against* monopoly and *for* social justice; *against* privilege, *for* the people; *against* bigotry, *for* religious freedom; *against* property values whenever they conflicted with human values. Wilson and others close to Brandeis nicknamed him Isaiah, because of his fanatical love of justice. He continued the struggle from the bench until he was eighty-two. Two years after resigning he died. This was 1941, when the present was shudderingly horrible and the future for Jews looked even more forbidding. Yet Brandeis, aged eighty-four, died an optimist, having a robust faith in the indestructibility of Jewish ideals and Jewish aspirations.

Stephen Wise, Fighter for Justice

Rabbi Stephen S. Wise was one of the greatest rabbinical figures America has yet produced. Some say *the* greatest. Few voices of social protest have spoken from any pulpit, anywhere, with such force and conviction. He was sometimes "God's angry man"; often he was likened to the ancient prophets. He believed passionately in Judaism as a revolutionary social force and had little patience with moral cowards, equivocators, and pussyfooters. He was a big man in every sense of the word. He stood six feet in his stocking feet but gave the impression of being much taller, bulking much larger. He was a big man, also, in his outlook on life. He always seemed to be looking over the heads of the world's Lilliputians, both literally and figuratively. He had, also, a big voice. One of the photographs his son and daughter cherish shows him standing on a platform set up one noon in 1918 in the middle of Wall Street, New York, addressing—without benefit of any mechanical devices—a crowd that filled the streets in the four directions of the compass as far as the eye could see. Wise, who before World War I had been a pacifist, was speaking that day on behalf of Liberty Bonds and he sent his voice booming and reverberating through the canyons of skyscrapers.

He was born in Budapest, the son and the grandson of rabbis, but was brought to New York when still an infant. He studied in New York with distinguished rabbis and then completed his education at Oxford University and in Vienna, where he was ordained. When he was just twenty-one he became assistant rabbi of B'nai Jeshurun, New York. Later, as rabbi, he remained with B'nai Jeshurun for five years. Then he accepted a call from Temple Beth Israel in Portland, Oregon, where he immediately became one of the leaders of a civic reform movement. He fought gambling, liquor, and prostitution interests, and accused police and city officials of being in collusion with them. He also helped obtain passage of state child labor laws, and fought discrimination against Chinese and Japanese immigrants.

After six years he accepted an invitation from Temple Emanu-El in New York to preach a series of trial sermons. After the first he was called before a committee headed by Attorney Louis Marshall to discuss conditions of employment. When Wise demanded as his one major condition for accepting the call to Emanu-El freedom of the pulpit, Marshall just as bluntly replied that "the pulpit of Emanu-El has always been, and is, subject to and under Control of the Board of Trustees."

Rabbi Wise returned to Oregon, but a year later was back in New York to establish what he called a Free Synagogue, which he defined as one with (a) absolute freedom of the pulpit (b) no distinction between rich and poor as to pews and membership privileges; (c) full participation of the synagogue in providing the community with social services, and, (d) complete identification with Judaism.

Explaining the final point, Rabbi Wise said:

"We mean to be vitally, intensely, unequivocally Jewish. Jews who would not be Jews will find no place in the Free Synagogue, for we, its founders, wish to be not less Jewish but more Jewish in the highest and noblest sense of the term."

Services were held first in a theater near Times Square, later in Carnegie Hall. The size of the congregation grew by the week. The Wise gospel was one of social justice, as he applied the ethical principles of Judaism to the situation of the day. When judges and other important citizens attended a public dinner to welcome Tammany Hall leader Richard Croker home from abroad, Rabbi Wise preached a sermon on *New York's Night of Shame*. He once branded a New York Police Commissioner as "a menacingly incompetent and incorrigibly stupid creature." He charged that the New York Police Department had "collected revenue for Tammany and even employed murderers to enforce its thievery." He demanded that Governor Franklin D. Roosevelt remove New York's mayor, James Walker, for abuse of his office. His colleague in much of this reform activity was the Reverend John Haynes Holmes, Christian minister.

Rabbi Wise was master of the rapier thrust. During the 1932 depression he opposed a city salary grab, under which Walker's own yearly compensation was to be boosted from $25,000 to $40,000. Walker protested that others had proposed the increase, and he asked: "What could I say to them?" Retorted Wise: "Your answer, Mr. Mayor, should have been, 'Is thy servant a dog that he should do this thing?'"

In 1919 employees of U. S. Steel went on strike for the right to organize. Wise, in investigating steel mill conditions, found that half the men worked an average of twelve hours a day for miserly wages, so he wrote to Gompers expressing his pleasure at the strike and offering his services. Then he locked himself in his study and prepared a sermon. The day he was to deliver it he told his wife, "My sermon this morning will light a million-dollar blaze." The object of his attack was Judge Elbert H. Gary, Chairman of the Board of U. S. Steel, who had charged that the strike was Communist-inspired, and whom the rabbi called "the most prolific breeder of Bolshevism in America." He accused U. S. Steel of "resorting to every manner of coercion and even of violence to prevent organization of the workers." At the time the Free Synagogue was in the process of raising funds for a building of its own, but as a result of the sermon some large pledges were canceled and many members of the congregation resigned. This was what the rabbi had predicted to his wife. As a result, the new building was not completed until after the rabbi's death, but this setback only spurred him on to more crusading.

He preached, argued, and fought for Negro rights and was one of the organizers of the National Association for the Advancement of Colored People. He talked and worked for fair employment practices, better working conditions for American labor, and the democratization of Jewish life. He was one of the founders of the American Jewish Congress and with his old opponent, Marshall, made such an impression at the Paris peace talks that they won the guarantee of minority rights that they sought, as well as making some progress toward the goal of establishing a Jewish home in Palestine.

The Congress was supposed to have disbanded after completing its peace mission, and it did—technically—but a meeting of the delegates was immediately reconvened and a permanent American Jewish Congress was set up, which, under the leadership of Wise, sought to put Judaism to work on both the national and international fronts. In a day when there was little talk of civil rights by anyone, Wise and his Congress did pioneer work in that field. Abroad, a World Jewish Congress was developed, and an attempt was made —in 1933—to organize a worldwide boycott of Germany, an idea fought in the United States by several national Jewish organizations that argued it would simply worsen the plight of German Jews.

Because he was critical of what he called the "separatist and sectarian tendencies" of the Reform movement, Rabbi Wise in 1922 founded the Jewish Institute of Religion, a seminary to train rabbis for Orthodox, Conservative, and Reform pulpits alike. The school was to be "liberal in spirit, wherein its teachers and students are not committed to any special interpretation of Judaism." A few of the graduates did serve as Orthodox and Conservative rabbis, but most of them joined the Central Conference of American Rabbis and later played important roles in Reform Judaism. In 1950 the Institute merged with Hebrew Union College in Cincinnati, with Dr. Nelson Glueck as president.

It was Rabbi Wise's passion for justice that convinced him that the Jews had a right to a land and a nation of their own, and for most of his life he devoted much of his tremendous energy to helping make the dream come true. He attended the second Zionist Congress in Basel in 1898 and was its English-speaking secretary. He was one of the founders of the Zionist Organization of America, and was for a long time its president. It was to him that President Wilson addressed the letter in 1918 giving American adherence to the principles of the

Balfour Declaration. Rabbi Wise's son and biographer, James Waterman Wise, considers "his passion for Israel as a people and as a nation
the cornerstone of his life's work."

Wise made enemies, not only among non-Jews but among his own
people as well. He was accused of being arrogant, vain, an op-
portunist, and a publicity seeker. But his friends and supporters knew
that he was a man of great dignity, real courage, high principle, rich
eloquence, and unswerving fearlessness. He believed that his people, the Jews, were divinely dedicated to Judaism's never-ending
struggle for justice. Whenever he experienced prejudice or injustice
he felt it was an equal affront to his dignity as an American and as
a Jew.

Stephen Samuel Wise died in 1949. His autobiography, *Challenging Years*, posthumously published, ends with this comment on the
second World Jewish Congress over which he had presided in Switzerland just a few months earlier, and the rebirth of Israel, which had
only recently taken place:

". . . a dignified and triumphant affirmation of the indestructibility
of the Jewish people, of its will to survive, and of its determination
to do all that one historic group can do to bring about a warless
world of freedom and democracy, of justice and peace."

Emil Hirsch, Opponent of Privilege

Emil G. Hirsch, rabbi of Sinai Temple, Chicago, was one of the
most forthright preachers in the Middle West. In the days when
Upton Sinclair was writing *The Jungle* to expose conditions in
Chicago's meat-packing industry, Dr. Hirsch one Sunday mounted
his pulpit bearing aloft a copy of a Chicago Sunday newspaper em-
blazoned with the heading:

THE PACKERS ARE STEALING THE WATER OF THE CITY

Grim of visage and stern of voice he began his sermon by saying:
"It has been announced that I will speak on a certain theme today,
but I have decided to change my topic to *Thou Shalt Not Steal!*"

While many in the congregation gasped in astonishment, he denounced the packing houses for robbing the city. He denounced them for what they were doing to Chicago's reputation. He denounced them for the shame they were bringing on the city. At the height of one of his most oratorical passages, he suddenly stopped, so the story goes, pointed his finger at a member of his congregation, Nelson Morris, and thundered: "Thou art the man!"

It was a sermon that no one present ever forgot. During the week that followed Morris resigned from the congregation and so did many of his close friends, and some others who had packing-house connections. The following Sunday Rabbi Hirsch smiled as he said from the pulpit:

"I have this week received notice that a number of members have resigned. I have always known that the Jews possessed one virtue— the virtue of resignation. But let me state that while the members are free to resign, the rabbi is also free to resign."

That good-humored threat ended the crisis. There were no more resignations and Dr. Hirsch continued for years preaching social justice from the Sinai pulpit.

Rabbi Hirsch wrote almost as powerfully as he spoke. In the *Reform Advocate* in 1893 he wrote: "Away with all this charity! Justice is what we need. Social justice everywhere!"

Sweatshops in those days were not confined to New York. Chicago had them too, and Hirsch described them as "an expedient of hell. God in heaven and Judaism protest that he that works shall not be robbed of his manhood."

David Philipson, Enemy of Corruption

David Philipson, rabbi of Congregation Bene Israel in Cincinnati, once wrote: "Judaism is not so much a church-going institution as a view of life; its teachings are concerned with the whole tangled web of existence."

The rabbi put this theory into sudden practice during his second year at Bene Israel. Cincinnati politics was then dominated by the Cox machine, which was often compared to Tammany Hall for its ruthlessness and corruption. From the pulpit Rabbi Philipson attacked the machine, naming specifics. At a meeting of the congregation one of the members, who was also a powerful force in the Cox machine, demanded a vote of censure, his argument being that a rabbi had no right to discuss controversial subjects from the pulpit.

The congregation voted against censure.

Ephraim Frisch, Political Liberal

Ephraim Frisch, rabbi of Temple Beth El in San Antonio, Texas, preached one Friday night in 1925 on *The Rising Tide of Illiberalism*. He discussed American imperialism in the Philippines and called for the independence of the islands. As the rabbi was closing the service with the benediction, a prominent member who had once been president of the congregation rushed to the pulpit, pointed his finger at the rabbi and shouted to the audience:

"That man is using the pulpit for political propaganda. What does he know about the Philippines? I have just come back from the Philippines as part of my trip around the world."

The rabbi was relatively new in the community. Sensing the perplexity of his congregation, he engaged in an exchange of questions and answers with his accuser and then, having demonstrated that he actually did know something about his subject, he declared dramatically as he thumped the lectern:

"This pulpit must be free or I shall no longer serve as your rabbi. If the congregation by a vote declares that it is not free, I'll resign immediately."

Instead of voting the congregation broke out in almost unanimous applause.

Samuel Goldenson, His Brother's Keeper

Samuel H. Goldenson, rabbi of Congregation Rodef Shalom, Pittsburgh, in the winter of 1928, during a serious general strike in the Pennsylvania coal fields, was invited to tour the mining area. After his return he delivered a sermon which he called *Am I My Brother's*

Keeper? Looking into the faces of a number of wealthy coal producers, he said:

"There are some who may not see the imperativeness of the morals involved because they are inclined to confuse the right to have with the right to share. By sharing I do not mean mere having, irrespective of any claim, but securing a part of the total output that one may rightfully claim as a result of his own labors. That, I submit, is the very essence of ethical thinking.

"Has the clergyman, then, the right to talk about these things? . . . no man in the entire world has as much right, and there is no man upon whom the responsibility to speak about such questions is so great as upon one who raises his voice in the name of ethics and religion."

Samuel Mayerberg, Dispeller of Fear

Samuel Mayerberg, rabbi of Congregation B'nai Jehudah in Kansas City, declared war on the Pendergast machine in 1932, when he delivered an address before the Government Study Club in which he accused the city administration of having an alliance with the underworld, charged that the City Manager was misusing public funds and in other ways violating the City Charter, and demanded immediate action by the City Council. From this small start came the organization of a Charter League made up of ministers, doctors, lawyers, and other distinguished citizens, with the rabbi as president. The Kansas City *Star* supported the reform movement, and the battle was on.

The telephones in the rabbi's study and his Charter League office were tapped. His files were ransacked. Important documents were stolen. He was offered sizable bribes to "lay off." Once his car was forced to the curb and a shot was fired at the window, but fortunately friends had equipped the car with bulletproof glass. The Governor assigned two men to serve as bodyguards for the rabbi who, as a double precaution, kept a loaded revolver on the floor beside his bed.

Every morning at three o'clock the rabbi received a telephone call from an underworld character, hostile to those in power, giving information about narcotics, illegal liquor, slot machines, and gangsters' movements. All this the rabbi passed on to federal agents, who then would make raids.

The fight went on for ten years, before Tom Pendergast was sent to prison, as were many corrupt election officials. Then a reform ticket was swept into office. As the rabbi described the results: "The spirit of our citizenry has changed completely. The pall of fear has disappeared. Heads are held erect and civic pride has replaced cringing shame. . . . Our community has learned the full significance of the saying of the Book of Proverbs: 'Righteousness exalteth a nation, but sin is a reproach to any people.' "

Judaism has been called a religion impelled by a vigorous social idealism. It is therefore not surprising that no righteous cause ever seems foreign to America's liberal rabbis. Sometimes they have risked the ire of their own congregations to join with humanitarians of other faiths in demanding an end to corruption and special privilege. The nine Jews whose life stories have just been sketched are just a few of the better known. Hundreds of others joined with them in their demands for a fair wage for labor, better working conditions, an end to child exploitation, improved housing, social security, prison reform, international peace, establishment of the League of Nations and later the United Nations, and support of Israel.

When David Ben-Gurion was in the United States in the spring of 1967, Sargent Shriver, first director of the Peace Corps, asked the former Israeli Prime Minister:

"How do you account for the fact that 40 percent of those in the Peace Corps are Jews and some 70 percent of those involved in civil rights and social justice causes are Jews?"

To which Ben-Gurion replied with a twinkle in his eyes:

"Because they are Jews!"

22

MOSAIC LAW—AMERICAN LAW

In the Book of Leviticus, after 24,529 words of laws, rules, and regulations, this summation appears: "These are the commandments, which the Lord commanded Moses for the children of Israel in Mount Sinai."

For thousands of years these religious laws have formed the foundation of Judaism. Every male child is still circumcised on the eighth day, because this was one of the laws given by God to Moses. Pork, shellfish, rabbit meat, and other forbidden foods are still not eaten because they are listed in Chapter Eleven of Leviticus. But many other Mosaic Laws have been reinterpreted, revised or modified, such as the commandments about sacrificing animals by fire, or cleansing lepers, or putting to death both men and women apprehended in the act of adultery.

Judaism is a religion based on law and the interpretation of divine commandments. The basic laws themselves are to be found in the Torah—the five books of Moses. But the simplifications and interpretations fill nearly two dozen volumes called the Talmud. For hundreds of years rabbinical scholars discussed, debated, and wrote their opinions. The process still goes on, for Judaism is a living religion, but the fundamental principle of the Hebraic commonwealth was that there are great moral laws that no monarch, no benevolent dictator, no democratic government has the right to amend or annul.

There are many reasons for Judaism being founded on law. (It is, in fact, the only major religion that is.) The most obvious is that so much of the Torah—so much of the conversation between Moses and

God—so much of the Covenant between God and the Jews—dealt with law. There is also the peoplehood of the Jews. For more than a millennium they lived as a geographical and national entity on their own soil, with their own set of moral and political principles, which were based on Mosaic Law.

Even after the Dispersal autonomous or semiautonomous Jewish communities in widely scattered places continued to regulate themselves by their national code. They even had their own courts of law in which disputes were settled according to The Law. Such religious courts functioned under the British in Palestine down to May 14, 1948, as they still do today in Israel.

Every Jew a Lawyer

Every religious Jew is at heart a lawyer, for when he reads and re-reads the five books of the Torah, he is reading mostly law. When he studies the Talmud he is studying law and how it can be, has been or should be interpreted. Much of his religious life is concerned with The Law. And even in such mundane matters as washing the hands before meals, cohabitation between man and wife, avoidance of gossip, how much to pay a hired man, and remembering which dishes to use for dinner, The Law must be considered. There is hardly a moment of an Orthodox Jew's waking hours when he is not thinking—consciously or subconsciously—in terms of law. As for the relationship of Reform Jews to The Law, while they no longer accept all of it as binding, they are still strongly motivated by the spirit of these ancient proscriptions.

Jewish scholarship down through the ages has been concerned primarily with The Law, one generation after another of scholars discovering anew the intellectual joy of matching wits with the learned Talmudic scholars of previous ages, in a field of so little interest to the *goyim* (non-Jews) that there was never any interference.

Law has also been of undiminished interest to Jews because, while Christianity focuses on the hereafter, Judaism's prime concern is the present and the immediate future. While Christianity is occupied principally with saving souls through faith, Judaism concentrates on saving mankind through acts of justice. While Christianity stresses the relationship between God and man, Judaism places on an even higher level the relationship between man and man. For the religious Jew belief is important only when it expresses itself in social action. For all those reasons The Law is important, for The Law clearly indicates what justice is, what the relationship between man and man should be, and exactly how belief can be transmuted into community action.

Since the Roman Conquest of the Middle East, The Law has been having its influence on the West. Medieval canon law was based largely on the Torah and it in turn had a profound influence on modern civil law. Many modern laws had their genesis in Hebraic law, including our present-day copyright law, which is based on a law evolved by medieval rabbis. The great jurists of the seventeenth century were influenced by bibilical and rabbinical writings. In the eighteenth and nineteenth centuries, on the Continent as well as in England, Jewish lawyers, advocates, and barristers played important roles in the development of secular justice.

In the Mosaic Tradition

With this background, it is not surprising that one of Judaism's principal contributions to America has been in the field of legal justice—a concern with law.

The legal profession in the United States has attracted Jews all out of proportion to their percentage in the general population. Jewish lawyers have acquired in America both fame and fortune. Those with a more altruistic ambition have led—or joined in—campaigns for prison reform, the rehabilitation of criminals, and abolition of capital punishment.

Although the Mosaic law fixes capital punishment for many crimes that at present are considered relatively trivial, in actual Judaic practice capital punishment was virtually eliminated during the Second Jewish Commonwealth. This was not accomplished by repealing the ancient law, which was considered divine and therefore eternal. Instead it was done by imposing so many restrictions that enforcement became almost impossible, and by substituting less drastic pun-

ishments, such as money fines. One example: a murderer was supposed to be put to death. But Talmudic rabbis hedged this law
around with these restrictions: the murderer had to know the nature of his act; he had to know the proscribed punishment; the
murder must have been deliberate; the murderer must have been
guilty of previous hatred for his victim; he must have used a deadly
weapon; and to commit the murder he must have "lain in wait."
All those elements of guilt had to be proven, and even then the
death penalty could not be imposed unless two reliable witnesses
testified that they had seen the deed performed.

It is therefore traditionally logical that many American Jews—
members of the legal profession and laymen alike—have taken the
lead in the campaign against capital punishment in this country, as
well as in many other attempts—some successful—to modernize
American jurisprudence.

Marshall and Legal Justice

In the chapter dealing with the World War I Peace Conference
Louis Marshall has already been introduced and more about him will
be found in the chapter on Judaism and Civil Rights. In many ways
he was the most outstanding legal mind America had yet developed.
And he was a proud Jew, who not only "identified," but was well
aware that his interest in law grew directly out of his Jewish roots.
He led the successful fight to obtain annulment of the American-
Russian Treaty of 1832. He helped obtain certain rights for the
Jews of Europe in the 1920s. He was one of the founders and at
one time president of both the American Jewish Committee and
the American Jewish Congress. He was chairman of both the Jewish
Theological Seminary and Dropsie College.

Supreme Court Justices

The first Jew to be named to the Supreme Court has also already
been introduced. As a student of Jewish history, Louis D. Brandeis
knew how Judaism had avoided strangulation by outmoded laws,

and so he devoted his twenty-three years on the Supreme Court bench to cooperation with Justice Oliver Wendell Holmes in a two-man campaign to keep the court from being shackled by dogmas of the past.

Brandeis was followed on the Supreme Court bench by four other Jews. Benjamin N. Cardozo of New York was sixty-two years old when he was appointed by President Hoover in 1932. He served until his death six years later, in that brief time acquiring a reputation as the philosopher of American jurisprudence. In 1939 President Roosevelt appointed a second Jew, Felix Frankfurter of Massachusetts, then only fifty-seven years old, but already one of America's outstanding legal authorities as professor of law at Harvard University and author of a number of standard works on political and constitutional matters. He served twenty-three years on the bench, with great distinction. Next came Arthur J. Goldberg, a Middle Western lawyer, who first had been noted for his skill in mediating labor-management disputes. He became general counsel of the Congress of Industrial Organizations (CIO) and of the United Steelworkers of America in 1948. He helped negotiate the merger of the CIO and the A.F. of L. in 1955. Then in 1961 President John F. Kennedy named him Secretary of Labor. A year later he was appointed to the Supreme Court, but he served only three years, resigning in 1965 to accept President Lyndon B. Johnson's appointment as chief American delegate to the United Nations, succeeding the late Adlai Stevenson. That same year, to fill the Goldberg vacancy on the bench, President Johnson appointed Abe Fortas of Tennessee, who had a reputation as a fighter for civil liberties.

One peculiar aspect of Roosevelt's appointment of Frankfurter was that a self-appointed committee of Jews called on President Roosevelt and urged him to withdraw the appointment on the ground that some assimilationist American Jews—including the members of the delegation, presumably—would be embarrassed by the attacks that would be made on the appointment in the course of the Senate debate on confirmation. Instead of withdrawing the appointment, Roosevelt lectured the delegation on the meaning of "freedom and equality under the law," and said he had named Frankfurter not because he was a Jew but because he had the necessary qualifications for the position. Discussing the incident later with Dubinsky, Roose-

velt (whom the Nazis without a shred of evidence, labeled a Jew)
said:

"I have never yet seen an Irish leader coming here to complain
when Irishmen are appointed to important offices. Jews need not be
so apprehensive, for this is their country no less than that of other
citizens. Frankfurter will surely be a credit to Jews and non-Jews
alike."

And indeed he was.

Five Individualists

It was not a coincidence or an accident of history that while the
court in modern times has been fairly evenly divided between liberal
and conservative justices, with the majority sometimes being on one
side and sometimes on the other, the five Jews appointed to the high
tribunal have all been classed as liberals and between them were
responsible for some of the most liberal decisions the court ever
handed down. It is true that had the five been on the bench all at the
same time, they might seldom have all stood together, supporting the
same opinion, for they were individualists. One of the five, when the
question of his confirmation came up in the Senate, was denounced
as a radical, yet before he finished his long service in the Court he
was sometimes denounced by the liberals for taking a conservative
position. And yet, taken as a group, these five men proved their
inherent Jewishness by supporting with their votes the sort of social
and legal justice advocated down through the ages by Judaism itself.

Jews in America have set a good example in their respect for law
and order. In every category of crime—from first degree murder to
petty larceny and juvenile delinquency—official statistics show the
rate for Jews to be considerably lower than for the population at
large. This is not surprising, remembering that Judaism is a religion
of law, and that its devoted followers spend much of their time
studying and memorizing not only the ten major commandments
but the hundreds of minor regulations that rule their lives.

23

NO MAN IS A STRANGER

Judaism holds that all human beings are equally children
of God, and, therefore, that all are equally entitled to both freedom
and respect. No exceptions are made. The religious Jew is told that
he may not oppress, exploit, or humiliate another person, regardless
of that person's race, color, creed, social position, economic class, or
other condition, and that he may not deprive any other person of
those rights and privileges which he claims for himself.

The Talmudic rabbis even ruled that it was oppression, exploitation, and humiliation to deceive another man, or to withhold truth
from him. Or, to restrain or inhibit him from reaching the heights to
which his natural ability and his ambition might take him.

Judaism, rejecting all distinctions, first gave the world the belief
that every human being is both sacred and equal to all others in
opportunity in the eyes of God.

In the Book of Amos, God reprimands his own people, saying to
them: "Are ye not as the children of the Ethiopians unto me, O
children of Israel? saith the Lord."

Him Thou Shalt Not Wrong

In another book of the Bible, written about a century after the
destruction of Solomon's Temple, the prophet Malachi rebukes the
Israelites for their sins, especially for their treatment of others, saying
to them: "Have we not all one Father? Hath not one God created
us?"

Although the word *stranger* appears frequently in the Bible, it is generally used in commanding that equal treatment should be accorded to everyone—that distinctions must not be made:

"One law shall be to him that is homeborn, and unto the stranger that sojourneth among you." Exodus 12:49.

"And a stranger shalt thou not wrong, neither shalt thou oppress him; for ye were strangers in the land of Egypt." Exodus 22:20.

The amount of repetition indicates how much biblical importance was attached to the idea of equality, which is stressed not only in most books of the Bible, but repeatedly in the writings and arguments of the Talmudic rabbis. A legend from the Midrash, widely quoted by rabbis in sermons and speeches asks: "Why did God create one man, Adam?" The answer given by the learned rabbis is that only one man was made—and he was created out of dust from the seven corners of the earth—so that thereafter no one could ever say to another: "My ancestors were greater than your ancestors!"

In a lesson on the unimportance of color, the Midrash tells the story of an Athenian in Jerusalem who asked a child to bring him eggs and cheese, and when the child had done so asked if the cheese came from a white goat or from a black goat, to which the child replied: "You are a grown man. You tell me which egg is from a white hen and which from a black hen."

Partly because it is a principle of their religion and partly because they themselves were so often denied civil rights in the various countries of their habitation, Jews have consistently been in the forefront of any movement aimed at complete equality for all people. This has been especially true in twentieth-century America.

Jews and NAACP

In 1909, when a small handful of white and Negro citizens met in New York to form the National Association for the Advancement of Colored People (NAACP) Rabbi Stephen Wise, who just two years earlier had established the Free Synagogue in a New York theater, was among the incorporators and gave his devoted service for the next forty years. More recently, Arthur Springarn and Kivie Kaplan, both Jews, served the NAACP as presidents, while many other Jews have served on the NAACP board of trustees and have helped contribute or raise the money with which the organization has financed its continuous campaign for state and federal enforcement of non-discrimination laws, passage of additional legislation to guarantee equal rights for all, educational work in brotherhood, and such direct action as sit-ins, demonstrations, and picketing.

Millions by Rosenwald

Julius Rosenwald, Chicago businessman and philanthropist, who once said it was easier to earn a million dollars honestly than to give it away wisely, contributed during his lifetime more than $63,000,000 to a wide range of educational, religious, scientific, and community organizations and institutions, with a lion's share of that amount going to Negro education. He tried to help groups rather than individuals and to give in such a manner as to stimulate others to give. The Julius Rosenwald Fund was created in 1917 to handle his contributions to the Negro community in the most scientific manner possible. Rosenwald did not believe in perpetual endowments, feeling that social conditions change too rapidly to warrant storing up great sums of money for a future the nature of which cannot possibly be discerned. The soundness of this theory was borne out by the fact that such charity as his assistance to Negroes was not only welcome but vital in the early part of the century, yet fifty years later had become completely outmoded by the drastically changed social and political conditions. In accordance with his theory, the Foundation was to spend principal as well as interest, and was to go out of existence when the money was gone. In the course of thirty-one years it spent $22,500,000, mostly to help build more than five thousand rural Negro schools, as well as innumerable Negro clinics. It promoted projects in general education and child study, and aided many Negro artists, writers, and musicians who later became famous. The Fund lasted for sixteen years after the death of Rosenwald, closing its books in 1948.

Marshall, Milgrim, Lehman

Attorney Louis Marshall was active in many aspects of civil rights. He was a member of the National Board of Directors of NAACP from 1924 until 1929 (his son, James, was a board member from 1932 to 1937) and spoke out often against segregation. He fought the Ku Klux Klan and on one occasion made it crystal clear that he would continue to use all his energies against the organization, even if it were to ease up on the Jews, as long as it remained "against the Negroes or any other part of our population." Marshall argued before the highest state and federal courts cases concerning segregation of Negroes, alien immigration, the abolition of private and parochial schools, and other aspects of the rights of minorities. One of his greatest legal triumphs in the United States Supreme Court was a decision that held invalid an Oregon law denying Catholics the right to send their children to a parochial school. This decision was a landmark, because it affirmed the constitutional right of any religious body to maintain its own schools.

Morris Milgrim, a pioneer in erecting interracial housing as a matter of high principle as well as good business, was a Jew, as were many others who campaigned for fair housing laws and practices.

Herbert Lehman, both as Governor of New York and as a member of the United States Senate, was constantly making public addresses and introducing legislation for more civil rights protection. In the lower house, Congressman Jacob Javits from 1947 until 1954 sponsored bill after bill designed to enforce civil rights, and when he went to the Senate in 1957 he continued his interest in the problem.

Jews on Segregation

The highpoint of the fight for desegregation of American public schools came on May 17, 1954, when the United States Supreme Court ruled that racial segregation in public schools henceforth would be illegal. In a public comment, the Union of American Hebrew Congregations urged all "congregants and congregations to join with forward-looking racial, religious and civic groups in the community in using their influence to secure acceptance and implementation of the desegregation decisions in every community in our land."

On the day that the Supreme Court announced its desegregation decision, the Rabbinical Assembly of America, representing Conservative rabbis, was in convention at Uniontown, Pennsylvania. There they adopted a resolution commending the justices for their "historic decision" and declaring that "the unanimity of their act and its courage will leave its indelible stamp not only in our country but the entire world."

The National Women's League of the United Synagogue of America in convention several months later passed a resolution pledging its full support "in the effort that lies ahead to give full and meaningful effect to this historic decision" and urging its sisterhoods to "do all that lies within their power to help make the transition required by the decision as harmoniously and as rapidly as possible."

The Vulnerable Minority Speaks Up

In some parts of the South officials began integrating the public schools without incident, but in other areas mass meetings, picketing, protests, and propaganda kept the public in a state of agitation. Governor Orville Faubus of Arkansas called out the National Guard to prevent Negro children from entering white schools. Southern Jewry was put in a difficult position, for everywhere in the South the Jews were a vulnerable minority against which the white non-Jewish majority could easily exert destructive pressures.

But the reaction of Southern Jewry as a whole wrote a bright chapter in the history of a people and a religion. Throughout the region rabbis mounted their pulpits and spoke out, fearlessly. Some even took part in public demonstrations. When White Citizens' Councils were formed, the names of rabbis were noticeably absent from the membership lists, despite all the pressures to which they were subjected.

It was a period of unrest and tension. Extremists vowed to lead a never-ending fight against any mixing of races. Racial bigots, representatives of white supremacy groups, and leaders of the KKK goaded unthinking people into militant resistance. Then the explosions began.

A school was dynamited. Then a church. Then the bombers turned their attention to Jewish religious buildings. On Armistice Day, 1957, an attempt was made to bomb Temple Beth-El in Charlotte, North Carolina. It failed. Three months later Leon Schneider, a member of Temple Emanuel in Gastonia, North Carolina, who had been mayor of the city, received a telephone call that his temple was going to be destroyed. Later a package of dynamite was found on the steps of the temple. Fortunately, the fuse had failed to go off. After the arrest of the man responsible, who was later judged insane, it was generally agreed that the case had had nothing to do with organized anti-Semitism or the civil rights movement.

Miami, Nashville, Jacksonville, Birmingham

On March 16, 1958, dynamite blasts did $30,000 damage to the school-recreation annex of Temple Beth-El in Miami, Florida, and the same day, in distant Nashville, Tennessee, an explosion ripped off the front of the Jewish Community Center. At the same time extremists threatened to shoot Federal Judge William E. Miller and a Nashville rabbi, Dr. William B. Silverman, one of the few religious leaders in the city to take a firm stand for the implementation of the Supreme Court decision, received a warning that his temple would be the next building destroyed. The rabbi obtained a permit to carry a gun and while armed guards were stationed at his home to protect him and his family, the other clergy of Nashville passed resolutions, offered to raise funds for the repair of the Community Center, and delivered angry sermons deploring the bombing. Rabbi Silverman helped organize the Nashville Community Relations Council, a bi-racial group. This brought on renewed attacks by the lunatic fringe. When he announced that on the next Friday night he would preach a sermon entitled *We Will Not Yield*, he received anonymous calls that if services were held that night the temple would be dynamited. Despite the threat the services were held and Rabbi Silverman spoke bluntly on the announced subject. Throughout the trouble he had the backing of a vast majority of his congregation.

The next trouble after Nashville was in Jacksonville, Florida, where the Jewish Center was dynamited. Then on April 28, a janitor at Temple Beth-El in Birmingham, Alabama, discovered a bomb in a window well on the west side of the building. It consisted of many sticks of dynamite and a burned-out length of fuse cord. Leaders of the Jewish community, who had been extremely active, behind the scenes, in promoting good human relations in the city, met at the home of the president of Beth-El and underwrote a substantial reward. This action received wide publicity, but resulted in no arrests. Subsequently a Negro Baptist church was bombed, killing five Negro children. Investigators found evidence that both bombings—the successful and unsuccessful one—might have been the work of the same criminals.

Then Atlanta

Atlanta, Georgia, was next.

For years Rabbi Jacob M. Rothschild, rabbi of the Temple, had been an outspoken defender of human rights for Negroes. As early as 1948 he had said in a sermon: "It becomes increasingly obvious that unless decent people take up the burden, the South faces a return to the most primitive kind of bigotry and race hatred."

Years of preaching that the Jewish religion considers "no man a stranger" had had its effect. Following the Supreme Court decision in 1954, a substantial portion of his congregation made efforts to implement the decision. That year the Temple president joined with the rabbi in issuing a plea to all members to vote against a proposed amendment to the Georgia Constitution which would have obstructed school integration. The following year both the Couples' Club and the Sisterhood presented programs dealing with civil rights. The Sisterhood then went a step further, inviting a Negro leader and his wife to take part in a discussion of desegregation at a public luncheon. This was unprecedented, then, but the Sisterhood resisted all the pressure that was applied to de-invite the Negro couple and the luncheon was a success, the first of many other such affairs at which Negroes have been both speakers and guests.

In sermons in Cincinnati and New York, Rabbi Rothschild declared: "There is a macabre and disqueting parallel between the South today and a totalitarian state. There is a curtailment of the right to speak freely and openly if what you say disagrees with the popular point of view."

One of the rabbi's sermons on civil rights was published in full by the Atlanta *Journal and Constitution* and by the *Congressional Record*.

Then it happened. At 3:30 A.M. on Sunday, October 12, 1958, an explosion of forty or fifty sticks of dynamite shook the foundation of the Temple on Peachtree Road, blew a twenty-foot hole in a sidewall, and did damage estimated at $200,000. Fortunately, no one was in the building when the explosion occurred, and the sanctuary itself suffered only broken panes, loosened plaster, and an unhinged door.

The next day the Atlanta *Constitution* said:

"It buried the little sky-blue robes of the children's choir under glass and plaster. The white collars lay gray and torn in water from broken pipes.

"It blew the vestibule wall and buried a bronze plaque commemorating men of the congregation who were killed in the military service of the United States flag.

"It shattered a little glass display case set up by the Sisterhood and spilled its contents onto the wet rubble. . . .

"It toppled Menorahs from the broken shelf and left those . . . lying bent and tarnished under the wreckage. . . .

"A small record album on one damaged shelf was named '*Thank You, God!*'"

As friends and strangers were expressing their indignation, Rabbi Rothschild and the president of the congregation received threats that their homes were next on the list. Janice O. Rothschild, wife of the rabbi, in *As But a Day*, a story of the Temple's first hundred years, published in 1967, wrote: "The blast was more than a shock. It was a shock treatment. For Jew and non-Jew alike the bomb released long-buried thoughts about themselves and each other. It blasted through the Southern moderates' wall of silence. All of the 'right people,' from Georgia Governor Marvin Griffin to President of the United States Dwight D. Eisenhower, had 'the right thing' to say about the bombing and said it for publication."

Atlanta *Constitution* columnist Ralph McGill wrote:

"This is a harvest. It is the crop of things sown.

"It is the harvest of defiance of courts and the encouragement of citizens to defy law on the part of many Southern politicians. . . .

"To be sure none said go bomb a Jewish temple or a school.

"But let it be understood that when leadership in high places in any degree fails to support constituted authority, it opens the gates to all those who wish to take the law in their hands. . . .

"It is a harvest, too, for those Christian so-called ministers who have chosen to preach hate instead of compassion. Let them now find pious words and raise their hands in deploring the bombing of a synagogue.

"You do not preach and encourage hatred for the Negro and hope to restrict it to that field."

Alexandria, Baton Rouge, Gadsden

Following the Atlanta bombing, Rabbi Emmett A. Frank of Temple Beth-El in Alexandria, Virginia, assailed the segregationist policies of Senator Harry F. Byrd and questioned whether "Byrdliness is synonymous with Godliness." When he was subjected to criticism, eleven Protestant ministers signed a "Freedom of the Pulpit Statement" defending the young rabbi.

In Baton Rouge, Louisiana, Rabbi Marvin M. Reznikoff of the Liberal Synagogue had long been an advocate of good human relations, with all that that phrase really means. He was a member of the executive board of the Baton Rouge Community Advancement

Corporation and a board member of the Baton Rouge Council of Human Relations, and a member of the state board. On July 27, he and the director of the Louisiana program of the American Friends Service Committee complained to authorities that their telephones were being tapped, and that someone was divulging private telephone conversations relating to civil rights and race relations. This led to the indictment of three men on charges of wire-tapping. Their trial helped to alert and educate the region in what segregationist forces were doing to try to intimidate those working in the field of civil rights.

Seventeen months after the Atlanta bombing, while members of Congregation Beth Israel in Gadsden, Alabama, were holding a dedication of a newly completed addition the service was violently interrupted by the explosion of a homemade bomb thrown at a window facing the crowded sanctuary. Fortunately, although it shattered the window, the bomb fell to the ground outside, where it exploded. Two members of the congregation who ran outside to investigate were shot and wounded by the bomb-thrower, using an automatic .22 rifle. Six hours later police arrested a sixteen-year-old boy, in whose suburban home they found a number of neo-Nazi pamphlets the boy admitted he had been trying to circulate. He was a member of his high school's band and a regular attendant of his local Baptist church, but somehow had conceived a hatred of Jews.

The following Friday citizens of all faiths joined the Jewish community in a service at Temple Beth Israel to declare their revulsion at the bombing and to show their feelings of brotherhood. In the pulpit, together with Rabbi Saul Rubin, were Episcopalian, Methodist, and Baptist ministers. The Gadsden Ministerial Association, meeting in special session the day after the bombing, passed a resolution deploring the bombing and declaring: "We view this attack upon a particular religious group as equivalent to an attack on all religions, Christianity included."

The boy, who had confessed both the bombing and the shooting, was released on $10,000 bail to await arraignment before the Grand Jury. Before the arraignment, he was killed in an automobile accident. At the request of one of the wounded members of Congregation Beth Israel, the case was dropped.

Miami Again, Then Jackson

On April 29, 1962, five sticks of dynamite attached to a lighted fuse were found in front of Anshe Emet Synagogue in Miami.

In the summer of 1964 Rabbi Arthur J. Lelyveld, who later became national president of the American Jewish Congress, was severely beaten by segregationists while serving as a volunteer minister-counselor for a team of civil rights workers in Mississippi.

Then there was the Jackson case.

Perry E. Nussbaum went to the Mississippi capital in 1953 as rabbi of Congregation Beth Israel. The Jewish population was then just 350 souls. Less than one year later the Supreme Court decision on segregation was handed down. From the start Rabbi Nussbaum was outspoken in his support of desegregation, as well as in his denunciation of McCarthyism, even though almost every right-wing movement in America was represented in his area. Writing in the Central Conference of American Rabbis' *Journal* in 1963, he reported: "Sometimes you were sure your phone was tapped. You wondered about some of the mail, delivered and undelivered. Talk about the clergy and mental health! Some of us were chapter and verse in the textbook of the paranoid. . . . When we were reasonably sure of one another, we dared voice what was treason (to the South) behind closed doors and was admittedly foolhardy and impractical from the pulpit."

In the beginning Rabbi Nussbaum had the friendship and cooperation of many Catholic and Protestant clergy and some college people. One by one, however, those who were outspoken disappeared. Twenty-eight ministers of one denomination were transferred to areas where they would cause less embarrassment. Two were assassinated. Commenting on the fact that he was the last liberal religious leader left in the community, Rabbi Nussbaum wrote: "So this last survivor is running scared. . . . Tell me, colleagues, how did Isaac feel when that knife was poised over his head?"

Chaplain to the Freedom Riders

Rabbi Nussbaum may have been "running scared" but he had the courage to become the secret chaplain of the Negro and white Freedom Riders, who were going about the South testing local segregation laws, although for several years he kept this connection unpublicized.

At about 10:30 P.M. on Monday, September 18, 1967, a bomb was exploded at Beth Israel's newly dedicated Fifth House, which had cost the small Jewish community almost half a million dollars. It had been planted in front of the door opening into the rabbi's study. Police roped off the building and sent for the FBI. A squad of bomb experts was flown in from Washington. One of the rabbi's chief concerns was for the thousands of books that might have been ruined by a broken water main.

Before going to bed that night Rabbi Nussbaum wrote a report to his congregation in which he said: "Last night a policeman said to me, 'I can't understand how anybody could want to destroy a church!' My own trauma was too much upon me to remind this well-intentioned sympathizer that over forty Christian churches have already been destroyed in Mississippi. . . .

"I sit in the middle of the night and pray for the light which will maintain Beth Israel in its Fifth House a symbol of Brotherhood and Love for all people, whoever they are, whatever they are."

130,000 Votes for a Bigot

In a later report to his congregation, Rabbi Nussbaum pointed out that in a recent Mississippi primary election, 130,000 voters had supported "a vicious bigot" and that "during these past months especially there has been a lot of bad anti-Semitic stuff passed around. The KKK, the John Birchers, and a host of anti-everything that is not white, Protestant, native Mississippi organizations have been meeting, speechifying and passing public resolutions." Then he said:

"In a climate which has depended on prejudice for generations, a prejudice which I have said for years is color-blind, generated and maintained by an Establishment, political, economic, and religious, which would have to go out of business otherwise—in such a climate this bombing was inevitable."

There were also bombings in Mississippi of a college building, the parsonage of a Negro clergyman, and the home of a white Christian who was dedicating his life to working for human equality.

On November 20, from Montreal, where he was addressing the biennial convention of the Union of American Congregations, Rabbi Nussbaum wrote to his congregation:

"Let all the decent peoples stand up to bigotry and racism, and demand that the authorities root out the vicious and the despicable. . . . Judaism insists that we all share out our blessings, the moral as well as the material."

Rabbi, My House, Too?

Then, at 11:10 P.M. on November 21, the Nussbaum home was bombed. The rabbi at the time was sleeping in a rear bedroom, and thus escaped injury. It was the twelfth bombing in Mississippi in less than ten months. Several days later a reward of $5000 was posted for the arrest and conviction of those responsible. Then the amount was raised to $25,000. Then to $50,000. Rabbi and Mrs. Nussbaum moved into temporary quarters elsewhere—hidden quarters, known only to police and the FBI. The rabbi's car was followed often, by mysterious characters. In a report to his people, the rabbi said: "It's not so funny when little children say to you: 'Rabbi, because you were bombed, is my house going to be bombed too?' Or when parents are desperately torn between keeping kids at home or sending them to Temple."

For weeks Rabbi Nussbaum, at FBI insistence, stayed in hiding. During the first ten days he was required to move to three different locations to thwart additional attempts on his life. In public statements he blamed the KKK as his attackers. (The Jackson bombings followed the conviction by a Federal jury of seven Ku Klux Klansmen on charges of conspiring in the 1964 lynching of three civil rights

workers, a verdict some observers thought would help curb terrorism.)

Congregation Beth Israel took advertisements in the papers to
announce: "We are proud of our rabbi, Dr. Perry E. Nussbaum,
and desire the citizenry of Jackson to know that we support him in
this bitter hour with every available resource of heart and mind."

The Jackson Ministerial Association issued *A Statement on Crimes
Against Those Who Work for Better Human Relations in Mississippi*
which called on all Christians "to search their hearts to determine
whether they, individually or collectively, have been guilty in some
way of contributing to this sickness of violent sin which is gnawing
at the foundation of society . . . to change their own attitudes
and outlooks and, in the particular case of the clergy and other
spokesmen, to try to communicate this repentant spirit to their
assembled congregations."

As a postscript to the Mississippi story, literature sent through the
mail to thousands of Jackson people read, in part: "The sane course
for all Christian American citizens to follow is to recognize the
instrument of organized Jewry for what it is—a religious device of
Satan."

Pointing the Way in Texas

Two rabbis and a Jewish layman helped to point the way in
Texas. Houston was fortunate to have the intellectual leadership of
Dr. D. H. White, editor and publisher of the *Jewish Herald-Voice*,
the oldest Anglo-Jewish newspaper in the South, founded in 1908.
Not only was he outspoken in his editorial comment but he provided
positive prodding within the organized Jewish community.

Rabbi Moshe Cahana, Congregation Brith Shalom, was persistent
in his efforts to mobilize the clergy of the area for affirmative
action. He himself marched in Selma and became better known
and more trusted by the Negro leadership than anyone else in the
religious field.

Rabbi Robert I. Kahn, Congregation Emanu-El, was equally
active but in other ways. His sermons carried an almost weekly

message on social justice. He quietly moved one of the largest congregations in the South to adopt a call to conscience. The statement was a guide for the congregation's practices regarding employment of Negroes, the attitude to be taken toward firms which discriminate, and suggestions as to the responsibilities of individual members. The mere adoption would have been a feat, yet it was not only adopted but printed and circulated in the form of a public commitment. The congregation held public meetings on equal employment opportunities, housed the first Head Start program, and in many other ways assumed community leadership.

The Southwest office of the Anti-Defamation League played the most significant organizational role in the area, serving as a catalyst in obtaining action by other groups and individuals.

Civil Rights Honor Roll

Other Southern rabbis commended by the Anti-Defamation League because of their involvement in the civil rights struggle are Rabbi Ariel Goldburg of Temple Beth Ahabah, Richmond, Virginia; Rabbi Harold Hahn of Temple Beth-El, Charlotte, North Carolina; Rabbi Charles Mantinband of the Reform Temple in Hattiesburg, Mississippi; Rabbi Julian Friedman of Temple Sinai in New Orleans, who in the 1940s opened his temple to Dr. Ralph Bunche when the Negro UN official could find no other place in New Orleans in which to speak.

At a critical moment in the race relations struggle, the Union of Orthodox Jewish Congregations at a biennial convention in 1960 passed a resolution declaring that "the only distinction permissible among men is the distinction by moral value, the distinction between good and evil; no other differentiation, be it by race or by color, is admissible in the life of a society which sees in man the image of the Almighty."

American Jewry was distraught in late 1967 when extreme Black Power groups, following the Six-Day war, made attacks on both Israelis and American Jews. Nevertheless, groups such as the Jewish Labor Committee continued to blame Negro disorders in Northern cities on "the failure of Congress to rally to a significant and massive attack on poverty," and liberal Jewish rabbis continued to work resolutely and fearlessly for better human relations in their communities.

24

AND EACH SHALL HAVE A VOICE

FAITH in the worth of the individual is an essential element of Judaism.

"Precious is man, since he is created in God's image," said Rabbi Akiba.

Judaism teaches that everyone has not only the right but the duty to express his own individuality. He is unique in the world, and is obligated to discover and develop that uniqueness.

He is also free to express or keep private the dictates of his soul and the thoughts of his mind. Judaism has often punished wrong conduct, but never wrong opinion. There were no Inquisitions in ancient Israel, and no autos-da-fé.

Two Golden Rules

In the first century, in the Sermon on the Mount, Christ said: "Therefore all things whatsoever ye would that men should do to you, do ye even to them."

But a hundred years earlier Hillel the Elder had put it differently: "What is hateful to yourself do not do to your neighbor."

It is often contended that the two disparate wordings of the Golden Rule illustrate a fundamental difference between Judaism and Christianity. Beyond question Hillel's admonition guarantees far more freedom and privacy than the later version, for Judaism's rule is, in effect, a suggestion that the neighbor not be proselytized, persecuted, put upon, or punished for his beliefs.

Job Even Argued with God

The Bible gives proof of how possible it was in the Jewish state to speak out, even against the highest constituted authority. Although King David was a popular and powerful monarch, the prophet Nathan publicly denounced him for having taken Bathsheba from her husband, and no one silenced or punished Nathan, or even questioned his right to voice his opinion. Other prophets on occasion angered the populace with their diatribes, but it was never suggested that they be silenced. Job even argued with God. The bare fact that the unpopular books of the prophets were preserved and placed in the canon itself is highly significant.

The *Gemara*—that part of the Talmud containing comments of the learned rabbis—is like a collection of the majority and minority opinions of the United States Supreme Court. Therein the authorities of one generation argue with the authorities of another generation, or contemporaries debate with each other the meaning and interpretation of religious laws, yet all the opinions are included in the *Gemara*, for future generations to study.

After Hillel founded his school of religious study in Jerusalem, a rival rabbi, Shammai, established a somewhat more conservative school of interpretation, and on many matters the two disagreed fundamentally, yet their ideas were given equal treatment in the Talmud and both men were respected as great rabbinical authorities.

Judaism has a positive religious outlook, yet it avoids dogmas.

No Centralized Control

An inherent respect for independence is seen in the organizational pattern of Judaism. Once there was a supreme rabbinical authority —the Sanhedrin. When it was dissolved in the fifth century some of its power was taken over by two Talmudic academies in Babylonia. But since the eleventh century, Jewish congregations and Jewish rabbis have been absolutely autonomous. No institutional authority has existed for the past nine hundred years to which individual synagogues or individual rabbis must be obedient. Although congregations may form associations and cooperate voluntarily in the interest of unity, each is entirely autonomous. Each chooses its own rabbi without dictation or interference. And the rabbis are likewise free from any centralized control.

Jewish liberalism is also evident in the attitude toward members of other religious groups. Judaism claims no exclusivity. It never contends, as Christians do in the words of St. Paul, that "He that disbelieveth shall be condemned." Instead, Judaism says that any good person—Jew, Protestant, Catholic, Buddhist, Moslem—is acceptable to God. This has a great bearing on the Jewish attitude toward those with divergent political, social, cultural, or ethical ideas.

Down through the centuries Jewish writers have accented Judaism's obsession with freedom—especially freedom of the mind. Heinrich Heine, German poet, wrote: "Since the Exodus, Freedom has always spoken with a Hebrew accent."

The Historical Motivation

Besides the religious reasons for Jews being advocates of unusual civil liberty there is a powerful historical motivation. Since the destruction of the Second Temple they have everywhere been victims of persecution, discrimination, suppression, censorship, and blacklisting. Book-burning in Hitler Germany reminded them of how often in times past angry mobs in various countries seized and burned the Scrolls of the Law. The denial of free speech in the time of McCarthy recalled to them how often during their long history they had been silenced. Whatever was done to deny modern men their rights had been done long ago to Jews. A thousand years before the birth of Senator McCarthy, Jews were fighting McCarthyism.

Thus it is no wonder that the history of Jews and Judaism in America is sprinkled with stories of rabbis and laymen who took great personal risks to fight for the rights of all Americans to freedom of ideas and freedom of action.

Civil liberties became a serious issue in the United States for the first time after World War I, when even the mildest form of radicalism was denounced and hundreds of innocent American citizens were victims of a form of witch-hunting the country had never before experienced. A few Jews were among the victims; many were among those who eventually were able to help reverse the trend.

Abhorrence of Interference

At the height of the witch-hunting in 1920, the Central Conference of American Rabbis passed and made public this resolution: "We declare our abhorrence of all interference, whether by private citizens or by officials, with the exercise of freedom of speech, oral or written, and of freedom of assemblage, both of which are guaranteed by the Constitution."

Shortly after the end of World War II, when history repeated itself and America began to be plagued by the same sort of illiberalism it had suffered a quarter of a century earlier, the Central Conference of American Rabbis expressed alarm over "the emergence of post-war hysteria indiscriminately directed against political non-conformists which intimidates the citizen in the exercise of freedom of speech, thought and press."

In 1950 Congress passed, over the veto of President Harry Truman, the Internal Security Act, also known as the McCarran Act, after the Senator from Nevada who had introduced it. Although it was designed "to thwart the worldwide Communist conspiracy," the Departments of Defense, State, and Justice, as well as the Central Intelligence Agency, warned that it would do more harm than good. It created a Subversive Activities Control Board, set up categories of "Communist-action" and "Communist-front" organizations whose members henceforth were to be suspect, and provided for "emergency detention camps" for those found to have dangerous ideas.

Many nationwide Jewish organizations were among the hundreds that petitioned Congress for repeal of the act, including the National Women's League of the United Synagogue of America, speaking for hundreds of thousands of Conservative women.

At its 1950 convention the United Synagogue passed a resolution condemning the act on the ground that it "flagrantly departs from American democratic principles and long-established practices."

The Rise of McCarthyism

When Senator Joseph R. McCarthy of Wisconsin attracted public
attention by accusing the Department of State of harboring a number of Communists—a charge which he was never able to substanti-
ate—the United Synagogue of America formally "deplored the
wholesale and irresponsible campaign of villification being conducted against government employees and men and women in public
life. The necessary effort to exclude the disloyal from positions of
responsibility can be exercised without defamation of the innocent."

As the McCarthy madness spread, hundreds of rabbis—Orthodox, Conservative, and Reform alike—in sermons and public addresses pointed out that Judaism is fundamentally antagonistic to
tyranny of all sorts, and is opposed to Communism as an ideology
and a way of life, because the party philosophy is hostile to the basic
beliefs of Judaism. But Judaism at the same time rejected domestic
tyranny foisted on the country in the name of false patriotism. As
McCarthy's methods became more and more unscrupulous—by
American standards—more and more Jewish leaders took a bold
stand against the McCarthy committee and its tactics.

The National Women's League of the United Synagogue of America urged its members to organize against McCarthyism and to work
for curbs on Senatorial immunity, "in order to prevent Senators
from engaging in irresponsible and ruthless character assassination of
loyal Americans." At the same time the League attacked the "sensational methods" of the House Committee on Un-American Activities
which "jeopardize the individual's standing in the community and his
means of earning a livelihood" and called on the Attorney-General
to withdraw from use his list of organizations "arbitrarily desig-
nated as subversive."

Alarming Trend Toward Suspicion

At its 43rd General Assembly, the Union of American Hebrew
Synagogues adopted a statement of basic principles and pledged itself

"to join with all freedom-loving forces in our community and nation to reverse the alarming trend toward suspicion, recrimination, fear and the equation of dissent with disloyalty.

"We pledge our unremitting vigilance to the end that neither Communist intrigue nor reckless demagoguery shall be allowed to corrode the fundamental liberties which have their origin in religious ideals."

At its biennial convention, the United Synagogue of America reaffirmed its faith "in the classic liberties of America—freedom of speech, freedom of press, freedom of religious conscience, freedom of assembly and petition," and rejected the concept that "the preservation of the national security and the effective countering of communist and other totalitarian ideas require the abandonment of our individual liberties."

Shortly before the Senate censured the Wisconsin Senator, a Gallup Poll showed that 56 percent of the Catholics and 45 percent of the Protestants polled approved of McCarthy, but that 98 percent of the Jews polled considered him a menace to the country. This was close enough to a unanimous vote to make possible a sweeping generalization that American Jews, true to the heritage of Judaism, are opposed to thought control and are champions of full civil liberties.

Tools of Tyranny

In the mid-1950s when the country was beset by a wave of loyalty oaths which teachers in twenty-three states were required to take, liberal forces opposed them because they were based on the concept of guilt by association, and because members of various religious groups, such as the Quakers, had religious grounds for not taking the oath, and because it was a device designed not to increase loyalty or to weed out those who might be disloyal, but to enforce conformity. In an opinion declaring the Oklahoma state oath unconstitutional, Justice Black said: "Test oaths are notorious tools of tyranny. When used to shackle the mind they are, or at least should be, unspeakably odious to a free people."

Denouncing test oaths and other threats to civil liberties, the

Union of American Hebrew Congregations declared in 1955: "We protest the irresponsible use of political informers by our law enforcement agencies. We deplore the view that citizens should be encouraged to inform against fellow citizens with respect to their opinions and political associations."

The Fight Against Oaths

Jews and Jewish organizations campaigned against loyalty oaths even when the principal victims seemed to be members of other religious groups, such as the Quakers. But in California Judaism became directly involved, for in 1953 the California Legislature, after a popular referendum, adopted a requirement that every church, synagogue, and other tax-exempt body must sign an oath swearing that it does not advocate the overthrow of the government by force and in event of hostilities would support the United States. Rather than sign the oath several Protestant groups gave up their tax exemption. Some synagogues joined with a number of churches in signing under protest. The Southern Region of the United Synagogue and the Board of Rabbis of Northern California were among those religious groups which publicly opposed the oath on the ground that by asking religious groups to sign, the state was casting suspicion on their loyalty and integrity. Eventually the United States Supreme Court declared the California law unconstitutional.

The Blight of Conformity

In 1952 the McCarran-Walker Act was passed. It tightened control of immigrants and aliens, and listed thirty-one reasons for keeping out an alien who wished to immigrate into the United States. At this time no substantial number of Jews were seeking to enter the United States and so the racist provisions of the act did not directly affect the American Jewish community, but many Jewish religious leaders opposed this second McCarran Act as they had opposed the first—on the ground that it contravened the ideals of justice and human equality that they as Americans had come to value.

All three branches of Judaism joined in these various fights against the blight of conformity, the stupidities of Neanderthal reactionaries, and the attempts to whittle away American civil liberties.

In 1965, making his presidential address before the 48th General Biennial Assembly of the Union of American Hebrew Congregations, Rabbi Maurice N. Eisendrath warned that a wave of "Neo-McCarthyism" had begun to sweep America. "It is stretching its tentacles onto the TV screen, into the universities and is affecting high precincts of American leadership." He called on his fellow Reform Jews not to permit "legitimate criticism of our present foreign policy to be branded as subversive and treasonable, the ready target for trigger-happy, character-assassinating witch-hunters."

"We have a duty to challenge the jibe of 'Communist' flung at almost everyone who presumes to differ from this day's Administration policy. Was it 'Communist' for some of us to seek a test ban treaty, so long opposed as unpatriotic and finally adopted because of the pressure of public opinion? When we opposed the Multilateral Force, acclaimed less than a month ago as indispensable to our so-called national security and now all but abandoned, was that 'Communistic'?

"I thought that the right of dissent, not merely in inconsequentials but in the clutch was a salient distinction between dictatorship and democracy. . . . As a religious Jewish community can we still our conscience and muffle our voice?"

25

LEARNING, THE HIGHEST COMMANDMENT

W HEN a Roman Catholic spends half an hour in a church or cathedral, he may count his beads, reciting Ave Marias and In Yemen, he said, he had not lived nearly as well as he now did in Pater Nosters, genuflect before a crucifix, or light a candle and pay homage to the Virgin Mary, for Catholicism is primarily a religion of adoration. When a Quaker goes into a Friends Meeting House, he may sit for half an hour in silent meditation. Other Protestants— from Holy Rollers to High Church Episcopalians—have quite different rituals and rules of religious behavior, but Protestantism in general is a religion of worship and prayer.

When an Orthodox European Jew goes to his synagogue he is likely to refer to it as the *schul*, the Yiddish word for school, which in turn is the popular word that Orthodox Jews in America as well as in Europe use for synagogue, and when he gets there he is likely to spend part of his time in what he calls *study*, which will consist of reading and rereading pages of rabbinical discussions in the Talmud, pondering over the subtleties of one scholar's argument; appreciating the inherent wisdom of the opposing opinion; weighing, thinking, cogitating, using the cells of his brain, as he lives up to Judaism's primary command: Study!

A Yemenite, interviewed several years ago after he had been brought to Israel in the mass immigration scheme called Operation Magic Carpet, complained that in the plastics factory near Tel Aviv where he had been put to work, he was not permitted to leave his machine when the urge came over him to "go to *schul* and study."

Israel, but at least he had had the freedom to leave his cobbler's bench as often as he felt the Talmudic urge, which was at least three or four times a day during the week and all day on Shabbat.

Less Than 1 Percent of the Human Race

Mark Twain, in a little-known magazine article written in 1898, tells how the great civilizations of antiquity—the Egyptians, the Persians, the Greeks, the Romans—all came and went, yet less than 1 percent of the human race, the Jews, "who properly ought never to have been heard of," have kept alive their culture and their civilization through all those thousands of years. He concludes with a three-letter question: "Why?"

Perhaps it is because, while others have been only adoring and meditating and praying (which religious Jews also do), the followers of Judaism have likewise been following intellectual pursuits—thinking and studying and sharpening their brains, as they remember the words of warning that Isaiah gave them:

"My people are gone into captivity for want of knowledge."

The Russian intellectual Ahad Ha'am, writing to Rabbi Judah Magnes, said: "Learning—learning—learning; that is the secret of Jewish survival."

Claude G. Montefiore, British scholar, put it a little differently: "It is the intellectual element in Judaism which enabled the Jews to go through unheard of degradations and persecutions, and yet never to suffer degradation of the soul."

Sigmund Freud, himself a Jew, said: "It was the Holy Book and the study of it that kept the scattered people together."

Because They Asked for Truth . . .

Emma Lazarus in one of her best poems, Gifts, tells what happened to the various great nations of history when they received the gifts they asked from God. The Egyptians wanted wealth. They received it, then vanished from history. The Greeks asked for beauty, but after being granted beauty they, also, disappeared. The

Romans requested power. They were given it and then they, too, were gone. The Jews asked for truth. Because they sought that and nothing else, they have lived from century to century, age to age.

One medieval rabbi said: "Synagogues and houses of study are Israel's towers."

Solomon Chose Wisdom

Starting with Mosaic times, learning was placed above all else. Moses asked God only to know. When the Lord appeared to Solomon in a dream and said, "Ask what I shall give thee," Solomon chose wisdom. When Rabbi Jochanan ben Zakkai was summoned before the commander of the troops laying siege to Jerusalem, he begged for—a school!

The ghettos and *shtetls* of the Diaspora were often islands of learning in a vast sea of ignorance and superstition. Down through the ages Jews developed a reverence for the life of reason. Learning was treated as sacred, the highest virtue; ignorance was the cardinal sin; study was a holy pursuit—the most holy.

Maimonides summed it up by saying that the goal of the religious life is the development of "the highest intellectual faculties and of such notions as lead to true metaphysical opinions."

Long before, Hillel told the impatient pagan: "Go forth and learn!"

In this intellectualistic religion the first qualification for a rabbi— as well as his continuing duty—was to be a scholar. Preaching could be done by others. He might have to take out the time to comfort the stricken and counsel the perplexed, but chiefly he was to concentrate on his studies, to solve scholarly problems for others, and to settle questions of ritual, observance, and faith in accordance with Judaism's teachings. The rabbi was not supposed to teach but to learn with his students. It was always a high compliment to say of a rabbi, "He knows how to *learn*."

The Talmud is strewn with admonitions about studying and acquiring knowledge.

"The prayer for knowledge is first among the Benedictions."

"No mercy for him who is without knowledge."

"With true knowledge it is as though the Temple were built."

"Without knowledge, how can there be discernment?"

"None is poor but he who lacks knowledge."

Moses Perles, seventeenth-century rabbi, said:

"Secular knowledge bears the same relation to the Torah as zero bears to one. Knowledge without Torah is zero; Torah without knowledge is one; the two together are 10."

And from the pen of the great Maimonides:

"One loves God only by dint of knowledge, and the degree of love corresponds to the degree of knowledge."

Maimonides also said:

"The advancement of learning is the highest commandment."

An old Palestinian Jewish proverb says:

"If you lack knowledge what do you have? If you have knowledge, what do you lack?"

Zechariah Frankle, nineteenth-century German Talmudist, said it briefly:

"Without learning, no Judaism."

The Rules for Study

Study was considered of such great importance that precise rules were laid down. Preferably it should be done in the synagogue. ("Who studies in a synagogue will not easily forget.") Studying alone was not recommended. ("God loves two students who arrange to study together.") Students were not to become so engrossed in their studies as to neglect their appearance. ("A scholar commits a capital offense if he appears with a stain of grease on his garments." "It is a disgrace for a scholar to walk with patched shoes." "You can tell scholars on the street by their walk, speech and dress." "A scholar, like a bride, should be without blemish and above reproach.")

The Talmud and other rabbinical writings contain many indications of the high esteem in which scholars were held. ("If need be sell all you have and marry the daughter of a scholar, and your daughter to a scholar." "The holy one avenges the offended dignity of a rabbinical scholar.") A scholar was even permitted to eat on a fast day, if going without food interfered with his studying.

It was considered an honor to have a scholar as a guest in the home. ("A table is not blessed if it has fed no scholars." "Great is the reward for hospitality to a scholar." "Who will not support a scholar will see no blessing.")

Truth was supposed to come through study—through effort expended. ("Were an angel to reveal to me all the mysteries of the Torah, it would please me little, for study is more important than knowledge. Only what man achieves through effort is dear to him.")

Even when scholars were not actually studying, they were supposed to have their minds on religious thoughts. ("Two scholars, traveling together, who do not discuss the Torah, deserve to be burned.")

The Talmud gives this description of the ideal scholar: "A scholar should be like a leather bottle, which admits no wind; like a deep garden bed, which retains its moisture; like a pitch-covered vessel, which preserves its wine, and like a sponge, which absorbs everything."

But the Mishna said there were three other types. "There are four types of students; the sponge, who absorbs all; the funnel, who lets it in one end and out the other; the strainer, who lets out the wine and retains the dregs; and the sieve, who lets out the fine and keeps the coarse flour."

Most American Jews were like the shoemaker from Yemen. Caught up in the everyday life of a country predominantly non-Jewish, they had to modify many of their religious habits. It was no more possible for an office worker in Detroit or a shopkeeper in New York to go to *schul* four times a day to study than it was for the man in the plastics factory at Tel Aviv. But centuries of this scholastic background left an impression, if not on individuals at least on the culture.

The People of the Book

It is meet and right that the Jews have become known as "the People of the Book." (It was Mohammed who first gave Jews this nickname.) Judaism is a book religion, for to a Jew the Torah is all-important. The holy of holies in a Jewish synagogue, before which burns the eternal light, contains—a book! The picture of a European Jew that most often comes to mind—the picture that seems typical and symbolic—is of a man with an other-world look in his eyes, bending over a book, which he is avidly reading.

Statistics of American publishers prove that "the People of the Book" buy books—especially hardcovers—all out of proportion to their numbers.

In 1964 the oldest book club in America—the Jewish Publication Society—celebrated its 75th anniversary. Unlike other book clubs, this remarkable organization from its inception has been a non-profit institution bent on spreading Jewish culture in America. Its board has included individuals from all wings of Judaism and has drawn its authors from great and distinguished personalities of the modern world—from Israel Zangwill and Solomon Schechter to Mordecai Kaplan.

While all American Jews may not have heeded the advice of the medieval scholar who said, "Make thy books thy companions, let thy cases and shelves be thy pleasure grounds and gardens, bask in their paradise, gather their fruit, pluck their roses, take their spices and myrrh . . ." still it is rare to find a Jewish home in America, however modest, without a library, or a wall covered with books, or a stand of books, or at least some evidence that the family reads and values books.

A Renaissance of Jewishness

In the post-World War II period many Jewish writers suddenly discovered their Jewish roots. Ludwig Lewisohn had said, "A Jewish book is a book written by a man who knows he is a Jew." By that definition there were suddenly many more Jewish writers in America writing Jewish books than ever before. There was Henry Roth's story of immigrant life, *Call It Sleep*, described as "the novelist's attempt to reconcile the promise of historic Judaism with the evidence of modern enlightenment—the search for elevation that fails."

Laura Z. Hobson in *Gentlemen's Agreement* and Arthur Miller in *Focus* dealt with anti-Semitism. Irwin Shaw in *The Young Lions* wrote of the experiences of an American Jew in the Army. Herman Wouk's *Marjorie Morningstar* may have lacked depth, but the same writer's *This Is My God* gave hundreds of thousands of American non-Jews a sympathetic understanding of Orthodox Judaism. The best comment on the novels of Philip Roth is from the pen of critic Marie Syrkin: "The umbilical cord which ties the author to his Jewish past is torn with such violence that the clinical details of the rupture obscure every other element." Leon Uris' *Exodus* told the story of the struggle to create Israel with such intensity of action that it made millions of American Jews much prouder to be Jews and much happier that Israel had survived its birth pains.

Saul Bellow, whose *Herzog* was read by millions of Jews and non-Jews alike, became a controversial figure, one Jewish critic contending that "Judaism in his work is a source of nostalgia, but also of guilt and anxiety, rather than an enlarging or emancipating force." Others thought him inconsistent about his Jewishness.

In the theater Lillian Hellman, Arthur Miller, and Paddy Chayefsky were Jews writing as Jews, sometimes about Jewish subjects, while *Fiddler on the Roof*, based on the short stories of Sholom Aleichem, gave more non-Jewish Americans an understanding of the religious background of Jews than a hundred books could have done.

Alfred Kazin, although a proud Jew, is a man of extremely catholic interests, who writes of life and literature from the point of view of a world citizen.

Lectures, Music

Because of Judaism's stress of learning, scholarship, and intellectualism, America at large has benefited in numerous ways. For example, there are many small cities scattered across the country in which the only lecture series that brings live speakers into the community was established by and is still financed by the Jewish community center or some temple or synagogue group.

In 1967 the leading lecture bureau in New York made a survey

of its bookings over a long period of years and found that more than
25 percent of all serious lectures throughout the country are sponsored by Jewish groups, although the audience may be mixed.

Does music fall into the intellectual category and does it have
anything to do with Judaism? In the case of Leonard Bernstein, yes!
This distinguished Jewish conductor and composer, in his *Third
Symphony*, also known as the *Kaddish Symphony*, gave his personal
reactions to the theme of the traditional Hebrew prayer which is
recited in mourning for a deceased parent, brother, sister, or close
relative. Critics praised the religious nature of the work and called
it "almost a religious drama." It was written for a symphony or-
chestra, three choirs, and a narrator. Faced by the threat of nuclear
annihilation, hundreds of performers join in praise of God—a Kaddish for the dead (who may well be themselves), followed by the
narrator saying, "Did you hear that, Father? . . . Great God, surely
You who make peace on high can handily supply a touch of order
here below." In the second part the narrator is identified as the
Daughter of Zion—"that part of Man you made to suggest immortality." She complains to God that she has been exiled by man,
who seems in love with death and bent on his own destruction. In
the third part the narrator asks God to believe in man: "Oh God
. . . believe in me and You shall see the Kingdom of Heaven, just as
you planned." Many music critics reviewed Bernstein's theology
rather than his music.

In 1968 Jews comprised 2.85 percent of the population of the
United States, yet the percentage of Jews in the country's symphony
orchestras and on symphony boards was five or ten or even twenty
times 2.85.

Jewish Education for Almost All

Thus far in the twentieth century the Jewish population of the
United States has increased by 500 percent, but the number of
Jewish children enrolled in Jewish schools has increased by 1200
percent. In 1900 most Jewish children in America received their
religious instruction from private teachers. By 1925 *Talmud Torah*

schools run by the Jewish community were common. But by the middle 1960s the situation had drastically changed. Of the 600,000 Jewish children in school, all but 10 percent were attending schools run by individual synagogues or temples. Slightly more than 50,000 children, nearly all from Orthodox homes, were attending Day Schools, inaccurately called Jewish parochial schools, although they did provide instruction in the general subjects of a public school as well as Jewish studies. A majority were in the New York metropolitan area. Such schools saved the children from exposure to oblique Christian teaching and instilled a deep sense of Jewishness by the concentration on Hebrew studies, but they had the disadvantage of depriving the pupils of the broadening experience of going to school with children of other religions and backgrounds. Nearly 300,000 children—about half the total—were attending Sunday schools. The majority of this group were from Reform homes. The disadvantages of Sunday schools were that the teachers, who often were the mothers of some of the pupils, were relatively inexperienced, and in the two to two and a half hours a week were able to give the children only a sketchy introduction to their historical background. The remaining 40 percent—some 241,000—were attending afternoon schools that held from two to five sessions a week. Most of these pupils were from Conservative homes. The disadvantage of such schools was that after attending public school all day, the young pupils were often too tired to concentrate on their religious studies.

Jewish educators were proud, in the late 1960s, that more than 80 percent of all Jewish children in America received some sort of Jewish instruction at some time during their elementary school life.

At a higher level, modern Hebrew was being taught in close to a hundred public high schools in sixteen cities, while some 15,000 students in approximately fifty colleges and universities were studying the language of the prophets. Although Hebrew as a college course dates back to Colonial times, it was not until 1930 that it was first taught in a public high school. The first ninety-five boys and girls in two New York high schools who signed up for Hebrew were warned they might get no credit for the course, that there were no up-to-date textbooks and that there were few qualified teachers. In 1944 the first chair of Modern Hebrew was established at New York University and now students were able to major in Hebrew, Jewish culture, or Jewish education and receive B.A.s, M.A.s or doctoral degrees.

Yeshiva University

Although fewer than three out of every hundred people in the United States are Jews, eight out of every hundred students in America colleges and universities are Jews.

The oldest Jewish institution of higher learning is Yeshiva University in New York, which grew out of a merger of Etz Chaim and the Isaac Elhahan Theological Seminary. At first the curriculum followed the course of studies in yeshivahs all over Eastern Europe. (The word *yeshivah*, Hebrew for a traditional Jewish school, is normally spelled with a final *h*, whereas the university in New York is officially spelled without the final *h*. The Hebrew plural for yeshivah is *yeshivot*.)

Down through the years the Yeshiva, as it has come to be called (or simply Yeshiva, without the article) has continued to teach Orthodox Judaism, stressing the religious concept that the Law is the word of God; that observance of the Law is piety, and that Jewish learning is the road to piety. For the devout Orthodox student it is of little importance into what society he happens to be born. From the divine perspective, ages are as a single moment and only the Torah and the word of God are eternal.

Gradually, however, Yeshiva lost its original concept. When students rebelled against the European idea of study for the sake of study alone and demanded that some of the secular subjects taught in American high schools and colleges be added to the curriculum and that Yeshiva prepare them for the rabbinate, adjustments were made and Yeshiva became not only a rabbinical seminary, but also a high school and a college of liberal arts and sciences, in which students could pursue their studies "in an atmosphere harmonizing the age-old truths and ideals of faith and culture with the fruits of modern knowledge."

In 1945 the New York State Regents conferred university rank on the college and Yeshiva became the first American university under Jewish auspices. Five years later its charter was amended to permit establishment of a medical and dental school. When Albert Einstein College of Medicine of Yeshiva University was opened, it became the first medical school in the entire history of the Diaspora under Jewish sponsorship.

Yeshiva has conferred honorary degrees upon such eminent Jews as Albert Einstein, Herbert H. Lehman, Benjamin Cardozo, Bernard Baruch, and Abba Eban and on such distinguished non-Jews as Jan Masaryk and Harlan Fiske Stone. Since its first commencement, its graduates have made notable contributions to Judaism, to America, and to humanity. Yeshiva has grown with America and, although clinging to the basic precepts of Judaism, has modified some of the nineteenth-century ideas of the immigrants from the Pale of the Settlement.

(While the New York Yeshiva remained until the present day the largest and most important institution of its kind in the country, numerous other yeshivot were established, some of them playing important roles in Orthodox Judaism.)

Brandeis, Stern, Dropsie

There were several post-World War II educational developments of great significance. In 1948 Brandeis University was established at Waltham, Massachusetts, largely through the efforts of Dr. Abram Sachar, former national director of Hillel Foundation, who became the university's first president. Unlike the Yeshiva, Brandeis is non-sectarian, although financed almost exclusively by Jews. Students are admitted without regard to race or religion, and professors are chosen on the same basis. Its department of Jewish Studies is by now world-famous, but no attempt is made to indoctrinate the students. In 1954 Stern College for Women was founded—the first liberal arts college for women in the United States under Jewish auspices. It is one of the colleges of Yeshiva University and is the counterpart of Yeshiva College, the arts and sciences college for men. In 1954 the student body numbered thirty-three. For the 1967–68 academic year there were in excess of six hundred students. A $4,000,000 apartment hotel was taken over as a dormitory for out-of-town students, and a police station more than a hundred years old was acquired and remodeled to provide classroom and administrative space.

Following the war Dropsie College in Philadelphia, established for graduate study in Hebrew and related friends, underwent considerable expansion.

Hillel Keeps Jews Jews

In the late 1960s, 350,000 Jewish students—about 80 percent of the Jewish college-age population—were attending colleges and universities in the United States or some foreign country. (There were, for example, many American Jews in the University of Geneva, Switzerland, studying medicine, because the quota system in some American medical schools denies admittance to all but a limited number of Jewish applicants.) On more than seventy American campuses Jewish students are kept aware of their Jewishness by a Hillel Foundation, with a full-time professional director.

Hillel was inspired by a Christian professor, at the University of Illinois, who, in 1923, was disturbed that several thousand Jewish students at the university had such little knowledge of, or interest in, their Jewish heritage. Some were even trying to pass as non-Jews. The challenge he threw out was taken up by Benjamin Frankel, a rabbinical student who was serving the Jewish congregation in the university town of Urbana as a part-time rabbi and who interested B'nai B'rith in organizing some Jewish activity on the campus.

The program was so successful at Urbana that it was extended to many other colleges in towns and cities that had too small a Jewish community to be able to care for the social and religious needs of the Jewish students. At first many Jewish students protested that a Hillel Foundation on their campus would unnecessarily draw attention to their Jewishness and would create anti-Semitism. In actual experience Hillel has improved the position of Jewish students on all seventy campuses, in addition to training many for Jewish leadership in their home communities after graduation. While most of the directors are rabbis, Hillel follows a non-denominational policy. Both Reform and Traditional services are provided, as well as various social and intellectual activities. In many colleges where the number of Jewish students does not warrant a full-time Hillel operation, a part-time counselor serves the students.

Late in the last century the Menorah Society was formed at Harvard and developed into the Menorah Association, with emphasis on the intellectual definition of Jewish life. The Avukah Society was organized on a number of campuses, principally to interest students, politically and intellectually, in Zionism.

Emphasis on Learning

Besides being a place of worship and prayer, every Jewish religious building in America—be it Reform temple or Orthodox or Conservative synagogue—is also an intellectual center. In most of them there are groups of people, young and old, every night of the week, engaged in studying, learning, improving the mind in one way or another. In extremely Orthodox synagogues there are still study tables placed where the light is best, giving the building much more the appearance of a study hall than a place of worship. Immediately after the destruction of the First Temple that is exactly what the meeting places of the Jews were, in Judea and Babylon—houses for the study of law. Only gradually did they become places in which prayers were said for the restoration of the Temple and then, finally, houses of worship. But they have never lost, even in America, their characteristic as places of study.

Even those American Jews who are not especially inclined intellectually themselves—and there are some, of course—as a rule have respect for learning, for learning and their religion are interwoven.

(The Talmud says: "The ignorant hate scholars more than the heathen hate Jews.")

26

SEEK YE THE PEACE!

In the Hebrew Bible, the word *shalom* appears 309 times. Often it is the cry of a war-weary populace, yearning for peace when there is no peace or even a distant hope of peace. Often it is the prediction of the prophet who holds out to his people God's promise of peace if they will mend their ways. Just as *shalom* today in Israel is more than merely the Hebrew word for peace but is said repeatedly throughout the day as a salutation, so in ancient times *shalom* meant much more than just the absence of slaughter and destruction. It described the wellbeing of individuals and groups alike. It meant personal harmony and tranquillity. It stood for freedom from fear and moral conflict. It encompassed public order and security.

In biblical times war was the normal way of life. Israel was not at all unlike other nations in this respect. She was almost continually involved in military activity. There were defensive wars and wars of adventure, civil wars, and revolutions. Again and again Israel fought battles in the name of God. If there were defeats it was because God was displeased. Israel's history, like that of her neighbors, was largely an account of wars lost and wars won.

The Vision—Peace

But even in those times the prophet Isaiah, who wrote so much about military matters, had his vision.

"And the wolf shall dwell with the lamb, and the leopard shall lie down with the kid; and the calf and the young lion and the fatling together; and a little child shall lead them. And the cow and the bear shall feed; their young ones shall lie down together; and the lion shall eat straw like the ox."

And then his most often quoted words: ". . . and they shall beat their swords into plowshares, and their spears into pruning hooks; Nation shall not lift up sword against nation, neither shall they learn war any more."

The prophet Micah, a contemporary of Isaiah, used the identical words, but added a picturesque vision of peace: "But they shall sit every man under his vine and under his fig tree; and none shall make them afraid; for the mouth of the Lord of hosts hath spoken."

It was the vision—the dream—of the wise men of Israel. Nevertheless, wars continued until finally Israel was utterly destroyed in the year 70 and the holy city Jerusalem was laid in ruins, and the Temple was no more. It was then that universal peace began to acquire real meaning for the people of Israel. Now they, like Micah and Isaiah, began to dream of a time when God would demolish the fortifications and destroy the armaments of man, and the treasures amassed by war and violence would be wiped out, and the pruning hook actually would replace the sword, and men really could sit under their vine trees instead of wasting their lives in military nonsense.

Peace—But with Justice

In the Midrash and the Talmud Judaism began to develop its concept of peace. Peace and justice must go hand in hand. Peace must be dynamic, constructive. Peace must be universal—not for Israel alone but for all nations. Gradually peace became one of the most sacred of Judaism's teachings.

Through all the centuries when those who merely talked of peace as a positive policy were often considered subversive, Judaism continued to preach and discuss peace in its synagogues and in religious and secular writings. Azariah Rossi, sixteenth-century Italian physician and scholar, wrote:

"All the peoples of the earth should know that while we, the remnant of Israel, live in dispersion, we are obliged, according to the words of the Prophets and the tradition of the Fathers, to pray for the peace and welfare of the state that rules over us. At the present time above all, when for our sins we are scattered to the four winds, it is our duty to supplicate Almighty God for the peace of all the inhabitants of the world, that no people may lift up the sword against another . . . and that He may remove from their hearts all strife and hatred, implanting instead peace in the world: for in their peace we too have peace."

Belligerency or Brotherhood

That was where Judaism stood on belligerency and brotherhood when history began forcing the Jews of America to take a position on questions of war or peace. In the Revolutionary and Civil wars, American Jews took sides just as other Americans did, and fought and suffered and died. Also in World War I. Yet between wars—and even during all the American wars—the pacifistic influence of Judaism made itself felt.

Rabbi Stephen Wise was one of a great many members of the Central Conference of American Rabbis who took a bold pacifist stand during World War I, until the United States became actively involved. Then he draped the pulpit of his Free Synagogue with an American flag and told his congregation it would remain there "until the morning of the dawn of peace for humanity." After the war he was one of those who helped draft a resolution passed by the Central Conference saying: "We give assurance to President Wilson of our fullest support in the establishment of the League of Nations and in his strivings to bring forth a just peace for mankind."

Wilson failed, however, in obtaining American adherence to the League. This and other events of the 1920s disillusioned Rabbi

Wise to the extent that he publicly apologized for having abandoned his pacifism and promised "without reservation or equivocation never to bless or support any war whatsoever again."

Straus and Peace

Oscar Straus, who became the first Jewish cabinet member when President Theodore Roosevelt appointed him head of the newly created Department of Commerce and Labor, was an ardent supporter of President Wilson's ideas for peace after the war, and worked with Wilson at Paris in 1918–19 to make the covenant of the League of Nations part of the Versailles Treaty.

After the Senate refused to permit the United States to join the League, Salmon Levinson, a Jewish lawyer in Chicago, published a plan for *The Outlawry of War*, which became the basis for the Kellogg-Briand Pact, signed at Paris in 1928 by fifteen nations that thereby solemnly agreed to renounce war in all their future relations with one another. In 1931 the Union of American Hebrew Congregations formally endorsed it.

Then Came Hitler

In the early 1930s American Jews joined with some non-Jews who were sensitive about what was happening in Europe and tried to campaign for a lowering of immigration bars to admit to America at least some of the hundreds of thousands of Central European Jews who wanted to get out before it was too late. They failed. Miserably. They had better success in raising money to help the relatively few who were able to escape what would so soon become Hitler's continent. Between 1933 and 1943—the critical years for European Jewry—the United States admitted only 168,000 Jewish refugees from Europe, less than 2 percent of the total. This immigration wave was unlike any that had come before. These were not "your poor, your huddled masses." These refugees were no "wretched refuse." Because the United States in most cases hand-picked just whom they would admit, the 168,000 constituted what one observer called "the greatest flight of talent the world had ever known." Among them were university professors, actors, actresses, scientists, musicians, and twelve future Nobel Prize winners. They were welcomed, of course, by all sections of American Jewry, for *these* immigrants could not possibly be a source of embarrassment for anyone.

Then came the fighting war. Rabbi Wise remembered his pledge with anguish. Was there no way to stop Hitler's madness short of war? The New York rabbi was not the only Jewish pacifist caught on the horns of that dilemma.

Jews As Belligerents

Never in any other American war had Jews played such prominent roles. Sixteen became either admirals or generals. Ten thousand of the 600,000 who fought on the various fronts were decorated for heroic action. Major General Maurice Rose, son of a synagogue functionary in Denver, Colorado, as commander of the 3rd Armored Division helped liberate Belgium, and was the first army commander since Napoleon to invade the German Reich from the west. His division was the first to breach the Siegfried Line and the first American unit to capture a German town. Sergeant Meyer Levin put a Japanese battleship out of commission early in the war. Lieutenant Frances Y. Slanger, a Jewish girl from Boston, was the first U. S. Army nurse killed on the Western Front, after having cared for three thousand men. Because of her, B'nai B'rith contributed $2000 to a nationwide campaign to erect a national Nurses' Memorial Home in Washington, D.C., in memory of nurses who gave their lives in the war.

Finally came victory and peace. But 1,500,000 people who had no place to go were in displaced persons camps, a sizable percentage of them Jews. Now Jewish individuals and organizations in America joined in another campaign to open the gates—a little. It was not until the spring of 1948 that a Displaced Persons Act was finally passed. In signing it President Truman said he did so with reluctance, because the bill was "flagrantly discriminatory," against Jews, as well as Catholics. By the time the act expired four years later only 63,000 Jews had been admitted.

These new immigrants were quickly absorbed. After a year or two the haunted look disappeared from their eyes, their bodies became almost normal again, and they found places in American Jewish society. It was only when a certain place in Poland or Germany was mentioned, or when a sleeve was rolled up and the tattooed numbers showed, that one would even guess.

Jews and Internationalism

Even before the fighting stopped, there was agitation within Jewish religious circles in favor of some sort of world body to try to keep the peace. The Central Conference of American Rabbis in 1944 adopted a resolution: "We hail preliminary plans announced for a democratic world organization to include small nations. We favor the establishment of an international assembly of nations which would create a body of international laws and which would have the power to enforce them. We urge such international cooperation on the highest religious grounds."

After the creation of the United Nations, it had no more ardent supporters than American Jews, who had many more reasons than non-Jewish Americans for being interested in the success of this new experiment in internationalism. A poll of a cross-section of Americans showed that the Jews questioned had a far greater interest in international affairs than the others. The American rabbinate—Orthodox, Conservative, and Reform alike—had consistently advocated international peace guaranteed by world government, for by tradition the absolute sovereignty of the national state is an obscenity in Jewish eyes. ("God alone is sovereign; no other sovereignty can be absolute.")

It is not an accident that after medicine, the greatest proportion of Jewish Nobel Prize winners have received the award for their services to peace.

During America's long involvement in Vietnam, rabbis and Jewish laymen alike were prominent in the opposition, delivering sermons, issuing statements, introducing resolutions, signing newspaper ads, helping to organize marches of protest—aimed at either halting the bombing of North Vietnam, stopping the escalation of the war, encouraging peace talks, or ending the entire adventure by bringing American troops home. Often, being the individualists they are, they disagreed on methods, but they were concerted in their desire to prevent what had once been a civil war in Vietnam from triggering World War III.

Orthodox rabbis often quote in their prayers for peace the words from the Book of Psalms which Prime Minister Eshkol used when he was greeted by President Johnson on his arrival in Texas in 1968: "Peace, peace shall come to the nigh and to the far. . . ."

27

SHE WORKETH WILLINGLY

ANCIENT Israel was part of the Orient and it is therefore not surprising that Jews in that time and in that part of the world were affected by the oriental attitude toward women. Yet the Bible gives proof that women often played important roles in early Jewish society. Two books of the Bible are titled with women's names. Stories of Jewish queens and Jewish heroines are sprinkled through the biblical narrative. The Talmud gives women certain special rights. In many historic periods the status of Jewish women in Palestine was superior to that of women in other societies—even the Greek.

But Orthodox Judaism, in America in modern times, as well as elsewhere in the past, has also imposed certain restrictions, the most obvious being the separation of men and women during religious services. The early American synagogues, copied after those abroad, were built with a balcony for the women and even there they were often hidden from any chance masculine stares by a screen or a curtain. This seating arrangement was often modified within a single synagogue with a change of rabbis. In one California synagogue, the women for years were seated in a curtained-off balcony. Then, after a change of rabbis, the curtain was removed. Later the balcony was demolished and the women were seated on the ground floor, but in two sections along each side of the synagogue, raised a few inches above the level of the men's pews. With another change of rabbis a railing that had separated the men's and women's sections was eliminated. Then the level of the seats was equalized.

Women in the Pulpit

Historians consider it possible that women functioned as lay readers
of separate women's services in such third-century and fourth-cen-
tury synagogues as Bet Alpha and Caesaria. In general, however,
no woman could function as a traditional rabbi because certain of
the commandments which the rabbi follows on behalf of the congregation are optional for a woman, and consequently she could not
properly represent those for whom they are mandatory. However,
there is no reason in Reform Judaism why a woman could not be
ordained and perform all rabbinical functions.

The first woman to be graduated from a recognized rabbinical
school in America was Helen Leventhal Lyons, who completed the
regular course of study prescribed by the rabbinate in the Jewish
Institute of Religion before it merged with Hebrew Union College.
Her father, Dr. Israel Leventhal, was rabbi of the Brooklyn Jewish
Center, and her grandfather, Rabbi Bernard Leventhal of Philadel-
phia, had been dean of the Orthodox rabbinate in America. Mrs.
Lyons, however, was never ordained.

In 1950, for the first time in America, a woman became the
spiritual head of a congregation. When Rabbi William Ackerman,
the rabbi of Temple Beth Israel in Meridian, Mississippi, died his
fifty-seven-year-old widow, Paula, was appointed to take his place.
The only precedent in the entire long history of Judaism, here and
abroad, was that for nineteen years an English Jewess, Mrs. Lily
Montague, had served as the spiritual head of a Reform temple
in London. In the case of Mrs. Ackerman, a special ruling of Reform
Judaism gave her the full powers of a rabbi and the State of
Mississippi gave her the right to perform marriages.

This narrative has already been sprinkled with the names of American Jewesses who have played important roles in the 314-year story
of Judaism in America. Emma Lazarus distinguished herself as a
Jewish intellectual; Henrietta Szold and Lillian Wald as humanitarians; others in related fields. America has offered Jewish women

an emancipation impossible abroad, and Jewish women, in return, have given America some noteworthy examples of leadership-for-the-good.

Where There's a Woman

Hannah Solomon, daughter of one of the earliest Jewish families to settle in Chicago, was only four feet six inches tall, but she had large ideas and great ambitions. In 1893 she was asked to organize the participation of the Jewish women of America in the world's fair called the Columbian Exposition. The Congress of Jewish Women which she formed, almost alone, the next year became the National Council of Jewish Women. In 1968, as it celebrated its seventy-fifth birthday, the Council had approximately 100,000 members, organized into some 287 units across the country.

Hannah Solomon, writing of the new-type American woman that she and her Council were helping to create, described her in these words: "She is the woman who dares go into the world and do what her convictions demand." The Council woman was doing something else: she was putting her Judaism to work in a manner that would have pleased the prophets of old: she was being "a light unto the nations."

A set of resolutions passed by the fledgling Council gave these aims: "To unite women interested in the work of Religion, Philanthropy and Education; to organize and encourage a study of the principles of Judaism, the history, literature and customs of the Jews, and their bearing on world history; to apply knowledge gained in this study to the improvement of Sabbath Schools, and in the work of social reform; to secure the interest and aid of influential persons to prevent persecutions."

This new force in American Judaism during its first seventy-five years worked with the poor and the homeless, with the blind, the deaf and the mentally retarded, with the sick and the aged, with refugees and immigrants, with those who dwelt in prisons, hospitals, slums, and D.P. camps; with Negroes, Mexicans, Puerto Ricans, and Orientals, as well as Jews; even with dope addicts and dropouts.

The members campaigned for better immigration and public health laws, for an end to prostitution and child labor, for anti-lynch laws, for improved public education. They enlisted in the fight for civil rights and in the war on poverty. Their pre-school program paved the way for Operation Headstart; their Golden Age Clubs led to the creation of the Senior Service Corps. They supported the League of Nations and then its successor, the United Nations, and missed no opportunity to work for world peace. They never seemed to worry whether a cause was popular or socially accepted.

When the scourge of McCarthyism swept the country, the Council spoke out boldly, at a time when many others were hiding behind noncommittal platitudes. In 1951, charging that "the greatest domestic problem in this country is not communism but McCarthyism," the Council launched a freedom campaign with the slogan: "Speak Up! Freedom Needs Exercise!" On the local as well as the national level Council members began administering antidotes to the poison. After a Minute Woman had gone through a library in San Antonio, Texas, stamping *Red Reading* on books that for some reason or another displeased her, the San Antonio Section of the Council put on an exhibition of great books that had been banned through the ages. The idea was an instant success and the exhibit went on the road, available wherever people wanted to resist blacklisting, censoring, and other forms of McCarthyism. "Freedom to Read" became one more Council motto.

As part of its seventy-fifth anniversary celebration the Council published a book, *Where There's a Woman*, demonstrating in dramatic words and photographs the unique role that this Jewish group has had in helping to shape the history of America from the days of bustles to the days of miniskirts.

The Healing of the Daughter of My People

Hadassah, the Women's Zionist Organization of America, was founded in New York City by thirty-eight American Jewish women, headed by Henrietta Szold. Today, with a membership of more than 318,000 in 1350 chapters and groups throughout the United

States and Puerto Rico, it is the largest individual Zionist organization in the world.

The nucleus for Hadassah was a small study group and its objectives were to carry on medical work in Palestine, enhance Zionism and the Jewish heritage in America, as well as to encourage members to fulfill their responsibilities of U.S. citizenship.

In 1913 Hadassah sent two American-trained nurses to Palestine, set up a small welfare station in the old city of Jerusalem for maternity care and the treatment of trachoma, the dread eye disease then the scourge of the Middle East. This marked the inauguration of a Hadassah health program which was directly responsible for the fact that Israel by 1968 would enjoy the highest health standards in the Middle East. In 1918, a medical unit sponsored by Hadassah and the Joint Distribution Committee, comprising forty-five physicians, dentists, nurses, and other technicians, reached the Holy Land and hospitals were opened in Jerusalem, Jaffa, Haifa, Safed, Tiberias, and Tel Aviv.

In 1939 on Mount Scopus, on the edge of Jerusalem, Hadassah opened an ultra-modern hospital, entirely financed by American Jewish women. Throughout World War II it was used by Allied authorities for research, diagnosis, and treatment of tropical diseases. In May 1948, following the murder by Arabs of Dr. Haim Yassky, director-general of the Hadassah Medical Organization, and seventy-six of his colleagues and members of the Hebrew University faculty, while en route to Mount Scopus, the Medical Center had to be evacuated. Later, Mount Scopus was placed under UN protection.

In 1949 Hadassah opened Israel's first undergraduate medical school. By 1968, with a student body of eight hundred, the school had already given Israel a corps of expertly trained physicians. From 1948 until the opening of the new Hadassah-Hebrew University Medical Center in 1961, Hadassah conducted its medical activities in five temporary hospitals in Jerusalem.

The new medical center is on a 300-acre site in the Judean Hills, overlooking the ancient town of Ein Karem. It comprises a 600-bed teaching hospital; clinics handling more than 250,000 patient-visits annually; a synagogue housing the world-famous stained-glass windows Marc Chagall created for Hadassah, and many other pavilions, schools, and installations. Hadassah medical teams are at work in such countries as Liberia, Ethiopia, Sierra Leone, and Tanzania, while medical and nursing students from those and other countries are being trained by Hadassah at Ein Karem.

Among the first shells fired by Jordan in 1967 into Israeli territory were those which hit the Hadassah-Hebrew University Medical Center. Hadassah doctors went into action in the Sinai, treating hundreds of civilian and military casualties, including captured Arab soldiers. In the aftermath of the victory, the installations on top of Mount Scopus, which had been empty for nineteen years, were returned to Hadassah and will be used as a rehabilitation center for civilians as well as military personnel.

There is much more to the Hadassah story. Plans are always underway for more extensive medical activities. The details are not pertinent to a history of Judaism in America, but it *is* significant that these 318,000 American Jewish women, recognizing their religion's emphasis on social justice, devote so much of their time, money, and energy to projects that serve as concrete examples of Judaism-in-action.

28

AMERICAN JUDAISM TODAY

Half of all the Jews in the world outside of Israel—approximately 5,721,000—were living in the United States in 1968. Most of them were in the large cities: in New York and its suburbs 2,687,680 or nearly 47 percent; in Los Angeles, Philadelphia, Chicago, and Boston another 23 percent of the total. Yet there were Jews in every one of the 50 states, even in Alaska (190) and Hawaii (1000).

There were 669 Reform congregations, 800 Conservative, and 3200 Orthodox, some of which, however, had a very limited membership.

Even before Hitler's attempt at genocide, the Jews of America had become the leaders of world Jewry by virtue of their numbers, their wealth, and the strength of their combined voice. Although they had failed in their attempt to open the country's gates more than a crack to let in victims of the Nazi madness, after World War II the Jews of the world looked to them for spiritual, moral, and financial help in dealing with all the post-war problems that international Jewry faced. And the American Jews bore the responsibility honorably.

At home a religious revival occurred, perhaps connected in some ways with the shock of what had happened to the six million in Europe, and with the euphoric effect of Israel's creation and survival. Hundreds of new congregations were organized, especially in the burgeoning suburban areas. A synagogue-building boom began unprecedented in the entire history of the Diaspora. Brilliant Jewish and non-Jewish architects vied with each other in designing structures that would be bold, inspiring, and beautiful. Vast sums were raised with little difficulty, not only for the synagogues themselves but also for ancillary buildings.

Thou Shalt Not Defame

The curve of anti-Semitism in America had many ups and downs during the 1930s, 1940s, 1950s, and 1960s. The high point came during the Depression years when Father Charles Edward Coughlin by air and Gerald L. K. Smith by the written word spread their poison across the country. Some people were actually led to believe that Franklin D. Roosevelt had changed his name from Rosenfeld, while his New Deal was nicknamed "the Jew Deal." As economic troubles slowly vanished, America was torn by conflicting opinions about Hitler and Mussolini. The America First organizations spread the whisper that no one would benefit from a war against the Nazis and Fascists except "the international conspiracy of Jews." After the war the extremism and stupidities of the McCarthy period led to another surge of anti-Semitism.

Late in 1959 and during the early 1960s the country was plagued by a swastika epidemic. The Nazi emblem was smeared on synagogues, temples, Jewish community centers and the homes of rabbis and Jewish laymen. Hate slogans were scrawled on school blackboards, store windows, and the walls of public toilets. Bricks and bottles were thrown through synagogue windows. Jews and those who expressed sympathy and understanding for the Jews received bomb threats—and some were carried out. Many of the incidents were traced to organizations of boys and young men who looked on the deceased Hitler as their hero.

The swastika epidemic was followed by something even more serious. Suddenly—almost like a man looking out the front window one morning and seeing his lawn covered with toadstools—the country awoke to the fact that the rich soil of American freedom had spawned an ugly crop of more than a thousand extremist right-wing organizations that were reaching millions of gullible people with their propaganda, especially by radio. Some were openly and obviously anti-Semitic. Others did it more subtly. This was the

Era of Neo-Naziism, not only in America but around the world. While the Orthodox, Conservative, and Reform branches of Judaism still disagreed—sometimes heatedly—on such matters as *minhag*, they closed ranks and presented a united front to these peddlers of hate. National organizations of Jewish men, women, and youth attacked with various weapons. One of the best-organized and most effective opponents of anti-Semitism was, and is, B'nai B'rith's Anti-Defamation League, organized in 1913 for the specific purpose of combating anti-Semitism by correcting falsehoods that are broadcast, printed or uttered in public, and by distributing accurate information about Judaism and Jews. Its mission was: thou shalt not defame!

Israel, a Stimulant

The American Council for Judaism was formed in 1942 by a group of rabbis but before long it became an organization principally of laymen, many of them wealthy. Their *bête noir* was the idea of Jewish nationalism. Immediately after World War II, when it became obvious that the promise of the Balfour Declaration was soon going to be kept, the Council concentrated its fire on the proposal for a Jewish state.

Extreme Orthodoxy in America, and even in Palestine itself, was against any man-attempt to reconstitute a Jewish state, on the ground that Israel would be revived by divine means, at the time of the coming of the Messiah. The two Reform bodies in America—the Central Conference of American Rabbis and the Union of American Hebrew Congregations—had both opposed Zionism for quite different reasons. They felt that the Jews had a mission in the Diaspora. They argued that millions of Jews had put their roots down in America and wished to remain here, and that agitation for a return to Palestine fanned the sparks of anti-Semitism into damaging flames. So both organizations passed resolutions against Zionism. But in 1935 the CCAR repealed its resolutions against Zionism, and two years later the UAHC did likewise. During the 1930s and 1940s, however, many individual American Jews remained anti-Zionist.

The American Jewish Congress, the Zionist Organization of America, Hadassah, many other organizations, and hundreds of individuals—rabbis and Jewish lay leaders alike—played important, sometimes spectacular roles in bringing Israel into being and making sure that she had the armaments and finances she needed to win the struggle for existence that began on the day of her birth. This is no place to retell that story, even though golden threads of American Judaism are woven through the fabric.

It is important to know, however, that what even discrimination and persecution had failed to do, the triumph of modern Israel now did. Nothing had ever united American Jewry like this. People to whom the very word *Zionism* had been anathema rejoiced with those who had worked a lifetime to help bring it about. Suddenly they were no longer Zionists and anti-Zionists, or members of Orthodox, Conservative, or Reform congregations, but Jews all of them —Jews who no longer needed to say, "Next year in Jerusalem!" Israel lived again and Jerusalem was her capital. Only a few extremists remained aloof from the celebrating—those who thought it was a mistake not to have waited for divine intervention, and those who wanted no Jewish homeland ever, under any circumstances, not even to give the homeless survivors of the Nazi fury a place to live out their lives in peace.

Help for Many Causes

At one time early in its existence, Israel had twenty-one political parties, and most of them had American counterparts—organizations, of men, often with affiliated women's organizations, that raised money for projects in Israel, sought recruits for their kibbutzim, and tried to spread the party's ideological precepts. The most successful fund-raisers have been the National Committee for Labor Israel and Pioneer Women, which send millions of dollars a year to Israel to support the vocational training, health, and immigrant welfare programs of the Israel General Federation of Labor—Histadrut. The Mizrachi and Mizrachi Women combine support of Israel with unswerving Orthodoxy. Israel's Revisionists had powerful and militant backing in the United States in the days when their underground arm, the Irgun, was engaged in such activities as smuggling shiploads of illegal immigrants into Palestine and in other ways harassing the British. Ben Hecht, the novelist and playwright, was the guiding light of the Revisionist organization in America and largely through his efforts a national committee was formed—the American League for a Free Palestine—which included several hundred Senators, Congressmen, Governors, and other leading citizens, Jews and non-Jews alike. This committee's work culminated in sending a ship called the *Altalena* to Israel during one of the 1948 armistices, loaded with 500 tons of arms and ammunition of the Irgun that had cost the committee members $4,000,000.

Six Voices That Speak As One

Despite differences of belief and practice between Orthodox, Conservative, and Reform Jews, the three groups came together in 1926 to form the Synagogue Council of America. This loose federation was largely the creation of Dr. Abram Simon, then president of the Central Conference of American Rabbis. He argued that while organized Jewish religion of America might continue to revolve around each individual synagogue or temple, there was need of a body which could speak for Judaism as a whole on issues about which all were in agreement. Six groups are represented on the Council: the laymen and the rabbinate of Orthodoxy and of Conservative and Reform Judaism. All six have the right of veto, thus assuring absolute unanimity when the Council speaks publicly. Throughout the years the Council has found many matters on which it could speak with a single, loud, clear voice for united Judaism.

On the local level Community Councils were formed, with all the synagogues and temples of a community cooperating, as well as all the Jewish clubs, societies, and other organizations. Such Councils engage in fund-raising, social service activities, and cultural and educational work. In the larger communities the Councils bring together Jews who might otherwise have had little or no contact with each other. Those Councils that are adequately financed employ a professional staff, and many have become paragons of efficiency.

Giving Without Precedent

Jewish federations were models for the hundreds of Community Chests formed around the country during the 1920s and 1930s. Jewish philanthropic organizations generally cooperated, but there were many causes that could not possibly share in the distribution of the Community Chest money, such as the relief of Palestine Jews, so in the large Jewish communities Jewish Welfare Funds were formed, to consolidate fund-raising for strictly Jewish causes. But there were still conflicts, especially in raising money for Palestine. In 1925 a number of Palestine-centered groups merged their fund-raising efforts and formed the United Palestine Appeal. More than $2,500,000 was raised the first year—much more than the total receipts of the constituent bodies the previous year. The conflict now was between UPA and the Joint Distribution Committee and local welfare drives. Finally, in 1939, the United Jewish Appeal was formed to consolidate fund-raising still further. In its first drive UJA raised $15,000,000—more than twice what American Jewry had given the previous year for the same work.

No five million people anywhere in the world have ever given as American Jews have in the years since 1939. There were peaks at the time of the creation of the State of Israel and during the crisis of 1956, but the ultimate in spontaneous, enthusiastic giving occurred in May and June 1967, before, during, and just after the Six-Day War, when outright gifts of more than $185,000,000 were made to UJA and $40,000,000 to Hadassah and several other organizations interested in Israel, while $175,000,000 worth of Israel Bonds were purchased during the emergency, a grand total of $400,-000,000. (These emergency figures are as reported by the New York *Times*. Nearly a year later no *official* figures had as yet been announced by any of the organizations involved.)

Despite all the consolidations of fund-raising, there are still many Jewish organizations that are not under the Welfare Fund or UJA umbrella and do their own soliciting. Between them they raise tens of millions of dollars a year. Notable among them are Hadassah, the Council of Jewish Women, Hebrew University, Yeshiva University, the Albert Einstein College of Medicine, the Yiddish Research Institute, ZOA, Histadrut. Then there is the Development Corporation for Israel, which in the first sixteen years of its existence sold well over one billion dollars' worth of bonds.

Swimming Pools and Sanctuaries

The Jewish Center movement, which blossomed during the mid-twentieth century, grew out of the desire of many American Jews to retain their Jewish identity, independently of any connection or lack of connection with synagogue or temple. A typical center has one or more swimming pools, a gymnasium, a library, an auditorium and rooms in which classes can be held in subjects ranging from Bible studies, Yiddish literature, and Jewish history to psychedelic art. Most centers have been helpful in encouraging Jewish group loyalty.

To compete with independent community centers, many Orthodox and Conservative synagogues and Reform temples have established their own centers, hoping that the proximity of a swimming pool to the sanctuary will encourage young American Jews to be more frequent in their attendance at religious services.

Kosher Is As Kosher Does

Despite the religious revival, the post-war period found fewer American Jews strictly observing the dietary laws. Some Orthodox families have adopted a dual standard, with a domestic policy and a foreign policy that are different. Within their own homes they live kosher, following all the laws, but outside the house they ignore the dietary laws because of the complications involved.

Many Jewish hospitals, supported by funds from Orthodox, Conservative, and Reform groups, have stopped serving kosher meals to their patients, unless a specific request is made. Even in such large cities as New York, each year there were fewer strictly kosher restaurants. But at the same time, the number of companies making rabbinically approved products has more than doubled. By 1968 more than 500 companies were manufacturing close to 3000 products under the supervision of the Union of Orthodox Congregations. On the list were even kosher chow mein and *Original Kosher Krispy Pizza.*

One strange influence of Judaism is in the food field. Sociologists call it *transculturation.* When Italians contributed spaghetti and pizza to the American gastronomy, religion was in no way involved. But when American supermarkets began selling *matzah,* kosher hot dogs, kosher corned beef, kosher pickles, and even kosher bacon (actually beef but resembling bacon in appearance and to some extent in flavor) it could be said that Judaism was directly affecting what non-Jewish America was eating. During the Passover season, hundreds of thousands of non-Jews in New York each year eat "Passover-type" dishes in "Jewish style" or "kosher type" restaurants. The Jewish culinary contribution also includes borsht, blintzes, and potato pancakes, although these have little if any religious connection. Some Jewish-style restaurants, however, have departed from anything that would be approved by an Orthodox rabbi. In the *Kosher Korner* of a Cleveland restaurant meat and dairy dishes were mixed indiscriminately, and the menu contained such items as shrimp cocktail and baked Virginia ham, along with cheese blintzes and sour cream, chopped liver with potato salad and stuffed kishke.

Orthodoxy, Hasidism, and Uniqueness

The ranks of Orthodox Jews in America were augmented and refreshed after World War II by the arrival of tens of thousands of extremely Orthodox Jews—the remnant of East European Jewry. In general they exerted a revitalizing influence on American Orthodoxy. The vast majority, while permitting nothing to vitiate their religion, did undergo rapid assimilation into American life, adopting the language, the daily customs, and the dress of other Americans.

However, the Hasidic Jews, settling in all-Jewish neighborhoods such as the Williamsburg section of Brooklyn, went on living their lives as if they were still in their old villages in Poland or the Balkan countries. They grouped themselves around a rabbi who had arrived with them and whose word was law in civil as well as religious matters. The men refused to shave off their long bushy beards or to shear their *payos* and the young women, upon marriage, cut off their hair and put on the *sheitel*, which may well have been the ancestor of the wig that suddenly became popular with most American women in the 1960s. The men continued to wear their broad-brimmed fur-trimmed hats or on Shabbat circular fur hats, and black coats that reach far below the knees. (Hundreds of years ago Polish men of distinction—non-Jewish—wore just such garments, but Jews, even if they were men of distinction, were forbidden to wear them, and so, generations later, after men's styles changed and such garments were no longer worn in Poland, they were adopted by Jews who took pleasure in finally being able to wear such elegant coats.)

Jews themselves tell the story of a Hasidic Jew from Williamsburg who made a trip to a small town in the Deep South. As he stepped off the bus, a crowd of local boys followed him down the street, laughing at his beard, curls, and peculiar garb. Bearing it as long as he could, the man finally wheeled around on the youngsters and in a heavy Eastern Europe accent asked:

"What's the matter, haven't you ever seen a Yankee?"

Religion was the essence and the substance of life for these Hasidic Jews—and still is for tens of thousands of them. They pray at frequent intervals and spend many of the remaining hours of the day in religious study. On certain religious holidays they devote themselves to wild, ecstatic rejoicing.

Judaism As a Civilization

In 1934 a Conservative rabbi, Mordecai Kaplan, a member of the faculty of the Jewish Theological Seminary, offered American Jews a new religious idea—a people-oriented theology. He called the 600-page book in which he set forth his principles *Judaism As a Civilization*. Thirty-four years later it was still in print and being widely sold. In it Kaplan frequently used the expression "Jewish peoplehood." He wrote that Judaism is not a religion, as most people understood that word, but a religious civilization. He defined

God as "the power that makes for salvation because we believe
in the power that makes for salvation." ("We can no longer believe
that God is a mighty sovereign, or that the universe is the work of
His Hands.") He considered Israel the hub of the Jewish world,
but believed that the Diaspora—the rest of the wheel—would always
exist for Jews.

In 1935 Kaplan founded the Reconstructionist Movement to
spread his ideas among Conservatives in particular and among all
American Jews in general. He was immediately labeled the "left-
winger of Conservatism." His ideas won many followers among his
students at the seminary and led to nationwide and even international
discussions in Jewish religious and intellectual circles, but he won
relatively few converts. When a Reconstructionist prayer book was
published, only five congregations in the country made immediate
use of it. Yet *Judaism As a Civilization* continued to go from one
edition to another, and *The Reconstructionist*, a bi-weekly magazine,
propagated the idea that religious Jews, as bearers of a civilization,
have the duty not only to engage in public worship, but also to
satisfy the aesthetic, cultural, educational, and social needs of the
Jewish community.

Reform Judaism and Unity

Reform Judaism has changed radically since its early American
days. The Pittsburgh Platform of 1885 committed the Reformers
to take an interest in "the contrasts and evils of the present organization of society," but this commitment was not universally honored
at the start. During the past quarter century, however, there has
been more and more social action on the part of the Reform group.
This has ranged from pronouncements, petitions, statements, and
sermons to participation by both rabbis and laymen in such group
action as civil rights demonstrations.

Reform Judaism has done much in recent years to bring about
some degree of Jewish unity, taking the lead in forming the Synagogue Council and community councils.

In many Reform temples services have acquired a more char-
acteristically Jewish flavor, as some of the old traditional customs
have been restored. Many Reform rabbis now wear a prayer shawl

and some even a pulpit hat. Traditional material has been added to the Union prayer book and some Reform temples have resumed the use of a cantor.

Everywhere Reform congregations are winning back to Judaism, by one means or another, many of those who had disaffiliated themselves from their religion years ago.

America and the Six-Day War

The reactions of most American Jews to what happened in the Middle East in the spring of 1967 were no different from the reactions of most American non-Jews. When the UN force on the Gaza frontier was suddenly withdrawn and it appeared likely that Israel would be invaded by at least three Arab armies, two of them equipped by the Russians and the third by the United States, American sympathy in general was with the underdog. As the David-Goliath story was being re-enacted in Sinai, along the banks of the Jordan and on the Syrian heights, most American cheers were for "David." But for those Americans who were also Jews, there were additional reactions that few non-Jews could possibly have had.

Even those who had once been anti-Zionists now had great concern for the survival of this small bastion of democracy, surrounded by military dictatorships, monarchies, and pseudo-republics. After all, this was the land of their ancestors, the birthplace of their religion, the home of their patriarchs. And so, long into the night many sat glued to television and radio sets, intent as they followed the war news and the Security Council debates. When it was confirmed that the Old City of Jerusalem had been captured, that Israeli troops were on the heights of Golan and on the banks of the Suez Canal, and that Hebron, Bethlehem, Nablus, Jericho, and Sharm-el-Sheikh, in the Gulf of Akaba, were all actually in Israeli hands, and that Israel not only was safe but that her soldiers in six days had won a military victory unprecedented in the annals of any nation, anywhere, American Jews reacted not unnaturally with relief, exuberant joy, and pride combined. At this precise split-second in history they were united as they never had been before—and might never be again. For that one week, anyway, a Jew could go out into the main street of wherever in America he lived and shout at the top of his lungs, "I am a Jew!" and be almost certain that someone would come up and congratulate him on what his co-religionists in Israel had just done. That week the anti-Semites were suddenly noticeable by their absence. It was not just a matter of peoplehood, but also of religion. Just as 200,000 Israeli Jews poured through the gates of the Old City to pray at the Wailing Wall, the first day it was permitted, even though many of them took pride in how un-religious they were, normally, so did hundreds of thousands of American Jews experience religious exultation over the fact that now any Jew—even an Israeli Jew—could say his prayers beside that small remnant of Solomon's magnificent Temple, and visit Rachel's Tomb, and no longer be denied access to any of his own religious shrines.

When the two most widely read American weekly news magazines, simultaneously and independently of each other, chose General Moshe Dayan as their man of the week and put similar pictures of him on their covers, it gave even the most insecure American Jew somewhat the feeling a mother has when one of her family finally gets the public recognition she feels he deserves. On some college campuses impressionable youth began going around with black patches over their left eyes, and there were jokes about Israel loaning Dayan to the United States to run the Vietnam war for a week. The day might come again—God forbid!—when malicious gangs would smear swastikas on the outer walls of American synagogues, but in the summer of 1967 the Jews of America were aware that once again they were reaping the benefits of what had happened in Israel.

It's Very "In" to Be a Jew

The Anti-Defamation League and other Jewish groups in America in the late 1960s were campaigning against certain unwritten rules which seemed to bar Jews from occupying high executive positions and membership on the boards of directors of corporations in certain areas of American big business. This was a far cry from the situation exactly three hundred years earlier, when some of the first Jews to settle in the Colonies were barred even from opening a butcher shop. There were still some colleges and universities in the East that covertly used a quota system which limited the number of Jews accepted, especially in graduate schools. There was still silent discrimination here and there. But what was important was that it was hidden. It was symptomatic of the times that it was neither good business nor good ethics to admit it.

The Israeli army's victory three times—in 1948, 1956, and 1967— over Arab armies that were greatly superior in both numbers and equipment did much for the morale of American Jews. Each time it happened they were able to hold their heads higher and walk more proudly.

But there were other, more constructive reasons for the greater security Jews felt in America during the last half of the twentieth century. Men who—unlike some of the early American Jews— neither converted nor changed their names nor in any way denied their Jewishness rose to positions of great importance in American life, and in distinguishing themselves they distinguished all Jews. There were Supreme Court Justices, Governors, cabinet members, high officials in every single branch of the federal government, men and women of esteem in the arts, literature, the theater, music. The more these people identified with their religion—the more they acknowledged proudly their Jewishness—the more they were respected by thinking people in the non-Jewish world, and the more dignity this gave to all American Jews.

The Courage to Look in a Mirror

One of Judaism's distinctive characteristics still very much alive in America in the last half of the twentieth century was the ability to be self-critical. It began in the Old Testament, a large portion of which is devoted to a recital by the Israelites of their own sinfulness, God's anger with them, and the punishment which they always acknowledged they very well deserved. It has frequently been pointed out by historians that the annals of man do not record anything remotely resembling this story of a people driven from their own soil and forced to wander about the world for almost two thousand years who in effect say: "It was just what we deserved because of our sins."

Sigmund Freud once commented: "I do not know whether one often finds a people that makes so merry unreservedly over its own shortcomings."

This willingness to look critically into a mirror is refreshing when it occurs in a Madison Avenue culture that often seems to be based on self-adulation. It explains a stream of novels written by American Jews about American Jews, starting with Ben Hecht's *A Jew in Love* and perhaps not ending with Saul Bellow's *Herzog*.

An example of Jewish self-criticism applied to Judaism itself is the following passage from *Giants of Justice*, by Albert Vorspan of the Union of American Hebrew Congregations:

"To applaud the reemergence of the synagogue in America is not to blink at the fact that the synagogue in America—Reform, Conservative, and Orthodox—as presently functioning—is frequently an inadequate vessel to hold so rich a wine as the Jewish tradition. . . . The synagogue is the repository of the totality of Jewish life, and should be the exemplar of all that is noblest in the Jewish tradition. But the synagogue itself is subject to secularization, class snobbishness, and materialistic pretentiousness. Too many Jews confuse the new building, the membership campaign, the bazaar, and the theater party—the means—with the purposes of the synagogue. Too many Jews believe that Judaism is an occasional thing which one acts out, prayer book in hand, within the four walls of the temple. To too many Jews the synagogue has become a kind of air-conditioned shrine where one goes, lightly and pleasantly, to pay obeisance to a proud Jewish past which expired some two or three thousand years ago. To too many Jews, the synagogue—and Judaism itself—has become irrelevant to life."

Intermarriage or Separateness

One manifestation of the new American attitude toward Jews was the ever-increasing rate of intermarriage between Christians and Jews. From the integrationist point of view this was commendable;

in the minds of many—perhaps most—Jewish religious leaders, it was a trend to be halted in every way possible, on the ground that intermarriage could ultimately destroy Judaism.

In the early days in America (before 1840) more than 15 percent of all marriages contracted by Jews were with non-Jews. During the latter part of the nineteenth and early part of the twentieth century the rate decreased, but after World War II it began to skyrocket. By 1968 the intermarriage rate for the Jewish community as a whole was approaching the 10 percent mark. In Washington, D.C., the rate has reached 13.1 percent. A survey some years ago in Charleston, West Virginia, showed that among the 367 married couples polled, there were 84 mixed marriages—22 percent. In twenty years in San Francisco, the rate of intermarriage rose from 10 percent to 17 percent. In Iowa the intermarriage rate was found to be 31 percent.

A study of intermarriage in Washington, D.C., by Erich Rosenthal, published in 1963 disclosed that intermarriage in the first generation (foreign-born) averaged 1.4 percent; in the second generation (native born of foreign parents) it had risen to 10.2 percent, and in third and subsequent generations (native-born of native parents) reached 17.9 percent.

A survey taken among Jewish college students showed almost one-third not opposed to the idea of intermarriage.

In 1934 Mordecai Kaplan wrote that "if nothing is done to prevent the tendency to intermarriage, Judaism can barely survive another century, and, even it if does survive, it will have become hopelessly devitalized."

In 1965 David Polish, founding rabbi of Beth Emet the Free Synagogue, in Evanston, Illinois, wrote that the Jewish people are in danger of disintegration "because both identity and purpose are being dissolved." He likened American Jewry to a man dying in a wintry blizzard and feeling warm as death approaches. "The unprecedented prosperity in which they (the Jewish people) live lowers both awareness of decay and resistance to it." With this prosperity, Rabbi Polish coupled intermarriage, quoting statistical charts which, he said, "give scientific validity" to Kaplan's foreboding about the suicide of the American Jewish community, by intermarriage.

Nathan Glazer, professor of sociology at the University of California, in his *American Judaism* wrote: "For a religion that looked forward to unity of mankind on the basis of prophetic justice, there would seem to be no possible objection to Jews marrying non-Jews, many of whom already accepted this outlook. Yet it was a rare Reform rabbi who took this position. Even radical Reformers like Einhorn opposed intermarriage."

The Central Conference of American Rabbis in 1909 declared that intermarriage is contrary to the traditions of the Jewish religion and should therefore be discouraged by the American rabbinate.

Kaufman Kohler, while president of Hebrew Union College, argued that because of the universalistic Messianic hope of the Jews, it is imperative that they continue their separateness and "avoid intermarrying the members of other sects."

Dr. Allan Tarshish, rabbi of Temple Jeremiah in Glencoe, Illinois, in his book, *Not By Power, a Study of the Growth of Judaism*, wrote:

"Ezra was shocked to discover the extent of intermarriage in Palestine. Four months after his arrival he convoked an assembly in Jerusalem at which representatives of the community voted overwhelmingly to dissolve such marriages. The Samaritans and others who had intermarried with the Jews were much affronted by this action. The whole question of this ban on intermarriage—more of an ethnic, national ban than a religious one—has caused much debate in Jewish life. Although the Samaritans and others had accepted the religion of Judaism, it evidently was felt by those who were born Jews that these severe regulations against intermarriage were necessary to preserve the vitality of the Jewish people. But in the light of history it seems most narrow, a reversion to the isolationism and tribalism of the earlier period. Later, there was the inevitable strong counter-reaction to this narrowness."

Those worried by the statistics on intermarriage saw two hopeful signs.

With more and more newly prosperous Jewish families moving to suburbia, and with the suburban synagogues and temples trying to weld their members into cohesive social as well as religious groups, and with more and more all-Jewish country clubs, the potential of intermarriage was lessening.

During the late 1960s close to three thousand Christians were converting each year to Judaism. Most were women who had married or were about to marry Jewish men and wished to establish Jewish homes. This figure is impressive. It indicates that Judaism today is so vital and its standing as a religion in the minds of Americans is such that at least a few thousand a year publicly and of their own free will convert.

This could not have happened in the United States in the early days. In many foreign lands it never could have happened in the past —and could not happen even now.

29

TOMORROW, NEXT WEEK . . .

THOSE are the American Jews. That is the story of Judaism in the New World. Nothing has been omitted intentionally. No person or group has been slighted purposely. But emphasis *has* been placed on those who seem to have best carried out Judaism's manifold teachings and admonitions about justice, for that certainly has been the contribution for which history will credit this religious group, and for that reason it has been the theme.

This is not, really, the last chapter of the story. Even as a printing press turns out these pages, the next chapter is being written by those who seek to walk in the rather large footprints of the Wises, the Cardozos, the Schechters, the Szolds, the Baruchs, and all the other great figures in the history of American Judaism.

Tomorrow, next week, the year after next, conditions may develop in America that will call for bold voices to speak out and for bold action to be taken to protect the freedoms that were won by an earlier generation of Jews and non-Jews alike. When that time comes some will hesitate, some will equivocate, but, as always, a giant here and there will stand up and demand to be heard, pointing out the way of the ancient prophets, and warning, as Jeremiah did:

Woe to him who builds his house by injustice!

ACKNOWLEDGMENTS

GRATITUDE is expressed to the following persons who read, critically, all or parts of the manuscript of this book, or who supplied information, or who checked the facts and figures:

Rabbi Kenneth Roseman, Assistant Dean, Hebrew Union College and Jewish Institute of Religion.
Stanley F. Chyet, Associate Director, American Jewish Archives.
Rabbi Emeritus Morris Silverman, Emmanuel Synagogue, West Hartford, Connecticut.
Professor Moshe Davis, Institute of Contemporary Jewry, Jerusalem.
Rabbi David Polish, Beth Emet the Free Synagogue, Evanston, Illinois.
Florence Wellins, West Hartford, Connecticut.
Rabbi Samuel Volkman, Temple Israel, Charleston, West Virginia.
James Waterman Wise, Tourrettes sur Loup, Alpes-Maritime, France.
Rabbi Samuel H. Vitzsick, Chaplain, Sinai Hospital, Baltimore, Maryland.
Morris Laub, United Synagogue of America.
Rabbi William B. Silverman, Congregation B'nai Juhudah, Kansas City, Missouri.
David A Brody, Director, Anti-Defamation League, Washington, D.C.
Rabbi Allan Tarshish, Temple Jeremiah, Glencoe, Illinois.
Dr. Miriam Freund, editor, *Hadassah Magazine*.
Rabbi Perry E. Nussbaum, Beth Israel Congregation, Jackson, Mississippi.
Beryl L. Reubens, the Mount Sinai Hospital, New York, New York.
Barbara Roth, National Council of Jewish Women.
Rabbi Zev Nelson, Temple Emeth, Chestnut Hill, Massachusetts.
Karl B. Friedman, Director, Temple Beth El, Birmingham, Alabama.

Rabbi Marvin M. Reznikoff, Liberal Synagogue, Baton Rouge, Louisiana.
Mrs. Abe Shurgin, Executive Director, The Temple, Atlanta, Georgia.
Rabbi Jacob L. Halevi, Temple Beth Israel, Gadsden, Alabama.
Paul Kresh, Union of American Hebrew Congregations.
Rabbi Allan L. Smith, Temple Emanuel, Gastonia, North Carolina.
Theodore Freedman, Houston, Texas.
John A. Morsell, Asst. Exec. Director, National Association for the
    Advancement of Colored People.
Rabbi Emanuel Feldman, Congregation Beth Jacob, Atlanta, Georgia.

SOURCES AND SUGGESTED READING

THESE are the books from which most of the facts have been gar-
nered that appear in this volume. Many are still in print and may be
purchased through local bookshops. All are worthwhile reading for
anyone interested in probing more deeply into any of the subjects
covered in the preceding pages.

CHAPTER I – UNWELCOME PIONEERS

Friedman, Lee M. *Jewish Pioneers and Patriots,* with preface by A. S. W. Ro-
senbach. (Philadelphia, The Jewish Publication Society of America, 5715–
1955.)
Gumbiner, Joseph H. *Leaders of Our People,* Book II, illustrated by David
Stone. (New York, Union of Hebrew Congregations, 1965.)
Marcus, Jacob Rader. *Early American Jewry.* The Jews of New York, New
England, and Canada, 1649–1794. (Philadelphia, The Jewish Publication
Society of America, 5721–1961.)
Roth, Cecil. *Personalities and Events in Jewish History.* (Philadelphia, The
Jewish Publication Society of America, 5721–1961.)

CHAPTER 2 – INSPIRATION FOR THE PURITANS

Friedman, Lee M. *Pilgrims in a New Land.* (Philadelphia, The Jewish Publi-
cation Society of America, 5708–1948.)
Gaer, Joseph, and Siegel, Ben. *The Puritan Heritage: America's Roots in the
Bible.* (New York, The New World Library, Mentor, 1964.)
Goodman, Abram Vossen. *American Overture.* Jewish Rights in Colonial
Times. (Philadelphia, The Jewish Publication Society of America, 5704–
1947.)

Kauper, Paul G. *Religion and the Constitution*. (Baton Rouge, Louisiana State University Press, 1964.)

Marcus, Jacob Rader. *Early American Jewry*. The Jews of New York, New England, and Canada. (Philadelphia, The Jewish Publication Society of America, 5721–1961.)

CHAPTER 3 – AT LAST, A RECOGNIZED RELIGION

Friedman, Lee M. *Early American Jews*. (Cambridge, Harvard University Press, 1934.)

Goodman, Abram Vossen. *American Overture*. Jewish Rights in Colonial Times. (Philadelphia, The Jewish Publication Society of America. 5704–1947.)

Learsi, Rufus. *The Jews in America: A History*. (Cleveland & New York, The World Publishing Company, 1954.)

Lebeson, Anita Libman. *Pilgrim People*. (New York, Harper & Brothers, 1950.)

CHAPTER 4 – AND LET THEM MAKE ME A SANCTUARY

Chyet, Stanley. (editor) *Rabbi Carigal Preaches in Newport*. The first Jewish Sermon Preached and Published in North America. (Cincinnati, American Jewish Archives.)

Friedman, Lee M. *Pilgrims in a New Land*. (Philadelphia, The Jewish Publication Society of America, 5708–1948.)

Gray, Ruth. *Jews in America*. A Short History. (New York & London. Basic Books, 1965.)

CHAPTER 5 – OUTPOSTS OF JUDAISM

Glazer, Nathan. *American Judaism*. The Chicago History of American Civilization. (Chicago & London. The University of Chicago Press, 1957.)

Goodman, Abram Vossen. *American Overture*. Jewish Rights in Colonial Times. (Philadelphia, The Jewish Publication Society of America, 5704–1947.)

Marcus, Jacob Rader. *Memoirs of American Jews, 1775–1865*, Volume I, and *Early American Jewry*, The Jews of Pennsylvania and the South, 1655–1790. (Philadelphia, The Jewish Publication Society of America, 5715–1955.)

CHAPTER 6 – CONTRIBUTIONS TO A REVOLUTION

Friedman, Lee M. *Pilgrims in a New Land*. (Philadelphia, The Jewish Publication Society, 5708–1948.)

Markowitz, Sidney L. *Jewish Religion, History, Ethics and Culture*. (New York, Citadel Press, 1955.)

McCall, Samuel Walker. *Patriotism of the American Jew*. (New York, Plymouth Press, 1924.)

CHAPTER 7 – JUDAISM MOVES WESTWARD

Marcus, Jacob Rader. *American Jewry*. Documents, Eighteenth Century. (Cincinnati, The Hebrew Union College Press, 1959.)

CHAPTER 8 – THE STRUGGLE FOR REFORM

Friedman, Lee M. *Pilgrims in a New Land*. (Philadelphia, The Jewish Publication Society, 5708–1948.)

Tarshish, Allan. *The Charleston Organ Case*. The American Jewish Historical Quarterly, Vol. LIV, No. 4, June, 1965.

CHAPTER 9 – ONE MAN'S CONQUEST

Marcus, Jacob Rader. *Memoirs of American Jews, 1775–1865*. (Philadelphia, The Jewish Publication Society of America, 5715–1955.)

CHAPTER 10 – THE WISE-LEESER FEUD

Friedman, Lee M. *Pilgrims in a New Land*. (Philadelphia, The Jewish Publication Society of America, 5708–1948.)

Gumbiner, Joseph H. *Leaders of Our People*. Book II. (New York, Union of American Hebrew Congregations, 1965.)

Heller, James G. *Isaac M. Wise*. His Life, Work and Thought. (New York, The Union of American Hebrew Congregations, 1965.)

Marcus, Joseph Rader. *Memoirs of American Jews, 1775–1865*. Volumes II and III. (Philadelphia, The Jewish Publication Society of America, 5715–1955 and 5716–1956.)

Raisin, Max. *Great Jews I Have Known*. A Gallery of Portraits. (New York, Philosophical Library, 1952.)

CHAPTER 11 – CHALLENGES OF THE NINETEENTH CENTURY

Friedman, Lee M. *Jewish Pioneers and Patriots*. (Philadelphia, The Jewish Publication Society of America, 5715–1955.)

Gumbiner, Joseph H. *Leaders of Our People*. Book II. (New York, The Union of American Hebrew Congregations, 1965.)

Levitan, Tina. *The First of American Jewish History*. (Brooklyn, The Charuth Press, 1952.)

CHAPTER 12 – THE STATE DIVIDES; THE JEWS DIVIDE

Korn, Bertram W. *American Jewry and the Civil War*. Introduction by Allan Nevins. (Cleveland & New York, The World Publishing Company, 1961.)
Rubinger, Naphtali J. *Abraham Lincoln and the Jews*. (New York, Jonathan David, 1962.)
Simonhoff, Harry. *Jewish Participants in the Civil War*. (New York, Arco Publishing Co., 1963.)

CHAPTER 13 – ANTI-SEMITISM LEAVES ITS MARK

Schwarz, Leo W. (editor) *Great Ages and Idea of the Jewish People*. Chapter entitled: *The American Experience*, Salo W. Baron. (New York, Random House, 1956.)

CHAPTER 14 – THE BIRTH OF CONSERVATISM

Davis, Moshe. *The Emergence of Conservative Judaism*. The Historical School in 19th Century America. (Philadelphia, The Jewish Publication Society of America, 5725–1965.)
Leibman, Charles S. *Orthodoxy in American Jewish Life*. (New York, American Jewish Year Book, Vol. 66, 1965.)
Wouk, Herman. *This Is My God*. (Garden City, N.Y., Doubleday & Company, 1959.)

CHAPTER 15 – GIVE ME YOUR TIRED, YOUR POOR . . .

Gumbiner, Joseph H. *Leaders of Our People*. Book II. (New York, The Union of American Hebrew Congregations, 1965.)
Simonhoff, Harry. *Saga of American Jewry*. 1865–1914. (New York, The Acro Publishing Company, 1959.)

CHAPTER 16 – SCHECHTER'S 1,400,000 FOLLOWERS

Gumbiner, Joseph H. *Leaders of Our People*. Book II. (New York, The Union of American Hebrew Congregations, 1965.)
Noveck, Simon. *Great Jewish Personalities in Modern Times*. (New York, B'nai B'rith, 1960.)
Raisin, Max. *Great Jews I Have Known*. A Gallery of Portraits. (New York, The Philosophical Library, 1952.)

CHAPTER 17 — NOTHING JEWISH IS ALIEN

Vorspan, Albert. *Giants of Justice*. (New York, The Union of American Hebrew Congregations, 1960.)

CHAPTER 18 — J.D.C., WAR BABY

Cohn, Norman. *Warrant for Genocide*. The Myth of the Jewish World, Conspiracy and the Protocols of the Elders of Zion. (New York, Harper & Row, 1966.)

Flannery, Edward H. *The Anguish of the Jews*. A Catholic Priest Writes of 23 Centuries of Anti-Semitism. (New York, The Macmillan Company, 1965.)

Handlin, Oscar. *Adventures in Freedom*. Three Hundred Years of Jewish Life in America. (New York, Toronto, London, McGraw-Hill Book Company, 1954.)

Parkes, James. *A History of the Jewish People*. (Baltimore, Penguin Books, 1964.)

Silver, Abba Hillel. *Where Judaism Differed*. An Inquiry into the Distinctions of Judaism. (New York, The Macmillan Company, 1956.)

Stember, Charles Herbert (and others). *Jews in the Mind of America*. (New York and London, Basic Books, 1966.)

CHAPTER 19 — HE THAT IS GRACIOUS UNTO THE POOR . . .

Roth, Cecil. *The Jewish Contribution to Civilization*. (London, The East & West Library, 1956.)

CHAPTER 20 — THE FOUR WHO LED LABOR

Friedman, Theodore, and Gordis, Robert. *Jewish Life in America*. (New York, Horizon Press, 1955.)

Epstein, Melech. *Profiles of Eleven*. (Detroit, Wayne State University Press, 1965.)

Ribalow, Harold U. (editor) *Autobiographies of American Jews*. (Philadelphia, The Jewish Publication Society of America, 5725–1965.)

CHAPTER 21 — SOCIAL JUSTICE, THE MAJOR CONTRIBUTION

Edelman, Lily (editor) *Jewish Heritage Reader*, with Introduction by Morris Adler. (New York, Taplinger Publication Company, 1965.)

Raisin, Max. *Great Jews I Have Known*. (New York, The Philosophical Library, 1952.)

Vorspan, Albert. *Giants of Justice.* (New York, The Union of American Hebrew Congregations, 1960.)
Wise, James, and Polier, Justine. *The Personal Letters of Stephen Wise.* (Boston, The Beacon Press, 1956.)
Wise, Stephen. *Challenging Years.* (New York, G. P. Putnam's Sons, 1949.)

CHAPTER 22 – MOSAIC LAW—AMERICAN LAW

Ribalow, Harold U. (editor) *Autobiographies of American Jews.* (Philadelphia, The Jewish Publication Society of America, 5725–1965.)
Roth, Cecil. *The Jewish Contribution to Civilization.* (London, The East & West Library, 1956.)
Steinberg, Milton. *Basic Judaism.* (New York, Harcourt, Brace & Company, 1947.)

CHAPTER 23 – NO MAN IS A STRANGER

Rothschild, Janice O. *As But a Day.* The First Hundred Years, 1867–1967. (Atlanta, The Hebrew Benevolent Congregation, 1967.)
Nussbaum, Perry E. *And Then There Was One . . .* (Philadelphia, The Central Conference of American Rabbis Journal, October, 1963.)
Vorspan, Albert, and Lipman, Eugene. *Justice and Judaism.* The Work of Social Action. Illustrated by Russell Roman. (New York, The Union of American Hebrew Congregations, 1959.)

CHAPTER 24 – AND EACH SHALL HAVE A VOICE

Vorspan, Albert, and Lipman, Eugene. *Justice and Judaism.* The Work of Social Action. Illustrated by Russell Roman. (New York, The Union of American Hebrew Congregations, 1959.)

CHAPTER 25 – LEARNING, THE HIGHEST COMMANDMENT

Finkelstein, Louis. *The Jews; Their History, Culture and Religion.* (Philadelphia, The Jewish Publication Society of America, 5721–1960.)

CHAPTER 26 – SEEK YE THE PEACE!

Gordis, Robert. *Judaism for the Modern Age.* (New York, Farrar, Straus & Cudahy, 1955.)

CHAPTER 27 – SHE WORKETH WILLINGLY

Fineman, Irving. *Woman of Valor.* The Life of Henrietta Szold, 1860–1945. (New York, Simon and Schuster, 1961.)

Graziani, Bernice. *Where There's a Woman.* 75 Years of History as Lived by the National Council of Jewish Women. Introduction by Dore Schary. Photographs by Ken Heyman. (New York, McCall Corporation, 1967.)

Levin, Alexandra Lee. *Szolds of Lombard Street.* A Baltimore Family. (Philadelphia, The Jewish Publication Society of America, 1960.)

CHAPTER 28 – AMERICAN JUDAISM TODAY

Bamberger, Bernard J. *The Story of Judaism.* (New York, The Union of American Hebrew Congregations, 1964.)

Eisenstein, Ira. *Judaism Under Freedom.* Foreword by Mordecai M. Kaplan. (New York, The Reconstructionist Press, 5717–1956.)

Fine, Morris, and Himmelfarb, Milton. (editors) *American Jewish Yearbook,* Vol. 68. (New York, The American Jewish Committee and Philadelphia, The Jewish Publication Society of America, 1967.)

Janowsky, Oscar I. *The American Jew.* A Reappraisal. (Philadelphia, The Jewish Publication Society of America, 5726–1965.)

Kaplan, Mordecai M. *Judaism as a Civilization.* Toward a Reconstruction of American-Jewish Life. (New York, The Reconstructionist Press, 1957.)

Memmi, Albert. *Portrait of a Jew.* Translated from the French by Elisabeth Abbott. (New York, the Orion Press, 1962.)

Polish, David. *The Higher Freedom.* A New Turning Point in Jewish History. (Chicago, Quadrangle Books, 1965.)

Rosenberg, Stuart E. *The Search for Jewish Identity in America.* Originally Published as *America Is Different.* (New York, Anchor Books, Doubleday & Co., 1965.)

Sklare, Marshall (editor) *The Jews.* Social Patterns of an American Group. (Glencoe, Illinois, The Free Press, 1958.)

Silverman, William B. *God Help Me.* From Kindergarten Religion to the Radical Faith. (New York, The Macmillan Company, 1961.)

Tarshish, Allan. *Not by Power.* The Story of the Growth of Judaism. (New York, Bookman Associates, 1952.)

INDEX

CIO (Congress of Industrial Organizations), 267, 291; Political Action Committee, 267
Circumcision, 32–33, 60, 287
Citizenship (naturalization), 13, 51–53, 63, 82, 137, 227
City of Refuge for the Jews, A., 145–50
Civil rights (civil equality; civil liberty), in colonial era, 13, 43, 51–53, 59, 62–64, 77; Judaism and, 293–308, 311–16; nineteenth-century, 136–37, 139
Civil War, 143, 151–89, 191, 192, 230
Cleveland, Grover, 195
Cleveland, Ohio, 114; orphanages in, 252; rabbinical conference (1855), in, 106; "The Temple" in, 241
Clothing industry, 258ff., 267–70
Coal mines, 284–85
Code Noir, 132
Cohen, Jacob, 12
Cohen, Mr. & Mrs. Abraham, 183
Cohen, Moses, 63
Cold Harbor, Battle of, 179
Colleges and universities, 120, 126–27, 326–29 (*see also* specific institutions, locations); colonial era, 16–17, 53–54; Hillel Foundation at, 328–29; quota system in, 357; rabbinical, 120, 126–27, 326–27 (*see also* specific institutions)
Colonial America, 1–14, 15–25, 27–38, 39–54, 55–67; religious schools in, 21, 33–35, 46, 95; Revolutionary War, 69–84, 133–34, 136
Color (in people), Midrash on unimportance of, 294
Columbian Exposition, 341
Columbus, Christopher, 3–4
Commerce and Labor, U. S. Department of, 334
Committee of Seventy, 192
Communism, 312, 313–14, 316
Community Chest, 251, 350
Community Councils, 349, 354
Confederacy (Confederate Army; Confederate States of America), 151–89 *passim*
Confirmation: bar *mitzvah,* 96, 224; bas *mitzvah,* 224
Conformity, 2, 275, 311–16. *See also* Individualism
Congregationalist, 134–35
Congregations. *See* Synagogues
Congress, U. S., 81, 94–95, 141, 142, 300; and civil rights, 308, 312, 313; and Civil War, 158, 159, 169; and

immigration, 227, 230; and Jewish chaplains, 158, 159
Congress of Jewish Women, 341
Congressional Record, 300
Connecticut, 24–25, 76–77. *See also* specific locations
Connecticut Valley, 24–25
Conservative Judaism, 197–203, 222–24, 243–44, 270, 297, 345, 354
Constitution, U. S., 81, 139, 140, 141, 315; Bill of Rights, 74, 94
Constitutions, colonial, 61–62, 65
Continental Army, 70–71, 79, 80
Continental Congress, 72
Conversion (converts), 2, 5–6, 16, 22, 23–24, 36, 50–51, 361
"Copperheads," Civil War, 173–74
Copyright laws, 289
Cordova, 2
Corporeal punishment, Uriah P. Levy and abolition in U. S. Navy of, 138, 141
Cosmos Club, 277
Cotton, John, 19
Cotton speculators, Civil War, 167–73
Coughlin, Charles Edward, 346
Council of Jewish Women, 243, 341–42, 350
Cox political machine, 283–84
Cresson, Warder, 173
Crime (criminals): incidence among Jews, 292; identification of Jews and, 165, 172, 181; Mosaic Law and, 287, 289–90, 292
Croker, Richard, 280
Cuba, 3, 4
Curaçao, 31
Curtiss, John C., 240
Cutters' Union, 268
Cyon, Dr. de, 239

Da Costa, Isaac, 63
Dandrada, Salvador, 12
Darmstadt, Joseph, 83–84
Dartmouth College, 17
David, King, 247, 310
"David the Jew" (colonial era), 24
Davis, Jefferson, 174
Dayan, Moshe, 356
Day Schools, 325
Dearborn (Mich.) *Independent,* 239–40
Deborah, Die, 125
Declaration of Independence (U.S.), 80
Declaration on the Rights of Man, 85
De la Caballeria, Alfonso, 3
De la Motthe, Jacques, 7–8
De Lucena, Abraham, 12, 30–31
De Lyon, Abraham, 59